W9-ADU-843

Darwin's Islands

1. Culpepper
2. Wenman
3. Narborough
4. Albemarle
5. Abingdon
6. Bindloe
7. Tower
8. James
9. Jervis
10. Duncan
11. N. Seymour
12. Baltra
13. Indefatigable
14. Plaza Islets
15. Barrington
16. Charles
17. Chatham
18. Hood

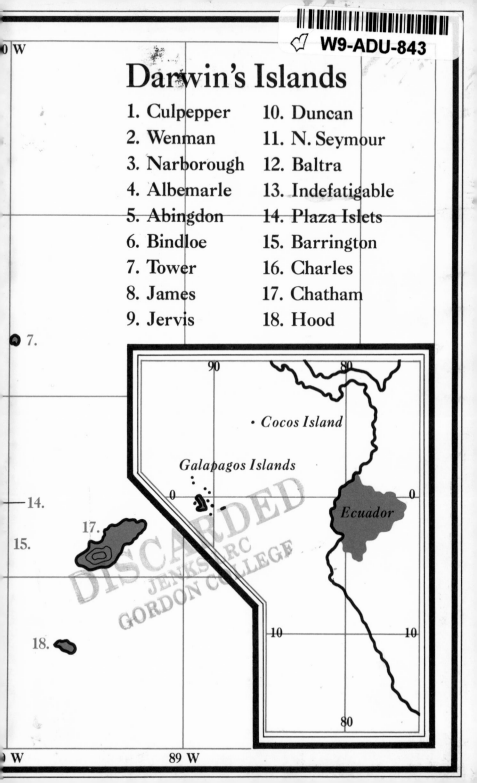

90

80

• Cocos Island

Galapagos Islands

0

Ecuador

0

10

10

80

DISCARDED
JENKS LRC
GORDON COLLEGE

The Library of

Barrington College

DARWIN'S ISLANDS

Ian Thornton was born in Yorkshire, England, and studied at Leeds University where he received his Ph.D. in insect ecology. In addition to his Galápagos expedition, Professor Thornton has done field work in Africa, the Middle East, Asia, and South America. He is currently Professor of Zoology and Dean of the School of Biological Sciences at La Trobe University in Melbourne, Australia.

WINN LIBRARY
Gordon College
Wenham, Mass. 01984

DARWIN'S ISLANDS
A Natural History of the Galápagos

IAN THORNTON

PUBLISHED FOR
THE AMERICAN MUSEUM OF NATURAL HISTORY
THE NATURAL HISTORY PRESS
GARDEN CITY, NEW YORK
1971

THE NATURAL HISTORY PRESS, publisher for The American Museum of Natural History, is a division of Doubleday and Company, Inc. Directed by a joint editorial board made up of members of the staff of both the Museum and Doubleday, the Natural History Press publishes books in all branches of the life and earth sciences, including anthropology and astronomy. The Natural History Press has its editorial offices at 277 Park Avenue, New York, New York 10017, and its business offices at 501 Franklin Avenue, Garden City, New York 11530.

Library of Congress Catalog Card Number 69–20061
Copyright © 1971 by Ian W. B. Thornton
All Rights Reserved
Printed in the United States of America

QH
123
.T48

Decorations by M. F. Gazze

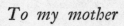

To my mother

Preface

"THE biological peculiarities are offset by an enervating climate, monotonous scenery, dense thorn scrub, cactus spines, loose sharp lava, food deficiencies, water shortage, black rats, fleas, jiggers, ants, mosquitoes, scorpions, Ecuadorian Indians of doubtful honesty, and dejected, disillusioned European settlers. Admittedly these are merely discomforts, but their effect is cumulative in a shut-in tropical island."

Although the British biologist David Lack wrote these words after a four-month stay in 1939, the Galápagos Islands have continued to excite the interest of biologists, students of evolution, and naturalists of every kind. It is true that the archipelago, straddling the equator out in the Pacific some six hundred miles west of South America, is no tourist paradise, but there is something about this strange, barren group of islands, with its unusual, often bizarre, animals and plants, that cannot fail to impress the visitor to its shores. Whether the impression is one of awe, excitement and wonder, or one of desolation and dejection, the islands leave their imprint. The early Spaniards called them "Las Islas Encantadas" and "encantada" is best translated in this context as "bewitched." The more prosaic Californian tuna boat crews of today refer to them simply as "the rock pile."

In fact, this archipelago has a place of very great importance in our contemporary culture. After being on board H.M.S. *Beagle* for more than three years, Charles Darwin wrote in a letter home from Lima, Peru, in July 1835, "I look forward to the Galápagos with more interest than any other part of the voyage." He was surely not disappointed. In his Journal he wrote:

> The natural history of these islands is eminently curious, and well deserves attention. Most of the organic productions are aboriginal creations, found nowhere else; there is even a difference between the inhabitants of the different islands; yet all show a marked relationship with those of America, though separated from that continent by an open space of ocean, between 500 and 600 miles in width. The archipelago is a little world in itself, or rather a satellite attached to America, whence it has derived a few stray colonists and has received the general character of its indigenous productions. Considering the small size of these islands, we feel the more astonished at the number of their aboriginal beings, and at their confined range. Seeing every height crowned with its crater, and the boundaries of most of the lava-streams still distinct, we are led to believe that within a period geologically recent the unbroken ocean was here spread out. Hence, both in space and time, we seem to be brought somewhat near to that great fact—that mystery of mysteries—the first appearence of new beings on this earth.

It was here, while observing the strange reptiles and birds of the islands, that the young Darwin first began to ponder evolutionary problems. His visit to the archipelago was largely responsible for setting up the train of thought that culminated in the *Origin of Species* twenty years later. The effects of this work extended far beyond the confines of biological science and touched off a major philosophical revolution in the world.

I am indebted to the staff of the Charles Darwin Research Station for assistance in many ways during my stay on the archipelago, as well as for information about the islands and their natural history. In particular, Roger Perry, Tjittes DeVries,

Miguel Castro, Bernhard Schreyer, and Rolf Sievers have all provided me with much valuable information in the course of informal conversation.

Mike Harris and Uno Eliasson, who were at various times my companions in 1967, generously shared their knowledge of the birds and plants respectively, and I am grateful to the latter for the use of several photographs.

For enabling me to move about from one island to another, I wish to thank Señor Bolivar Aguere, owner of the *Santa Marianita*, also "Conejo," the "patron" or skipper, and "Chappie," the crewman. They were all very patient and pleasant, often in unpleasant and difficult circumstances. The visit to the far northern islands, Wenman and Culpepper, could not have been achieved without the vital assistance of Miguel Castro, who generously put his vast experience of seamanship in Galápagos waters at my disposal, and dealt calmly with several unpredicted emergencies with resourcefulness and considerable skill.

My colleague in Hong Kong, Doctor Alan Wright, was kind enough to read carefully through an early manuscript, and offered many constructive suggestions.

I have drawn fully from the works of the authors listed in the bibliography, and my dependence on them is very great. However, any errors of fact or interpretation remain my own.

Contents

In conclusion, it appears to me that nothing can be more improving to a young naturalist, than a journey in distant countries. It both sharpens, and partly allays that want and craving, which, as Sir J. Herschel remarks, a man experiences although every corporeal sense be fully satisfied. The excitement from the novelty of objects, and the chance of success, stimulate him to increased activity. Moreover, as a number of isolated facts soon become uninteresting, the habit of comparison leads to generalization. On the other hand, as the traveller stays but a short time in each place, his descriptions must generally consist of mere sketches, instead of detailed observations. Hence arises, as I have found to my cost, a constant tendency to fill up the wide gaps of knowledge, by inaccurate and superficial hypotheses.

But I have too deeply enjoyed the voyage, not to recommend any naturalist, although he must not expect to be so fortunate in his companions as I have been, to take all chances, and to start, on travels by land if possible, if otherwise on a long voyage. He may feel assured he will meet with no difficulties or dangers, excepting in rare cases, nearly so bad as he beforehand anticipates. In a moral point of view, the effect ought to be, to teach him good-humoured patience, freedom from selfishness, the habit of acting for himself, and of making the best of every occurrence. In short, he ought to partake of the characteristic qualities of most sailors. Travelling ought also to teach him distrust; but at the same time he will discover, how many truly kind-hearted people there are, with whom he never before had, or ever again will have any further communication, who yet are ready to offer him the most disinterested assistance.

CHARLES DARWIN

Journal of Researches
into the natural history and geology
of the countries visited during the voyage
of H.M.S. Beagle *round the world.*

CHAPTER ONE

The Historical Setting

THE first human beings to set foot on the Galápagos Islands may have been the Incas. Means (1942), in a study of pre-Spanish navigation off the Andean coast, suggests that the Galápagos Islands were discovered in the latter half of the fifteenth century by the Cuzco prince, Tupac Inca Yupanqui, later to become the tenth Inca, and one of the most renowned of the Inca kings. He was grandfather of the famous Quito Inca, Atahualpa, who was put to death by Pizarro.

For all their civilization, the Incas had no written language. Systems of knotted strings, or "quipus," were used as aids to ancient chants and memories, but our knowledge of Inca history is largely dependent on stories handed down by word of mouth from generation to generation. Sarmiento de Gamboa spent seven years, during the first generation of the Spanish conquest, studying the history of Peru, obtaining his information from native historians who could still personally recall events dating from the days before the Spanish arrived. Over forty of these historians met and approved Sarmiento's chronicle of names and events, which was published in 1572 as a *History of the Incas.* Cabello de Balboa, who arrived in Peru in 1566, wrote an independent *History of Peru* in 1586.

Both these chroniclers record how Tupac Inca marched down

to the coast with his army to somewhere near present-day Guayaquil. Sarmiento's history states that Tupac Inca heard rumors from merchant mariners of two inhabited islands to the west, called Ava Chumbi (Outer Island) and Nina Chumbi (Island of Fire), where there was much gold. The Inca constructed a vast fleet of balsa rafts with sails, and set out with twenty thousand chosen men to find the islands. The fleet was away for nine months or a year, and Tupac Inca returned with "black people, gold, a brass chair, and the skin and jaw-bone of a horse." These trophies were deposited in the Cuzco fortress until the arrival of the Spanish.

Cabello's independent chronicle corroborates this story in large measure. According to Cabello, the voyage lasted for a year or more, and two islands, Hagua Chumbi and Nina Chumbi, were discovered in the South Sea, which the Inca named Mamacocha, "mother of lakes." The trophies reported were similar to those in Sarmiento's account, except that silver was included, the chair was of copper, and there were the skins of animals similar to horses.

The uninhabited Galápagos Islands could not have been the source of black people, silver or gold, a chair of brass or copper, or horses. However, various authorities, including Heyerdahl (1952), believe it likely that the Inca's expedition made a raid on the continent north of their point of departure, on their return voyage, and could have obtained the prisoners, gold and the chair on this mainland raid. But before 1519, when Cortés landed at Vera Cruz with sixteen horses, this animal was unknown in the New World, and the reference to skins like those of horses is difficult to explain. It is at least possible that the parts of a "horse" were in fact the remains of a bull sea lion, obtained from the Galápagos Islands. Heyerdahl is convinced that a large fleet of hundreds of balsa craft, spread out in line abreast, could have found the Galápagos Archipelago. If so, "Island of Fire" would have been an apt name for one of these volcanic islands. However, Heyerdahl provides a good deal of circumstantial evidence that the islands reached by

Tupac Inca may have been Mangareva and Timoe, even farther away, in the Gambier group.

Whatever the truth may be about Tupac Inca's voyage, the contemporary official Ecuadorian government map of the Galápagos proudly bears the name Nina-Chumpi over the island of Albemarle, and Huahuachumpi for Chatham. Markham (1892), however, supposes that Huahuachumpi, Outer Island, must have referred to Narborough.

Heyerdahl discovered ceramic evidence of pre-Colombian expeditions from the mainland to the Galápagos (Heyerdahl and Skjolsvold, 1956; Heyerdahl, 1963), but this has been objected to on the grounds that the pottery may have been brought there more recently by buccaneers. However, Heyerdahl points out that a Galápagos cotton plant, which has a spinnable lint, is very closely related to a domesticated cotton and is not dispersed by ocean currents or by birds (but see also CHAPTER 10). It is certainly quite possible that the Galápagos cotton was transported by man from the American continent.

The Galápagos Islands bear no archaeological remains of habitations or structures, and permanent settlement in prehistorical times is unlikely, because of the difficulty there would have been in obtaining a regular supply of fresh water. There is only one small permanent stream on the archipelago. Nevertheless, the islands are known to have been visited by balsa rafts in historical times, and it seems that pre-Colombian visits of short duration may well have been made.

The islands were first discovered, as far as is definitely recorded, by Fray Tomás de Berlanga, the Bishop of Panama, in 1535, when his ship was caught in the South Equatorial Current (FIGURE 1) and was swept some 500 miles off course on a voyage from Panama to Peru. The bishop wrote an interesting account of his adventures to his emperor, Carlos V of Spain. His account included descriptions of the giant tortoises (galápagos) and the iguanas, and he mentions the remarkable tameness of the birds on the islands. His comments on the landscape, however, were uninviting: . . . "most of it is full of very big

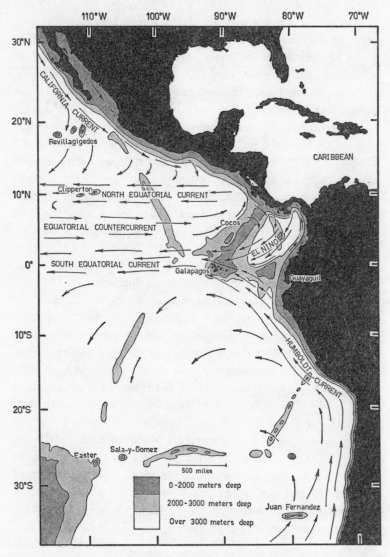

FIGURE 1. East-central Pacific Ocean, showing main ocean currents and submarine ridges.

stones, so much so that it seems as though at some time God had showered stones." The bishop's party eventually succeeded in finding water, but only after considerable difficulty. The shore parties were reduced to chewing cactus for the moisture it contained, and two men and ten horses died of thirst before the ship reached Puerto Viejo in Peru, a month later.

About eleven years afterward, a renegade Spaniard, Diego de Revadeniera, fled with about a dozen men in a stolen vessel to escape the wrath of both his deserted commander, Centeno, and Pizarro, the conqueror of Peru. Like the Bishop of Panama, he was carried off course and after twenty-five days sighted the volcanoes of the Galápagos, where he landed to search for water. The group eventually succeeded in reaching what is now Guatemala, but only after suffering terribly from hunger and thirst, living on sharks caught with hooks made from their own spurs. Like the bishop, Revadeniera noted the Galápagos tortoises, iguanas, and the tameness of the birds, and he was the first to mention the Galápagos hawk.

In the seventeenth century, British buccaneers and privateers, with instructions to war against the Spanish, used the archipelago as a safe base from which they were able to attack the Spanish gold-bearing galleons which were leaving the west coast of South America, and also to sack and pillage the coastal towns of the continent. One of the most well-documented of these visits is that of the ships *Bachelor's Delight* and *Nicholas*, in 1684, when Dampier, Cowley, Wafer, Davies, Eaton, and Cook discovered that James Bay, on the island of James, was an anchorage with firewood, water in the rainy season, salt, and plenty of tortoises. In 1709, another privateer, Woodes Rogers, having rescued "Robinson Crusoe" (Alexander Selkirk) from Juan Fernandez, and appointed him second mate on the *Duke*, sailed north, sacked Guayaquil, and then repaired to the Galápagos. He found "nothing but loose Rocks, like Cynders, very rotten and heavy, and the Earth so parch'd that it will not bear a Man, but break into Holes under his Feet, which makes me suppose there has been a Volcano here; . . . yet there's not the least Sign of Water, nor is it possible that any can be contained on such a Surface." He had to return to the mainland to water his ships. A few months later he sailed back to the Galápagos to take on tortoises and wood, and then returned again to the continent to continue the looting and burning of the coastal towns.

The islands of James and Charles seem to have been favorite haunts. On James, various finds of smashed South American pottery bear witness to uninhibited carousing near James Bay, and it is more than likely that Buccaneer Bay was aptly named. On Charles Island, caves rough-hewn by buccaneers served as temporary first dwellings for the early settlers. There are stories, too, of buccaneer vessels that were wrecked on Indefatigable's somber shores and whose crews, in their long searches for water, were forced to abandon and cache their heavy gold loot. Such tales, of course, do not die easily.

The buccaneer, Edward Davies, wrote in his journal that with more than a hundred Spanish captives on board "wee sailed away to the Westward to see if wee could find those Islands called the Galipoloes, which made the Spaniards laugh at us telling us they were Inchanted Islands, and there was never any but Captaine Porialto that had even seene them but would not come neare them to anchor at them, and that they were but shadowes and noe reall Islands." The islands were thought by the Spaniards to move about in the sea and have no fixed position—to be "enchanted" or "bewitched." Even today uncertain winds and unpredictable currents make sailing in Galápagos waters a hazardous business, and several small fishing boats have sailed away from one or another of the islands never to be seen again.

From personal experience I can quite understand how such a belief could be fostered. In March of 1967, I was on watch aboard the Research Station's vessel, *Beagle*, at 3 A.M. with the captain, Mr. Bernhard Schreyer, in the Bolívar Channel between Narborough and Albemarle. We were sailing north at no more than three knots because a thick mist was enveloping us. The water temperature was 68° F., and we were shivering, despite our thick sea jackets. At 3:30 A.M. the moon set and shortly afterward an island, which we thought at first to be Narborough, appeared to port as a large, dark shape against the gray mist. As we watched, the island gradually enlarged and increased in height, then quite suddenly was no longer there. Shortly before dawn the mist cleared, and we were able to see, quite distinctly, all the seven volcanoes of the islands of Narborough and Albemarle, and to realize that what we had seen earlier in the night could not possibly have been Narborough. The only explanation we could offer to account for the phenomenon was that the "island" we saw was, in fact, the shadow of Narborough's volcano cast on the blanket of mist by the setting moon, which was almost full. As the moon sank, the shadow would have increased in height, to disappear completely and quite suddenly once the moon had set below the horizon—a sort of "Spectre of the Brocken" effect. Whatever the real explanation may be, there is no doubt that such phenomena might well augment the belief that the islands were "enchanted" or "bewitched."

It is clear from Edward Davies' journal that in 1684 the islands were already known to the Spaniards, not only as "Las Islas Encantadas," but also as "Las Islas Galápagos"—the Tortoise Islands. The giant reptiles were used not only by the buccaneers but also in the late eighteenth and nineteenth centuries by British and American whalers and sealers as a living stock of food. These seamen hunted in the rich, upwelling waters of the Humboldt Current, which flows northward from the Antarctic along the west coast of South America and then turns westward to sweep through the Galápagos archipelago (FIGURE 1). Thus the Galápagos area was a favorite spermwhaling ground from the late eighteenth century until the decline of the whaling industry in the 1860s. Also during the nineteenth century, tens of thousands of the Galápagos fur seal (*Arctocephalus*) were killed. One of the sealers, Captain Benjamin Morrell, states that he took five thousand sealskins in about two months (Morrell, 1932). Thousands of giant tortoises were removed from the islands during this period, as provisions. They were stacked, alive, one on top of the other, in the ships' holds, to be brought out and slaughtered as required, for their fresh meat and fine oil. It is said that the animals could survive for over a year in these conditions without food or water. Whalers' logs inspected by C. H. Townsend (1925) showed fifteen thousand giant tortoises recorded as being removed in this way by whaling ships between 1811 and 1844 alone. Probably well over a hundred thousand were taken; indeed, in large part the Galápagos tortoises made the Pacific whaling industry possible (Koford, 1966). The low, lava-walled "corrals" made by the sealers and whalers at this time for holding live tortoises are still to be seen near many beaches and anchorages in the islands.

About this time too, the islands were frequently visited by both British and American naval vessels sailing to and from the west coast of North America round the Horn. One of the most famous vessels in the Galápagos' history (always excepting H.M.S. *Beagle*) was the U.S. frigate *Essex*, which was a thorn in the side of the British whaling fleet in the early nineteenth century. In August of 1813, a midshipman (acting lieutenant) of the *Essex*, John Cowan, had an argument with a brother officer on board, Lieutenant Gamble of the marines. They went ashore at James Bay, James Island, to settle their differences in the time-honored manner on the beach, and as a result of the ensuing duel, young Cowan was killed. He was buried with full military honors, and Captain Porter of the *Essex* buried a bottle at the grave head. The bottle contained a letter for his first lieutenant, who, however, never returned to James. The grave was visited in the following year, but since then no one has been able to locate it. The bottle, with its contained letter, presumably must still be there, but all attempts to recover it have so far failed. Such episodes, often flavored with intriguing mystery, abound in the short history of the Galápagos.

Gamble was later given command of one of Porter's prizes, the *Greenwich*. One of the midshipmen on board this vessel was a young man, William Feltus, who kept a most interesting journal of his experiences with the fleet in the Galápagos. Feltus was later killed by natives at Nukuhiva in the Marquesas, but Gamble eventually returned to America and brought the boy's journal with him. The *Essex* itself was captured in Valparaiso by the British in March 1814, after it had practically destroyed the British whaling fleet in Galápagos waters, but no papers whatever were found on board. Gamble's own journal was destroyed in the fire following the San Francisco earthquake of 1906, but Feltus' journal, which Gamble brought back, survives.

Late in the eighteenth century a strange kind of "post office" was established on the island of Charles. This consisted of a barrel mounted on a post at what became known as "Post Office Bay." The barrel is marked on a chart, which is dated 1793, made by James Colnett of the Royal Navy. Letters left in the barrel by outgoing ships would be collected and delivered to England by the first inward-bound ship to call. In this way, letters could be posted to an address ten thousand miles away and delivered perhaps a year later. J. R. Slevin (1959) states that in 1832–33 thirty-one ships called at Charles, so that presumably the barrel was much used. It was kept in good repair by any ship that found its condition to be deteriorating, and was replaced from time to time. There is still a barrel at Post Office Bay, and it is still used occasionally in the original manner. The bearers of this unusual mail today, however, are the round-the-world yachts of various shapes and sizes that pass through the Galápagos on their way southwestward across the Pacific. Their skippers regard it as both an honor and a duty to carry this "mail" as far as they can, and then pass it on to another yacht whose course takes it toward the letter's destination. Passed on from one yacht to another, the letters are eventually delivered to addresses as far away as Europe.

In 1832 the archipelago was annexed by the newly independent country of Ecuador, and the islands were given

TABLE I.

Names of Galápagos Islands mentioned in text.
Name in common use by inhabitants is italicized.

ENGLISH NAME	OFFICIAL NAME	OTHER NAMES
Abingdon	*Pinta*	Gerandino
Albemarle	*Isabela*	Santa Gertrudis
Bainbridge		
Barrington	Santa Fe	
Bartholomew	*Bartolomé*	
Bindloe	*Marchena*	Torres
Brattle	*Tortuga*	
Caldwell	Caldwell	
Champion	Campéon	
Charles	Santa María	*Floreana*
Chatham	*San Cristóbal*	Dassigney, Grande
Cowley		
Crossman	*Los Hermanos*	
Culpepper	Darwin	Guerra
Daphne Major	Mosquera	
Duncan	Pinzón	Dean
Eden	Eden	
Enderby	Enderby	
Gardner-by-Charles	Jardinero	
Gardner-by-Hood	Jardinero	
Guy Fawkes		
Hood	*Española*	
Indefatigable	*Santa Cruz*	Bolivia, Norfolk, Porter, Valdez, Chávez, San Clemente
James	San Salvador	*Santiago*, Olmedo, Gil, York
Jensen	Coamano	
Jervis	Rábida	
Narborough	*Fernandina*	Plata
Onslow	Onslow	
Plaza	Plaza	
North Seymour	Seymour	
South Seymour	*Baltra*	
Tower	*Genovesa*	Ewres
Watson	Watson	
Wenman	Wolf	Nuñez, Gasna, Genovesa, Ewres

Ecuadorian names. Since English names, commemorating English royalty, aristocracy, admirals, naval vessels etc., had been given to them as early as 1684 (Slevin, 1955), each island now had at least two names. Some also already had names given to them by the Spaniards (for example, the name "Isabela" [Albemarle] dates from 1744), and the result today is that several islands have three or more names, and one even has eight. There is now a set of "official" Ecuadorian names, used by the government in correspondence, etc., and a set of English names, which are usually used in scientific works for the sake of continuity (TABLE 1). The local inhabitants have a "common" name for each island, which may be a name included in neither of the above sets. For example, the official name of the island called "Charles" by the English is "Santa María." However, no one in the Galápagos ever calls the island anything but "Floreana." In 1892, in honor of Christopher Columbus, the Ecuadorian government officially renamed the whole archipelago "Archipielago de Colon"; however, the group of islands is now so well-known by the apt name "Galápagos" that the official name is only used in government correspondence.

The most important episode in the history of the Galápagos was without doubt the short visit of Charles Darwin, who in 1835 spent five weeks in the islands as a young twenty-six-year-old naturalist on H.M.S. *Beagle,* the British survey vessel. During this short period of time, this remarkable observer and thinker was struck by the fact that although the Galápagos were similar to the Cape Verde Islands in climate and physical characteristics, the fauna and flora of the two archipelagos were quite different; however, in each case they were clearly similar to, but not identical with, those of the nearest continental areas. He concluded that living things had not been divinely created to fit their environments, nor were environmental conditions the only determining factor in the molding of new species. He also noticed that many of the recently introduced animals and plants were more successful in the Galápagos than the archipelago's original inhabitants. He thus realized that the latter were by no means perfectly adapted to all conceivable conditions, but rather that when their environment was changed, as by the introduction of other species of animals of plants, the indigenous living things were not particularly well adapted to the new and changed conditions.

Darwin noted, too, that although the Galápagos animals and plants were clearly related to those of the South American mainland, they nevertheless usually differed from them, sometimes in quite remarkable ways, sometimes only slightly. He found that different islands of the archipelago often carried their own distinct forms of particular groups of animals or plants, which, however, were clearly related to those forms on other islands of the archipelago. These facts he found explicable only on the theory that species can and do change, and are not fixed for all time, as they should be according to the theory of special creation. He realized that the Galápagos fauna and flora must have originated from those of the continent, and must later have become modified by the various environmental conditions on the separate islands. The Galápagos Islands were thus responsible for one of Darwin's major contributions—the demonstration that species are not unchangeable, specially created entities, but that they are subject to the process of evolution.

Darwin's second great contribution was the discovery of the way in which evolution occurs—by natural selection, although this idea did not crystallize until three years later, and was not published until twenty-one years after that, when he had amassed a huge body of supporting facts. However, his consideration of the Galápagos fauna, especially the finches, was largely responsible for the development of his theory. Two years after his visit he wrote: "In July opened first notebook on Transmutation of Species. Had been greatly struck from about the month of previous March on character of South America fossils, and species of Galápagos Archipelago. These facts (especially latter) origin of all my views."

The Galápagos Islands can thus lay claim to being the birthplace of modern biology. But they can surely claim more than that. With the publication of Darwin's "views," not only did biology become an integrated, evolutionary science, but, as the idea of evolution was applied to almost every field of knowledge, a real revolution in human thought was begun. A chain reaction was started, which, throwing off new sciences such as genetics, biochemistry and social anthropology on the way, has culminated in a new and harmonious view of mankind's own true significance in the universe.

Other notable visitors from the turn of the eighteenth century included Captain George Vancouver, who in His Majesty's ship-of-war *Discovery*, visited the islands in 1759. Lord Byron, in command of H.M.S. *Blonde*, dropped anchor in Tagus Cove, Albemarle, in 1825, on the way to the Hawaiian Islands with the bodies of the Hawaiian King Kamehameha II and his Queen. Both of them, not having been exposed to the diseases of civilization, had died of measles while on a short official visit to England. Herman Melville visited the Galápagos in 1841 and made it the setting for his short work *The Encantadas*, a fantastic interpretation of the islands, published in 1856.

The first permanent inhabitant of the Galápagos was an Irishman named Patrick Watkins, who lived on Charles in 1807 or thereabouts. He was either marooned or asked to be put ashore there, and he subsisted by growing vegetables which he traded with the whalers for sufficient rum to keep himself permanently intoxicated. Captain Porter, of the *Essex*, describes his "ragged clothes, scarce sufficient to cover his nakedness, and covered with vermin; his red hair and beard matted, his skin much burnt, from constant exposure to the sun, and so wild and savage . . . that he struck everyone with horror." Watkins had the habit of capturing visiting sailors at gun point and forcing them to be his slaves. Midshipman Feltus (see above) mentions in his diary that Watkins left Charles in 1809 by stealing a whaleboat while its crew were searching for water and tortoises ashore. He took with him five of his slaves, but reached Guayaquil alone. Whether he ate them, or simply disposed of them by pushing them overboard to conserve water, is not known.

The islands remained uninhabited until 1832, when General José Villamil, a native of Louisiana who had served Ecuador in the war of liberation, was granted permission by the newly independent country to found a colony on the islands. He chose Charles Island, and the colony prospered, selling meat and vegetables to the whalers, until, at the time of Darwin's visit three years later, about 250 people were on the island. Many of these were undesirables, convicts and the like, and Villamil and most of the original settlers soon afterward abandoned the colony and moved to Chatham, leaving only a few convicts and guards behind. Colonel Williams, in charge of the remnants, flogged them unmercifully and hunted them with dogs. During the inevitable revolt, Williams fled and the colony soon broke up completely. Within three years of the founding of the Charles colony, the domestic animals, which escaped into the wild, as well as the colonists, had reduced the tortoise population of that island to such an extent that expeditions were made to other islands for food.

In 1869, Chatham Island was recolonized by Manuel Cobos, who, with slave labor, founded a colony optimistically named "Progreso." The tyranny and cruelty of Cobos, who flogged and executed his workers when he saw fit, resulted in his being killed in his bed by the machetes of his slaves. Progreso remains today as an agricultural settlement on Chatham about three miles above Wreck Bay, the seat of government. A rough lava road, the only one of any length in the Galápagos, connects the two villages.

In about 1870, a certain Señor Valdizan obtained a concession to collect "orchilla," a lichen used to make dye and known as "dyer's moss," which was commonly found on many of the islands and was of considerable value. His colony of convicts was based on Charles. However, like Cobos, he was murdered, and his employees, after an orgy of violence, killing, and rape, either returned to Ecuador or joined the Chatham colony.

In 1893, Don Antonio Gil, a prominent citizen of Guayaquil, investigated Charles Island for the purpose of colonizing; but he decided against it and instead built a small village, Villamil, on the shore of southern Albemarle. He established a second village, called Santo Tomás, at about 2000 feet in the moist zone of southern Albemarle. By 1909 cattle had been introduced and roamed wild about the upper slopes of the volcano Sierra Negra. Two hundred or so colonists lived on the mountain and subsisted by selling cattle to the mainland and digging sulphur from the crater wall, transporting it to the beach by donkey.

In the early twentieth century, there was a promotion hoax. Norwegians were lured to Charles to start fruitgrowing and canning. After discovering that the island was not the fertile paradise that it had been painted, they stuck it out for only about a year; then some moved to Chatham and a few to Indefatigable, where they lived by selling vegetables to the tuna fleet that visited quite frequently. A few of them still remain on the islands of Indefatigable and Chatham.

During the Great War of 1914 to 1918, the Galápagos saw little excitement, the only visitor being the German Admiral von Spee who, while on the way to the Falkland Islands, stopped at Villamil to obtain fresh meat for the German Asiatic Fleet.

For the extraordinary sequence of events that occurred on Charles Island after the arrival of its first real settlers, Doctor Ritter and Dore Koewen, in 1929, the reader is referred to the biographical account of Mrs. Margret Wittmer, one of the small group of settlers who still lives on Charles with her family (and who, incidentally, personally supervises the mail service at Post Office Bay). The short "reign" of a polyandrous baroness, self-styled "Empress of the Galápagos," and the mysterious disappearances and unexplained deaths of several of those associated with her, make a fascinating story (Strauch, 1936; Wittmer, 1961).

The first aircraft to visit the archipelago came in 1934 in a dramatic rescue operation. William Robinson, a naturalist on the yacht *Svaap*, was stricken with appendicitis in Tagus Cove,

Albemarle. He managed to contact the *Santa Cruz*, a tuna boat in the vicinity, which used its radio to call for help to Panama. The U. S. Navy sent two seaplanes with doctors, and the destroyer *Hale*, to Tagus Cove. An emergency operation was performed on board, and Robinson's life was saved through the use of the newly discovered system of radio communication (Robinson, 1936).

During the Second World War the United States was permitted to build a strategic air base on Baltra, from which the approaches to the Panama Canal could be patrolled. A fine airstrip that survives today was built, but unfortunately most of the island's indigenous fauna was exterminated. Efforts by the United States to lease or purchase the islands were resisted by the Latin American countries, and the United States flag was eventually hauled down in 1946.

There are still small settlements on Charles, Chatham, and southern Albemarle. On Indefatigable there are small farming communities in the moist zone at Bella Vista and Santa Rosa, as well as quite a thriving community at Academy Bay. The airstrip at Baltra is still used occasionally, and an Ecuadorian military unit is stationed on that island. For the last few years two men have been stationed on James as custodians of the disused equipment and rights of an abortive commercial venture to extract high-quality salt from a crater near James Bay. Over a hundred men were originally employed in this concern. In all, there are now about 3500 inhabitants of the archipelago, most of whom are on Chatham, with smaller numbers on southern Albemarle, Indefatigable, and Baltra, and two families on Charles. The rest of the archipelago is uninhabited.

The strong and unpredictable currents, particularly in the northwest, deter most local skippers, who do not possess sextants, from venturing to distant islands in small craft which are equipped only with single engines of low speed. Sail is little used in the islands, for winds are unreliable and often very light. However, when the Charles Darwin Research Station's new research vessel is completed, interisland transport should cease to be a problem. Getting ashore can be difficult on some islands that lack suitable beaches, such as the cliff-girt northwestern islands, Culpepper and Wenman, particularly if there is a high swell. For beach landings, a light, flat-bottomed dinghy or "panga" (PLATE 1) is ideal; it can be maneuvered in very shallow water and easily pulled clear onto the beach and later refloated.

In general, the only certainty about transport, both between the Galápagos and the mainland and within the archipelago, is its uncertainty, and a strict time schedule is impossible to maintain. A very large allowance of time should be made for unpredictable contingencies.

In spite of these difficulties, it is possible to get almost everywhere on the archipelago given time and sufficient determination, and the rewards are well worth the effort.

In addition to Darwin's visit on the *Beagle*, there have been many visits of scientists and scientific expeditions to the islands. The first extensive plant collection was made as early as 1825 by the famous botanist David Douglas, on board the *William and Mary*, a brig of the Hudson's Bay Company. The great Harvard zoologist Louis Agassiz, a vigorous opponent of Darwinism, spent nine days on the archipelago on the *Hassler* in 1873. He returned to lecture at the California Academy of Sciences, not on evolution, but on the importance of natural history museums, and died in the following year, evidently without changing his views as a result of his Galápagos visit. George Baur, an early proponent of the theory that the present islands were formed as the result of the subsidence of a once much more extensive land mass, spent three months visiting twelve of the islands in 1891 and wrote extensively about the natural history of the archipelago. Six years later, the Webster-Harris Expedition was organized on behalf of Lord Rothschild, of Tring, England, who had become interested in the giant tortoises of the world. The expedition stayed for about eight months and returned with sixty living tortoises. Additional tortoises were secured for Lord Rothschild's private collection by Mr. Rollo Beck, on the schooner *Mary Sachs* in 1901.

The Stanford zoologists Edmund Heller and Robert E. Snodgrass accompanied a sealing schooner to the Galápagos in 1898, and returned with large collections of reptiles and plants from many of the islands; only 224 sealskins were obtained in a stay of over six months, and this was the last commercial sealing expedition to the Galápagos.

The most extensive survey of the archipelago ever undertaken was that of the expedition of the California Academy of Sciences, whose director, like Agassiz, was an opponent of the theory of evolution. Under Rollo Beck's leadership, the party sailed in the 85-foot sailing schooner *Academy* (after which Academy Bay on Indefatigable is named), and remained in the Galápagos for twelve months during 1905–6. Many young American biologists on board this vessel, such as E. W. Gifford, F. X. Williams, J. R. Slevin, and J. S. Hunter, subsequently became famous scientists. The collections they made were the most comprehensive ever, and remained so until recent years. During the visit, the 1906 San Francisco earthquake occurred, destroying the academy's museum and most of its collections; however, the material secured by the expedition was of such scope and value that the institution's position as a leading research-center was immediately restored. Since then the academy's interest in the scientific aspects of the archipelago has become traditional; its Galápagos collections are the largest in the world and its publications on Galápagos biology include many important scholarly works. The academy is generally considered the center of the research into the archipelago's natural science.

William Beebe, the great writer-naturalist and tropical biologist, journeyed to the Galápagos in the *Noma* in 1923, and again two years later aboard the *Arcturus*. His entertaining books, *Galápagos—World's End* and *The Arcturus Adventure* (Beebe, 1924; 1926), describing these voyages, were the inspiration of many subsequent visitors to the islands and a number of settlers.

Hans Hass led a Submarine Research Expedition in 1954, and

one of its members, I. Eibl-Eibesfeldt, was later asked to make a survey of the islands on behalf of UNESCO. He was joined by R. I. Bowman, and the result of their 1957 mission was the establishment of the present research station. A noteworthy by-product was Eibl-Eibesfeldt's excellent book *Galápagos—Noah's Ark of the Pacific.*

In 1959, appropriately enough on the centenary of the publication of Darwin's *Origin of Species,* the Charles Darwin Research Station was founded on a site near Academy Bay, Indefatigable. It was formally dedicated in January 1964, during the visit of over fifty scientists who were taking part in the Galápagos International Scientific Project. This expedition, which unfortunately stayed for only about five weeks in the Galápagos, included specialists in a wide variety of subjects.

The research station now provides facilities for visiting scientists, promotes the conservation and study of the Galápagos fauna and flora, and operates weather, seismographic, and oceanographic stations. The station is organized and operated by the Charles Darwin Foundation, an international foundation with headquarters in Brussels. The government of Ecuador has proclaimed the whole Galápagos archipelago a national park, and legislation protecting the fauna has been passed. These actions of the Ecuadorian government, together with the establishment of the research station, have given grounds for hope that this unique area of such absorbing interest to educated and inquiring man will be preserved in its natural state for the enjoyment and instruction of future generations.

CHAPTER TWO

The Islands

THE Galápagos Islands lie within an area about two hundred miles square, and the easternmost island, Chatham, is some six hundred miles west of the coast of Ecuador. The archipelago straddles the equator (which passes through the crater of Volcan Wolf, at the northern end of Albemarle) and extends to about 1° 20′ South (Hood Island) and 1° 40′ North (Culpepper Island) (FIGURE 2). The total land area is about 3000 square miles, the largest island (Albermarle) being about 75 miles long and somewhat greater in area than all the other islands together. There are four fairly large islands, Narborough, James, Indefatigable, and Chatham, eleven smaller ones, and numerous smaller rocks and islets.

"These islands at a distance have a sloping uniform outline, excepting where broken by sundry paps and hillocks; the whole black Lava, completely covered by small leafless brushwood and low trees. The fragments of Lava where most porous, are reddish like cinders; the stunted trees show little signs of life. The black rocks heated by the rays of the Vertical sun, like a stove, give to the air a close and sultry feeling. The plants also smell unpleasantly. The country was compared to what one might imagine the cultivated parts of the Infernal regions

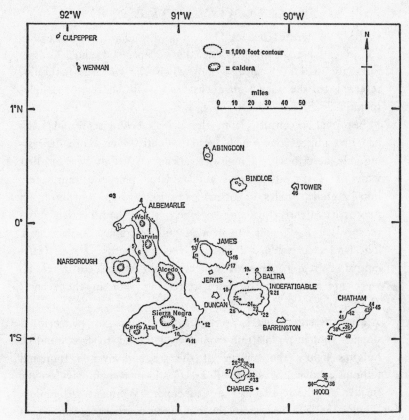

FIGURE 2. The Galápagos Archipelago, showing places mentioned in the text.

1. Punta Espinosa	17. Bainbridge Rocks	32. Caldwell Islet
2. Punta Mangle	18. Eden Islet	33. Gardner-by-Charles
3. Redonda Rock	19. Daphne Islet	34. Punta Suarez
4. Punta Albemarle	20. North Seymour	35. Gardner-by-Hood
5. Caleta Black	21. Plaza Islets	36. Punta Cevallos
6. Tagus Cove	22. Jensen Islet	37. Wreck Bay
7. Bolivar Channel	23. Academy Bay	38. El Progreso
8. Iguana Cove	24. Bella Vista	39. El Junco
9. Santo Tomás	25. Santa Rosa	40. Freshwater Bay
10. Villamil	26. Tortuga Bay	41. Sappho Cove
11. Brattle Islet	27. Black Beach	42. Cerro Brujo
12. Crossman Islet	28. Post Office Bay	43. Cerro Pitt
13. James Bay	29. Onslow Islet	44. Punta Pitt
14. Buccaneer Bay	30. Champion Islet	45. Pitt Islet
15. Sulivan Bay	31. Enderby Islet	46. Darwin Bay
16. Bartholomew Islet		

to be." So wrote Charles Darwin in his diary on September 16, 1835, when he first sighted the Galápagos Islands. Captain Fitz-Roy of H.M.S. *Beagle*, on which Darwin was naturalist, referred to the Galápagos coast as "a fit shore for Pandemonium."

Just over a century later, the British ecologist David Lack had first impressions which were evidently even more depressing. He describes the "inglorious panorama" that was his first view of Chatham: "Behind a dilapidated pier and ramshackle huts stretched miles of dreary, greyish brown thornbush, in most parts dense, but sparser where there had been a more recent lava flow, and the ground still resembled a slag heap. The land rose gradually, with no exciting features, to a sordid cultivated region, beyond which, partly concealed in cloud, were green downs, the only refreshing spot in the scene." (Lack, 1947).

The present islands rise from the Galápagos platform, a sloping submarine plateau from two hundred to five hundred fathoms below the surface of the sea and over a thousand fathoms above the ocean floor. A deep trench divides the smaller northern islands of Culpepper, Wenman, Abingdon, Bindloe, and Tower, from the remaining southern group which includes all the larger islands (FIGURE 3). The largest of these, Albermarle, consists of six separate volcanoes, five of them typical "shield" volcanoes with immense summit calderas (collapsed craters), while all the others, with the exception of Chatham, consist of a single large volcano and its subsidiaries. The volcanoes of Albermarle and Narborough are in a mature, active stage of development; the rest have progressed beyond this stage to varying degrees, and most of them lack summit calderas.

There is evidence of local uplifts, submergences, tilting and and erosion; the most recent uplift was in early 1954, when the west shore of Albermarle at one point rapidly rose fifteen feet, prior to the eruption some months later of the adjacent

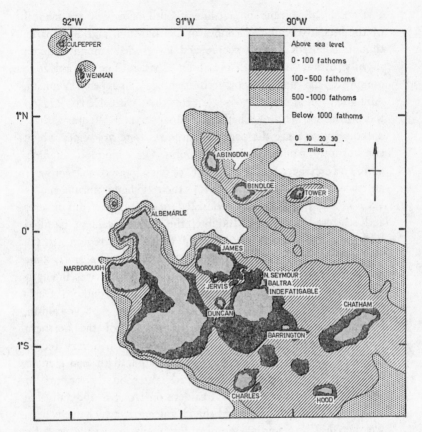

FIGURE 3. Bathymetry of the western part of the Galápagos platform.

Volcan Alcedo. Many local uplifts probably accompanied the growth of the Galápagos volcanoes.

McBirney and Aoki (1966) recognize three zones of the archipelago, each including islands with similar structure and rocks. The first of these is in the southwest and includes Narborough, Albermarle, and Charles. Charles differs from the other two islands, however, in the structure and composition of its lavas, and McBirney and Aoki found no evidence of either a large shield volcano or a caldera, both of which are typical of the recently active volcanoes of Narborough and Albemarle, though Richards (1962) recognized an eroded summit caldera slightly over a mile in diameter on Charles. The second zone comprises the line of northern islands, Culpepper, Wenman, Abingdon, Bindloe, and Tower, together with Cerro Pitt on the northeastern tip of Chatham. Culpepper and Wenman, these authors suggest, are the peaks of large separate volcanoes which rise abruptly from some 1200 fathoms. On Abingdon, Bindloe, and Tower, they found evidence of two periods of activity: an early period, responsible for their general form, and a very recent period, which consisted of eruptions from fissures and scattered vents. On Bindloe, the former caldera is filled with lava from recent eruptions in the summit region (PLATE 2), and this has overflowed down the slopes. The third zone comprises the central group of islands, James, Jervis, Indefatigable, Duncan, Baltra, Barrington, Hood, and southern Chatham. These are the products of an early phase of volcanism, possibly coincidental with the early activity of the northern group of islands. Of this group, only James has had very recent eruptions—the rest are extensively vegetated, with conspicuous faulting. There is a poorly preserved crater on the summit of Jervis, and a fairly well-defined caldera on Duncan. Indefatigable and south Chatham are broad-shield volcanoes which have been weathered; Baltra and Barrington are blocks of lava caused by faulting and do not have central volcanoes.

The highest volcano of the archipelago, Volcan Wolf (PLATE 3), is approximately 5400 feet high, while Cerro Azul, at the other end of Albemarle, is only slightly lower. All the volcanoes of Albemarle are over 3500 feet in elevation; that on Narborough is about 4900 feet and those of James and Indefatigable reach almost 3000 feet.

The summit calderas of the active volcanoes of Narborough and Albemarle are impressive. The Narborough crater is four miles wide across its major diameter and had a depth of about 2000 feet until 1968 when the floor of the caldera dropped hundreds of feet as a result of an explosive eruption in June. The largest caldera of Albermarle, Sierra Negra, is about eight miles across its major diameter and about 350 feet deep; the smallest, Cerro Azul, is two and three quarter miles across its major axis and possibly over 2000 feet deep. The active volcanoes are all of the shield type, with craters very wide relative to their heights, giving them a flat-backed, whalelike appearance in outline. The sides, notably of Narborough, Cerro Azul, and Volcan Wolf, are sometimes very steep; Wolf rises over 5000 feet in 1.8 miles, and slopes 35° in the upper 2000 feet. The flanks of these volcanoes are extensively covered with recent lava flows.

ORIGIN OF THE ISLANDS

Quite obviously, the Galápagos Archipelago is volcanic. Mc-Birney and Aoki described it as "a large archipelago second to none in the magnitude of its recent volcanism." Though all authorities are agreed on the volcanic nature of the islands, the actual mode of origin of the group is still shrouded in mystery, and controversy rages even today.

Most students of the Galápagos, whether geologists or biologists, fall into one of two camps. On the one hand, there are those who believe that the archipelago has at some time in the past been connected to the continent, while on the other hand there are those who maintain that the Galápagos Islands are truly oceanic and have never been connected to a continental land mass since the time that they emerged from the sea as a result of volcanic activity.

Recently, the latter school has gained the wider general acceptance, although it is itself divided into two groups. One group postulates that a larger land mass, originating in isolation from the continent, has partially subsided, thus resulting in the present group of islands. The other maintains, as did Darwin, that the present islands are the result of separate volcanic building processes.

Many authors have suggested former land connections between the Galápagos and the South American continent, or at least a series of island "stepping stones," to account for the present distribution of animals and plants. For example, E. C. Van Dyke (1953) suggested that the submarine ridge, Cocos Ridge, which extends at depths of less than 1200 fathoms from Costa Rica almost to the Galápagos Islands (FIGURE 1), was an isthmus connecting the Galápagos to the continent until the rise of the Andes. Recently a second submarine ridge, the Carnegie Ridge, has been discovered. This extends eastward from the Galápagos to the continent, with a depth of less than 1400 fathoms, and is separated from the continent only by the deep Peruvian trench and the continental shelf (FIGURE 1). The Carnegie Ridge has provided an additional basis for speculation on former continental connections.

K. W. Vinton (1951) has put forward the theory that the present group of islands is the result of the submergence of one large island of the Miocene era (from 28 million to 12 million years ago) and that this large "primitive Galápagos" was bathed by currents from the Caribbean flowing through the strait of Panama (there being no Panama isthmus at that time). Vinton also suggested that the Cocos Ridge was above the sea during Oligocene and Miocene times (from 40 million to 12 million years ago), and extended as a peninsula to within one hundred miles of the "primitive Galápagos" land mass. The ridge then became inundated, and it was only in Pleistocene times that Cocos Island was built on the crest of the ridge. Vinton's theory receives some support from the studies of Leleup on the cryptozoic fauna (see CHAPTER 4). Vinton estimated the age of Cocos Island as Pleistocene from the thinness of the soils, scarcity of beach deposits, and the character of the streams. The botanist A. Stewart (1911) had earlier concluded that Cocos Island was younger than the Galápagos Islands and that it has a typical oceanic flora, there being no evidence of a former connection between Cocos Island and the Galápagos. Vinton's theory is not at variance with Stewart's conclusions, and would account for the Central American and West Indian affinities of many Galápagos organisms.

G. B. Dalrymple and A. Cox (1968) recently analyzed lava samples from Cocos Island, and they found that the rocks are oceanic in character. It is thus unlikely that the Cocos Ridge is a submerged continental peninsula, which could have acted as a land bridge in the past. However, these investigators dated three flows on Cocos Island by the potassium-argon method, and found their ages to be about 2 million years. There is thus some overlap in the duration of volcanic activity in the Galápagos area (see below) and on Cocos Ridge, so that it is at least theoretically possible that Cocos Island may have served as a stepping stone for organisms in their dispersal from Central America to the Galápagos.

The distribution of several groups of animals and plants is harmonious on the archipelago, or at least on the central group of large islands. That is, representatives of the various groups of organisms occur on most of the islands, without any notable absences or disproportionate representation on any of them. Stewart believed that the Galápagos flora as a whole showed such an internal harmony, and examples can be seen in many of the endemic plant groups. The distributions of native rats, reptiles, and land birds too, are harmonious, as are the distributions of many of the insects, such as the ants, grasshoppers, beetles, and cryptozoic insects. Thus on *purely biological* evidence, the hypothesis that a once-continuous land mass has been dissected into several islands receives some support. This is particularly strong if one assumes that the northern line of islands, Culpepper, Wenman, Abingdon, Bindloe, and Tower, and the southeastern peripheral islands, Charles, Hood, and Chatham, were independent of the large central mass.

Banfield, Behre, and St. Claire (1956) found no evidence supporting either the theory that there were former continental connections or Vinton's theory of a once-continuous Galápagos land mass later split up into separate islands by subsidence. Instead, they put forward a "steppingstone" theory whereby volcanism has progressed successively southwestward from the South American continent, the earliest such volcanic islands being long since planed down by erosion after they became extinct.

However, as yet there is no evidence of former islands now beneath the sea between Galápagos and the South American continent. No guyots (flat-topped seamounts) have been found that would represent volcanic cones truncated by marine abrasion. Soundings along and across the Cocos and Carnegie ridges are insufficient at this time to provide evidence either for or against the steppingstone hypothesis. Moreover, there is as yet no geological evidence of either a general rise or a general subsidence of the Galápagos archipelago itself, however attractive such theories may be to the biologist wishing to account for the present-day distribution of species on the archipelago.

J. T. Wilson (1963) has proposed the theory that volcanic islands form over mid-ocean submarine ridges, that the volcanoes are initially active as they form over the ridges, then become extinct as they move away from them due to the convection currents set up by cooling. According to this author, such islands are moving at a rate of 3.5 cm. per year away from their parent ridges. On Wilson's theory, the Galápagos Islands have been moving away from the Cocos Ridge in an east-southeasterly direction, that is, toward the South American continent. However, the geological studies of Banfield and his colleagues led them to suggest a movement in the opposite direction.

Wilson's theory thus implies that not only the Galápagos Islands were originally farther away from the continent than they are now, but that they also should be progressively older toward the southeast. It is true that the southeastern islands, Hood, Chatham, and Charles, are the most eroded, and that the most recently active and highest volcanoes are those in the west, on Narborough and Albemarle. Volcanic activity in the past two hundred years has also occurred on the northwestern islands of Abingdon, Bindloe, and James. Nevertheless, the recent studies of Cox and Dalrymple (1966) suggest that this picture of progressive ageing in one direction, as is clearly shown in the Hawaiian Islands, cannot be substantiated by palaeomagnetic data.

Cox and Dalrymple have estimated the ages of samples of volcanic rocks from all the main islands of the Galápagos except Tower, Barrington, and Chatham. The estimates were made by using a combination of palaeomagnetic stratigraphy and potassium-argon dating.

The first of these methods is based on the fact that the earth's magnetic field has not always been as it is now, directed toward the north, but there have been in the past four million years two major periods (called polarity epochs) when the earth's field was completely reversed in direction, that is, oriented toward the south. These two epochs of reversed polarity were separated by an intervening epoch of normal polarity which lasted for almost a million years. The ferromagnetic minerals which are present in lava flows act as small magnets and become polarized when the lava cools. By examining the direction of polarity of a particular lava flow, it is possible to find out whether the earth's magnetic field was normal or reversed at the time when the flow cooled. The lava has a "magnetic memory" and can thus yield important information as to its age.

Because there was more than one epoch with normal polarity and more than one with reversed polarity, an ambiguity arises. A particular polarity could have been formed in either a late or an early epoch of that polarity, and additional independent evidence is required to assist in placing flows in the correct polarity epoch. The amount of erosion and faulting and the extent of vegetational cover often provide such additional evidence for young rocks, but in the Galápagos, which are arid and free from frosts, erosional differences of this kind are slight and thus of only limited value as corroborating evidence.

Cox and Dalrymple made potassium-argon analyses in order to obtain additional information. Radioactive potassium-40 decays to argon-40 at a constant rate, and by analyzing rocks for their contents of these isotopes, the ages of the rocks can be determined within certain limits. By combining this method with palaeomagnetic analysis, Cox and Dalrymple assigned lavas taken from forty-five sampling sites on fourteen islands to their polarity epochs. All but one of these samples were dated as having cooled within the past 2.4 million years, and the greatest age found by the potassium-argon method was 1.47 million years. One sample, from the Plaza Islets close to Indefatigable, which showed reversed polarity, was assigned to an older polarity epoch.

From Wilson's theory of oceanic island formation it would be expected that the oldest islands would be at the southeast of the group. The age relations of the various flows do not show such a clear-cut progressive ageing in one direction (TABLE 2). Although the older lavas do generally occur in the southeastern quadrant of the archipelago, nevertheless samples from the northwestern island, Wenman, consist only of rocks of the older group. Moreover, the oldest rocks of all occur near the center of the archipelago, and both young and old lavas occur on some islands, notably on Indefatigable, where some of the oldest and youngest flows in the Galápagos occur side by side. Sampling of the archipelago was not uniform; three islands were not sampled, and the western and northern islands were sampled less intensively than James, Indefatigable, and Charles.

Cox and Dalrymple point out that it is necessary to be cautious of interpreting these results as indicating the sequence of emergence of the islands. Older lavas may be completely overlain by more recent flows and thus inaccessible for study, and some of the lavas that have been sampled may have been formed beneath the sea a long time before the emergence of land.

All that can now be said about the geological history of the Galápagos Islands is that they probably originated not earlier than the late Miocene, about fifteen million years ago—marine fossils found on Indefatigable are possibly Miocene

(Durham, 1965)—and that the present subaerial volcanoes were probably built mainly during Pleistocene and Recent times, two and a half million years ago or less. Exactly when the volcanic activity first began, and the sequence in which the various volcanoes rose above the sea, is still not known.

TABLE 2

Relative ages of lava samples from the Galápagos Islands, showing number of samples in various polarity epochs (modified from Cox and Dalrymple, 1966).

POLARITY EPOCH OF SAMPLES

Islands (arranged roughly in order from NW)	Brunhes normal < .85 million years	Matuyama reversed .85–2.4 million years	Older (reversed)	Relative age of samples
CULPEPPER	1	—	—	young
WENMAN	—	2	—	older
NARBOROUGH	2	—	—	young
ALBEMARLE	2	—	—	young
ABINGDON	2	—	—	young
BINDLOE	2	—	—	young
JAMES	8	—	—	young
TOWER		not sampled		—
JERVIS	1	1	—	young & older
DUNCAN	—	2	—	older
BALTRA	—	2	—	older
INDEFATIGABLE	6	1	—	young & older
PLAZA	—	—	1	oldest
BARRINGTON		not sampled		—
CHARLES	5	4	—	young & older
CHATHAM		not sampled		—
HOOD	—	3	—	older

R. I. Bowman (1961) has made a useful division of the islands into two groups, based on ecological grounds. The first group consists of large islands, with a diverse flora, much of the area being above 1500 feet, and with two or more vegetative zones. This includes Albemarle, Indefatigable, James, Chatham, Charles, and Abingdon. Typical of this group is Indefatigable, on which Bowman recognizes seven vegetative zones. In the second group he places small islands, with fewer than a hundred species of vascular plants, most of the area below 1000 feet, and possessing only the arid vegetative zone. Islands placed in this group are Hood, Barrington, Baltra, Tower, Jervis, Culpepper, and Wenman.

Three of the islands do not fit nicely into either of these categories. Narborough is similar to the islands of the first group, but possesses a poor flora. Although it is 4900 feet in height, only eighty species of vascular plants had been found on the island by 1961, and twenty-nine of these species are also found on Albemarle. However, Narborough has been very little explored, and Bowman believes that its poor flora may be due in part to the recent volcanism and the fact that it lies in the rain shadow of Albemarle. As recently as June 1968, a multimegaton explosion occurred in the Narborough crater; it blew out a new hole a mile across and over 500 feet deep and resulted in a new lake (Colinvaux, 1968a, Anon., 1968). Vast areas of vegetation were overlain with volcanic ash. The effects of this eruption on the island's ecosystem are now being investigated. Bindloe is the seventh largest island of the archipelago, yet it is rather low (1125 feet) and has a poor flora of only forty-seven species of vascular plants. Because it is low, it receives less rain and has but one vegetative zone; moreover, much of its area is covered with recent lava flows. Thus Narborough may be regarded as an exception to the first group, and Bindloe to the second. The position of Duncan, however, is peculiar. It is small, but of moderate height (1502 feet); it possesses two vegetative zones and a varied flora of over one hundred species. There have been no recent lava flows.

The archipelago lies in the path of the Humboldt Current, which sweeps up the west coast of South America bringing with it the upwelling colder waters of the Antarctic, so rich in marine life that off the coast of Peru they support populations of sea birds of such density that their guano is a major natural resource of that country. Near the equator, this current swings out into the Pacific and passes through the Galápagos Archipelago (FIGURE 1). However, it is periodically displaced from December to May, when a warmer, less saline current, named "El Niño" (The Infant) because of its appearance at Christmastime, comes from the north. In about a dozen years of the last century and a half, "El Niño" has extended much farther south than usual, resulting in the death of large concentrations of fish close to the continent. This, in turn, has affected the vast populations of sea birds on the South American coast. During such a "Niño" year, unusual winds, storms, and cloudbursts occur in the Galápagos. From June to December, the Humboldt Current sweeps through the Galápagos, and the archipelago experiences its cool season. At this time, precipitation is low (average monthly rainfall less than 0.8 inches), sea temperatures are between 55° and 73° F, and air temperatures seldom rise above 77° F. During this season a fine mist covers the heights, and, although the moisture does not fall as rain, it thoroughly wets the vegetation. This is locally called the "garua," and June to December is known as the garua season. On the other hand, from December to May when the "Niño" has sway, precipitation is high (average monthly rainfall 1.0 to 6.0 inches), sea temperatures are high (77–95° F) and air temperatures higher than in the garua season. The rain during this season, though heavy, is intermittent, with dry, sunny spells, and precipitation varies tremendously from year to year. For example, in 1950, total rainfall at Wreck Bay, Chatham, was twenty-five times as great as it was in 1953. The buccaneers of the *Bachelor's Delight* even reported rivers on the islands in 1684; as Lack says, this was a "wet year"! There is also a considerable localization of this rainfall. N. Leleup (1965) quotes an example on Indefatigable where the summit received nine times as much rainfall in four days as did the Research Station on the south coast.

Low islands receive less precipitation than high islands, even in the form of garua. The prevailing winds are from the southeast; thus the southern slopes of the high mountains are moister, whereas the northern slopes are arid, like the low islands. Because of the porous nature of the volcanic rocks, the rain, where it falls, is rapidly absorbed, and not retained at the surface. The result is that there has been relatively little of the usual weathering process, and the soils are thin in general. There is only one permanent stream on the archipelago, at Freshwater Bay on Chatham, and on the other islands potable water is available for any length of time only on James, Charles, and two of the Albemarle volcanoes. The crater lake of Narborough has been known to dry up completely; although its water is sulphurous, it is drinkable. On all the smaller islands there is no fresh water, and large areas of the larger islands are virtually waterless.

Many of the higher islands have an interesting zonation of vegetation from shore to summit, particularly on the exposed southern slopes. Indefatigable demonstrates this to the greatest extent. There is a very short littoral (shore) zone, with the mangroves *Rhizophora* (red mangrove), *Avicennia* (black mangrove) and *Laguncularia* (white mangrove) predominating. This is followed by an arid belt, which extends up to about 500 feet and is characterized by the giant candelabra cactus *Jasminocereus*, the prickly pear *Opuntia*, and the usually leafless "palo santo" tree (*Bursera*), with the low grayish-leafed bushes *Croton* and *Maytenus*. A transitional zone follows, with the trees *Pisonia*, *Psidium* and *Piscidia* mixed with the cacti, and this is succeeded by a very dense and shady moist zone, in which *Psidium* and *Pisonia* are mixed with the cat's-claw tree ("uña gato") *Zanthoxylum* and the interesting woody composite *Scalesia* (a treelike relative of the sunflower and daisy), which is often dominant in this zone and found only on the

34

Galápagos. A so-called "brown zone" occurs above this, consisting chiefly of bushy *Psidium*, a smooth-barked guava. At about 1300 feet the *Miconia* belt begins. *Miconia robinsoniana* is a bush about six to ten feet high with leaves resembling cacao and is called "cacaotillo" by the inhabitants. It occurs nowhere else in the world, and forms pure stands of almost impenetrable vegetation. This zone is followed above 1600 feet by the "pampas," an open grassy summit zone with bracken (coarse ferns) and isolated clumps of tree ferns. The summit pampas zone is secondary, the result of widespread fires in the 1930s and 1940s.

The north face of Indefatigable, facing Baltra, is in the lee of the mountain, and here the dry zone is very much deeper, extending for about six miles from the shore.

Most of the high volcanoes have at least four recognizable zones, dry, transitional, moist, and grassy, but they do not all follow the same pattern. For example, a *Miconia* belt is present only on Indefatigable and Chatham. The lowest zone of Cerro Azul's south face at Iguana Cove is very thick, moist vegetation, which gradually clears through a bracken zone to ash and thick patches of *Scalesia* on the summit. A true summit pampas zone is absent from James, Narborough, and the volcanoes Cerro Azul, Alcedo, Darwin, and Wolf; and the summit of Abingdon is covered with an impenetrable mass of bracken and ferns, although small grassy patches occur about 400 feet below the summit. The lower, dry islands are characterized by prickly pears and palo santo, except that palo santo is absent from Duncan.

CHAPTER THREE

Sea Birds

SEA birds were possibly one of the earliest forms of life to colonize the barren Galápagos Islands. The birds depend for their sustenance, not on the land, but on the life in the sea. Some of them require plants for nest building, and these must have been later arrivals, but the majority make only a token nest on the ground and do not use plant material. Rocky plantless islands, which had no predaceous animals, would have provided colonial nest sites for these species, from which they could make their foraging expeditions. It is quite possible that they were instrumental in bringing to the islands plant seeds, small animals, etc., either externally, adhering to their feet or feathers, or internally, in their alimentary tracts.

THE BOOBIES

Perhaps the commonest, and also some of the most interesting, sea birds in the Galápagos are the boobies. These have recently been studied extensively on the islands by Doctor Bryan Nelson, who lived with them for twelve months. Much of the following section on the Galápagos boobies and frigate birds depends upon his observations.

"Bobo" is Spanish for clown or dunce, and presumably the

name "booby" derives from the rather "silly" way these birds have of allowing one to approach very close to them and the obvious difficulty they experience in taking off unless they are on the edge of a cliff or other prominence.

Most birds usually develop "brood patches" at the laying season. These are areas of the underside of the bird, and, in general, occur only in the sex that broods, unless both sexes sit on the eggs, in which case both develop brood patches. The patches are without feathers and are well supplied with blood vessels; in the sitting position they lie over the eggs, allowing heat to be transmitted from the bird's body to the eggs. Usually, the number of brood patches developed by a particular species is related to the number of eggs laid. Boobies never develop such brood patches. Instead, boobies and gannets incubate their eggs under their feet, which are well supplied with blood vessels and webbed between all four toes, whereas most other sea birds' feet are webbed only between three toes.

They are quite large birds, living in colonies of hundreds of individuals, and the young feed by taking their food directly from the crop of the parent. The adults fish by making spectacular plunge-dives into the water. A bird may be seen to stop in mid-flight, hover for a second or two, close its wings slightly and then dive perhaps fifty or sixty feet straight into the water like a javelin. Contrary to popular belief, the fish is not speared by the booby in its dive, but by the dive the booby gains speed and attains greater depth under water; it can then attack the fish from below. The fish is seized in the beak as the booby rises and is usually swallowed under water.

In the Galápagos three species of booby occur, the blue-footed (*Sula nebouxi*), masked (*Sula dactylatra*), and red-footed (*Sula sula*). Often two or sometimes all three of these species have closely adjacent colonies, and interesting comparisons can be made.

The Blue-footed Booby (PLATE 4), as its name implies, is characterized when adult by having bright, startlingly blue feet. It lives in dense colonies and "nests" on the ground. The nest is actually non-existent, although pairs do indulge in "nest-building" activity. The male brings material, a twig or feather, holds it up for the female to see and then carefully places it on the patch of ground regarded as the "nest." Both will solemnly play about with this, altering its position and so on. This behavior suggests that in the past the ancestors of this species built real nests, and it is still thought to have an important function in forming the pair-bond that will ensure that the pair stays together long enough to raise offspring. A behavior pattern that is advantageous to the species has thus been preserved.

Blue-footed Boobies often fish in groups, making synchronized dives into the water; there are even reports that the dive is made on a whistle signal given by one of the group. Dives can be made into very shallow water only a few feet deep, and there is one record of a blue-foot diving from a height of fifty feet into two feet of water, safely. Nelson (1968a) has suggested that the unusually long tail of the blue-foot allows the plunging bird to change direction extremely rapidly under water after its dive. Blue-footed Boobies restrict their fishing to the inshore shallows and can thus make short and frequent food-gathering trips of less than one hour's duration, enabling them to feed and rear two or even three chicks per brood.

The average egg-sitting stint of one of the parents is eighteen hours. The male is smaller than the female, about two-thirds of her weight, and yet has the same tail length. He can dive into shallow water faster than the female without hitting the bottom, and does his share of the fishing when the chicks are small. As the chicks get older and require more food, the female takes over almost completely. She can travel farther and bring back more food, and by this time the chicks are big enough to wait a little longer. Thus a division of labor develops between the sexes. The sexes also differ in the appearance of the eye. That of the female has dark pigment on the iris surrounding the pupil, which thus appears larger than that of her mate. They also differ in call: the male whistles, the female honks.

Near Cerro Brujo, on the northwest coast of Chatham, in

May 1967, we observed a very large school of yellow-fin tuna going after bait fish with such voracity that the water boiled and foamed. Blue-footed Boobies soon noticed this and not needing to plunge-dive, came down on to the surface in scores to gorge the bait fish. The bait fish were thus trapped between the predators above and below them.

In contrast to the blue-foots, Red-footed Boobies do actually make a nest, consisting of a platform of twigs, on the branches of bushes a few feet from the ground or even on branches on the ground itself. The nest is built by the female, from material brought by her mate. Two types of adult are found, in the same colonies, and both have bright red feet. Although the chicks are white (PLATE 5), the juvenile birds are brown and, as they age, some birds turn white again (PLATE 6) while others stay brown. In the Galápagos, the majority of adults are brown, with a blue bill and red feet and face. Nelson noticed that birds in the white phase tend to pair together, although W. L. Beebe (1924) remarked that mixed pairings were common. On Wenman and Culpepper there appear to be more birds of the white phase than on other islands. Exactly what the mechanism is that determines whether or not a bird will go through a white phase is not known.

The red-foots, again in contrast to the blue-foots, make long fishing trips several miles out to sea; they feed to a large extent on flying fish. Only one egg is laid, and because the sitting bird has to wait so long for the return of its mate (the average egg-sitting stint is 60 hours—maximum, 144 hours) the egg is often deserted, so that many chicks are starved because of the long trips and often poor catch. Thus one egg is probably as much as the parents can deal with. There is less social behavior than in the other two species, probably because colonies are not so dense and competition for nest sites is less severe. (A young Red-footed Booby will grip, when set on one's arm for example, whereas young of the other two species fall off; this is an obvious adaptation to a tree-nesting habit.) Colonies of Red-footed Boobies seem to inhabit the peripheral islands of the archipelago, Culpepper, Wenman, Tower, Chatham (Cerro Pitt), Gardner-by-Charles, Redonda Rock, and Punta Moreno of western Albemarle (FIGURE 4). At Cerro Pitt and Gardner-by-Charles, all three species occur. Possibly the peripheral distribution of the red-foots is related to the distance they have to fly to their feeding grounds.

The Masked Boobies are strikingly colored black and white,

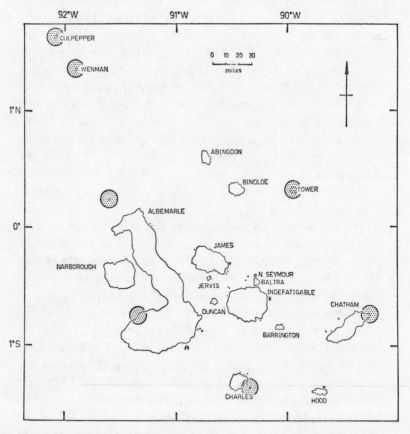

FIGURE 4. Distribution of Red-footed Booby colonies in the Galápagos.

with grayish feet, a yellowish beak and a black "masked" face (PLATE 7). In flight they are easily mistaken for the white phase of red-foots, although the red-foot has a continuous black band around the end of the tail, whereas the Masked Booby has the black tail feathers arranged in a V.

In most respects the behavior of the Masked Booby is intermediate with the other two species. Fishing is carried out about a mile or so from the shore, at distances more or less between those of blue-foots and red-foots. The female often lays two eggs, but they are laid five days apart, and one hatches five days before the other. The first-hatched chick is thus larger and stronger than the second, and physically evicts it from the "nest" so that it dies of starvation. The result is that only a single chick is raised. Nelson (1968a) noted that this sibling murder was carried out whether or not food was scarce at the time. Thus an interesting fratricidal instinct has evolved as a behavior pattern in the Masked Booby and ensures that one chick is raised to maturity. In contrast, the chicks of blue-foots were observed to quarrel only when there was a shortage of food, resulting in the death of the weaker.

In all three species, although the chicks grow tail feathers at fourteen weeks, they may not fly until the twentieth week, and even after that they return daily to their parents for food. Watching these birds for any length of time, one soon notices two fixed and striking behavior patterns. The first is "sky pointing," which occurs during courtship. The male slowly raises his beak and points it at the sky, at the same time half-opening his wings and rotating them so that the tips point upward. The second is a recognition signal given on alighting on the nest. The relieving bird will rock and nod its head from side to side, and thus be accepted to the nest and not treated as an intruder.

THE FRIGATE BIRDS

On the Galápagos, frigate birds are constantly in company with the boobies. Two species of frigates, the "vultures of the sea," occur on the islands—the Great Frigate Bird, *Fregata minor*, and the Magnificent Frigate Bird, *Fregata magnificens*. Although very light birds, they are fairly large, with a wingspan of about seven feet; when sitting they cross their wings swallowlike over their backs. Although their feet are small, unwebbed, and useless for walking or swimming, frigates can perch with great ease on twigs and branches, either with two toes forward and two back, or three forward and one back. The beak is about four inches long, strongly hooked, and has a sharp tip. It is perfectly adapted for snatching fish from just below the surface, picking up floating organic debris, or lifting twigs from the ground or from another bird, while in full flight.

Frigates are experts at using air currents and can soar for minutes on end without the least flapping of the wings. They have been recorded soaring at a height of 4000 feet, and have been seen as far as 1000 miles from land. They specialize in harassing boobies that have made a catch, sometimes even capsizing them in flight by seizing the tail or a wing tip and forcing their unfortunate victim to disgorge the contents of the crop in mid-air; they then swoop down to catch the loot before it reaches the sea. Apparently frigates have no way of telling when they first begin a chase whether their chosen victim has made a catch or not. However, Nelson (1968a) suspected that after the chase had been going on for a short time, the frigates in some way came to know whether or not the booby had a full crop. If it had, the frigates persisted in the chase, and were invariably successful in robbing the bobby of its meal. Nelson points out that the calls of full and empty boobies differ —after some time he was able to distinguish them himself— and suggests that the nature of the booby's call may serve as a clue to the marauding frigates.

From the very large populations present on some islands, for example Wenman, it seems almost certain that frigates also supplement this method of feeding by catching, in flight, fish that rise to the surface, and they have been reported catching flying fish before they drop into the water. They cannot do more than this, however, for a frigate cannot rise from the water, and certainly none ever land on the surface. Their very small preen gland is incapable of properly waterproofing the feathers, which become waterlogged if immersed. In the air, however, they are unsurpassed experts at effortless, graceful, soaring flight, yet are able to put on a turn of speed good enough to catch a fast-flying booby. Their characteristic long, forked tails can be trimmed this way and that, and opened and closed like scissors, to facilitate their elegant maneuvers. They are such efficient flying machines that practically half their weight is in the flight muscles, and their wingspan-to-weight ratio is the greatest of any sea bird.

The males are black, with iridescent green feathers and a red bare patch under the throat. Immature birds are easy to recognize since they have a white or yellowish head. The males of the two species differ very slightly in appearance, and only a real expert could tell them apart in flight. However, females of the two species can be distinguished fairly easily; the *minor* female is white from bill to chest and has a red ring round the orbit (PLATE 9), whereas the breast of the *magnificens* female is white, but with black on the throat and a black orbital ring (PLATE 8). Both species occur on Tower, Wenman, Culpepper, James (chiefly *minor*), Cerro Pitt on Chatham (chiefly *minor*), and western Albemarle, but only *magnificens* seems to be present on North Seymour, Daphne, and the islets near Charles, and only *minor* at Punta Cevallos (Hood). Where both species occur, the populations are kept separate and do not mix freely in the nesting areas.

R. W. Risebrough (1968) believes that the affinities of the Galápagos *minor* population lie to the north and west, whereas those of the *magnificens* race lie to the east. Since *minor* is "tamer" than *magnificens* in the presence of man, A. Brosset (1963) suggested the latter was the more recent arrival. Rise-brough discusses the coexistence of the two species on Tower, and suggests that certain species characteristics result in a re-duction of competition between them. *F. minor* in other areas nests in trees and bushes, or, where these are absent, on the ground. On Tower, *minor* invariably nests on low bushes or a small elevation of the ground, whereas *magnificens*, which elsewhere in the archipelago is a tree nester, always nests at a height at least three feet above ground. Individuals of *magnificens* are larger than those of any other frigate species, and those of the Galápagos race are larger than those of any other *magnificens* population. Thus the *magnificens* individuals have more difficulty in taking off from the ground or low nests than do those of *minor*. As well as this difference in nesting sites, there also seems to be some segregation of feeding grounds. Although *magnificens* is outnumbered ten to one by *minor* on Tower, it is the commoner coastal feeder, *minor* being much more pelagic.

Wonderful as these birds are to watch in the air, their behavior at mating surpasses even this as entertainment. At this time, the male slowly inflates the bare patch under the throat by transferring air from his air-sac system, until a taut, bright red balloon the size of a melon is developed under his chin (PLATE 9), the whole process taking about twenty minutes. He sits with his head propped skyward by the pouch, with wings outstretched, and waits until a female of his species flies overhead. The white throat markings of the females of the two species make them distinguishable from below, and males of one species do not react to overflying females of the other species. When the right females do fly over, he upturns and vibrates his outstretched wings, and rocks his head from side to side, at the same time uttering a peculiar, high-pitched, clucking sound. If the female ignores him, he relaxes and waits for the next. The presence of one displaying *minor* male will attract others, and over the trees and bushes close groups are formed of such males, all displaying and ululating together as the females pass overhead.

At last a female is enticed down to such a group, for the visual and auditory stimulation of the combined display must be tremendous. As soon as the female arrives, a harsh rattling sound is included as a component of the display of the excited males.

She selects one of her competing suitors—who, incidentally, are not antagonistic toward one another—and begins to respond by making a poor imitation of his sounds and wagging her head from side to side. Some of the unsuccessful males may now move off, perhaps to join another more effective group, or, less likely, to form the nucleus of a new one, while others may stay and persist in their efforts to entice a female.

It is only after pair formation has begun that the nest is built. It consists of an untidy platform of twigs (PLATE 9) usually constructed on any low shrub, although on North Seymour and on Hood frigates have been seen nesting on the ground. The nest material is collected in flight, sometimes torn from bushes, but more usually robbed from a Red-footed Booby or even another frigate. Until the single egg is laid, the collection of nest material is done by the male, although the female does most of the actual building.

Incubation in *minor* takes fifty-five days, and the male takes a good share of this duty, although the female's initial stint prior to and immediately after egg laying may be as long as a fortnight. Male and female each take three spells during incubation, and each time they lose a fifth of their weight. During incubation, the male's pouch deflates slowly, until it is just a small shriveled patch of skin under the throat, although, occasionally, males can be seen flying about with the pouch inflated.

Nelson has concluded that the crucial factor in the breeding biology of frigates is the scarcity of their food supply, which brings enormous problems in the feeding of the young. *F. minor* breeds only every other year on Tower, and part of the colony breeds one year, part the next, thus halving the difficulties of a very bad food supply in any one year. According to Risebrough (1968) reproduction is well synchronized in *minor* but continuous in *magnificens*, which is less pelagic. The young frigate has a slow, long period of growth, and takes food only from the crop of its parents until it is almost a year old. Even after this, while it is gaining flight experience and proficiency in piracy, it still feeds partly from its parents for some time. The long breeding cycle means that it is difficult for pairs to stay together for successive breeding cycles, and the fidelity to both nest site and mate over the years, as well as the defense of territory, are much less developed in frigates than in boobies.

In April of 1967, while camped on the edge of the *Junco*, an upland fresh-water lake in a crater on southern Chatham, with Doctor Uno Eliasson, a Swedish botanist, and his wife, we noticed that the frigates kept diving to the surface of the lake and skimming the surface for a second, as though fishing. The presence of fresh-water fish on these oceanic islands in this upland body of fresh water would have been interesting to say the least, and we soon realized that they were in fact drinking or bathing. After touching the water, a bird would again gain height, take two or three quick flaps while "marking time," as it were, then "shrug" its shoulders and fall, with its wings half-folded and held at a backward angle of 45°. The wings rustled and quivered as they moved through the air without resisting it and the air rushed through the opened feathers— the sound was reminiscent of a snipe "drumming" in Britain. The bird would flatten out near the surface, and give the tail one or two shakes. When this maneuver was performed over the lake, small droplets of water could be seen ringing the calm surface, and we realized that the bird was simply drying off in this way, rather as a dog shakes itself after getting wet. Birds would also "slide" down to the lake at an angle, against the wind, with half-closed wings. Their line of approach was immediately over our tents, and the sound was rather like jets coming in to land, and quite different from the sound made during the "drying" maneuver. About twenty frigates performed for us in this way each morning and evening.

THE BROWN PELICAN

The Brown Pelican, *Pelecanus occidentalis*, is a feature of the landscape around the Galápagos shores (PLATES 10 and 11).

Although the smallest of the pelicans, it is one of the largest birds in the islands, with a wing span of six to seven feet, and like most of the "wild" animals and birds, will allow a very close approach. It is to be seen near wharves and anchorages, and even nests within twenty yards of the Research Station's dining room at Academy Bay on Indefatigable.

The Brown Pelican nests in mangroves, usually *Rhizophora*, although I have seen it nesting on rocks on the shore of Barrington sound, when Doctor DeVries and I nearly stepped on two chicks after dark one evening. The bird is majestic in flight with its neck folded over its back, using its great wings sparingly, two or three flaps to gain height, then a long shallow glide, and again a few flaps. It plunge-dives rather awkwardly and slightly spirally into shallow water, and bobs up quickly to drain the pouch of sea water by tilting its bill; then flinging up its great beak, it releases the fish which is caught and swallowed. Thus the pouch is not used to store food, merely to catch the fish and retain it until the pelican surfaces. The bird also fishes by swimming on the surface and shooting its head down into the water. Adults can be distinguished easily, since they have a white head, while the immature birds have a brown head. The form in the Galápagos is slightly different from that on the mainland and has been described as an endemic subspecies.

TERNS

The Noddy Tern, *Anoüs stolidus*, breeds on the archipelago and is fairly generally distributed. This dark bird, with a somewhat paler head, can be seen often in small groups on rocky shores but more usually in small flocks hovering over the water as they gather food from the surface. The Sooty Tern, *Sterna fuscata*, has a large breeding population on the plateau of Culpepper, where it is difficult to walk without treading on the birds or their eggs (Cavagnaro, 1965; Fosberg, 1965). This bird sometimes also breeds on the neighboring island of Wenman.

The Audubon's Shearwater, *Puffinus l'herminieri*, is most usually seen in flocks of fifty or so at sea, as it skims along with rapid wingbeats close to the waves, often between troughs. This, like the Brown Pelican, is regarded as being an endemic subspecies, confined to the archipelago.

THE RED-BILLED TROPIC BIRD

Nesting in cliffs on Hood, Tower, Indefatigable, South Plaza and other islands, and on the outer slopes of the crater which is Daphne Island, is the world-wide Red-billed Tropic Bird, *Phaëthon aethereus*, which lays its single egg in holes or burrows in the cliffs. With its long, streaming "tail," consisting of two long white feathers, and its rather hurried, pigeonlike, fluttering flight, this white bird reminds one of the fairground "birds" with long revolving tails which children used to swing on the end of a string. The tropic bird is a plunge-diver, and is named after Phæthon, the son of Apollo who fell from the sky into the sea. It is wide-ranging; birds banded in the Galápagos have been recovered off the coast of Peru and in the Gulf of Panama (D. W. Snow, 1967). D. W. Snow (1965b) found evidence of a definite breeding season (September to January) in the small population of probably less than fifty pairs on South Plaza islet, whereas no such pattern was discernible on Daphne, where a considerably larger population breeds, and where there is competition for a limited number of nest holes.

PETRELS

Three species of storm petrels occur in the Galápagos—the Madeiran Storm Petrel, *Oceanodroma castro*, which is worldwide, the Galápagos Storm Petrel, *Oceanodroma tethys*, which has distinctive races in the Galápagos and off the coast of Peru, and Elliot's Storm Petrel, *Oceanites gracilis*, the Galápagos population of which is also an endemic subspecies. All are velvety black, about the size of a swallow, with a white patch on the rump and forked tail (PLATE 12), and have a musky smell. *O. gracilis* has a batlike, flitting and gliding flight a few inches above the waves, and when feeding, the birds hover, paddling lightly on the water with their webbed feet, and occasionally dive. The word petrel, incidentally, is supposed to derive from St. Peter, who walked on the waves. This species is the commonest of the storm petrels in inshore waters and surprisingly has not yet been found breeding. In Peru, it has a close relative that also has not been found breeding. *Oceanodrama castro* and *Oceanodroma tethys* are truly oceanic, and have different flight and feeding behavior. Both of these petrels breed on Tower, and sometimes also at Isla Pitt, North Chatham. *O. castro* also breeds on Plaza, Daphne, Cowley, Onslow, and Guy Fawkes, an islet just north of Bartholomew. The two *Oceanodroma* species were intensively studied by Harris from 1965 to 1967 (Harris, 1967, 1969d). He suggested that the two species are ecologically isolated, and do not actually compete for food. Their times of feeding are certainly different, *O. tethys* being a night feeder, and the type of food taken and the feeding areas may also differ. *O. tethys* takes smaller fish, and probably restricts its feeding to the cooler waters of the Humboldt Current, whereas there are indications that *O. castro* might prefer the more oceanic waters to the west of the Galápagos.

Harris has shown that on Plaza, *O. castro* exists as two apparently morphologically identical populations, which each breed annually, but six months out of phase, so that one population breeds in the cold season and one in the warm season. Moreover, the two populations use the same nest sites, and even failed breeders and non-breeders remain faithful to the cycle. Thus it is possible for a large number of birds to make use of a limited number of nest sites. Harris points out that this situation, which may well be unique among birds, could give rise to divergence of the two populations without any spatial isolation. In contrast, *O. tethys* breeds in the colder months, although a very few eggs were laid by the large Tower colony in the hot season.

O. tethys has a very dense population on the small islet Isla Pitt, near Cerro Pitt, North Chatham. Since it is a night feeder, its display and mating behavior occurs during the day, and can be more easily studied than that of the other storm petrels, which usually display at night. This small rocky islet is extraordinarily rich in animal life. It is the home of several sea lion families, including some of the largest bull sea lions in the archipelago with their harems, Fork-tailed Gulls, Red-footed Boobies, frigate birds and marine iguanas. In the early morning a dark cloud is formed over the islet by the small, White-rumped Petrels returning to their nests. They nest in holes under stones, but as the population density builds up and all these sites become occupied, they will nest even under bushes.

Nelson (1966b, 1968a) has described very dense prolonged flights of individuals of both *tethys* and *castro* on Tower, which he noted were not "house-hunting" flights or mating flights. The birds inhabit a mass of passages and chambers beneath the thin lava crust, and a constant noise of muted calling can be heard from under the lava. Above the lava, hundreds of twisting, turning birds fly about like a cloud of gnats, occasionally even colliding with one another, so dense is the swarm of birds. This occurs from dawn until dusk, daily, for months, and individuals remain in flight for long periods without alighting. Nelson suggested that these peculiar flying displays *could* possibly be a form of "epideictic" behavior, whereby a population indulges in some form of activity in order to obtain information about itself and thus regulate its size before the wasteful method of food limitation sets in. However, Nelson believed that both species were involved in the flights, and thus discounted this explanation. Harris has also observed these displays, and believes only one species to be involved—*O. tethys*. He points out that the huge population of this species occupies only a small fraction of the available habitat on Tower. One possible explanation is that these dense flights affect the gonads of individuals either visually or auditorily via the endocrine system, so that some birds do not lay when normally they should. Such individuals would not consume energy in wasteful egg laying and rearing, but would produce fewer offspring than they would if the population were regulated by food limitation —in fact, they would not lay at all. Thus the behavior would be disadvantageous to the population in the short term as far as actual numbers are concerned. In the long term, however, probably the two regulatory mechanisms would achieve about the same end result, although the behavioral-limitation mechanism would be less expensive in terms of mortality and energy than would regulation by food limitation.

Some authorities believe the large congregations of starlings in certain British towns to be such epideictic groupings. V. C. Wynne-Edwards (1962), who is chiefly responsible for elaborating this theory, also suggests that the vertical movements of plankton may be an example of the same phenomenon.

There is no evidence for this explanation of the dense flights of these petrels in the Galápagos. It seems that the birds involved in the peak of display on Tower are in fact non-breeders, and on Isla Pitt there is no evidence that any birds at all fail to breed. Thus the display has no obvious advantage either for individual birds or for the population. The functional significance of the behavior, which of course involves the consumption of a great deal of energy, is, as yet, unknown.

The Hawaiian Petrel, *Pterodroma phaeopygia,* which is otherwise restricted to the Hawaiian Archipelago, nests in thick vegetation on the wet uplands of Indefatigable, Chatham, Charles, James, and Albemarle, although eggs have only been found on Indefatigable. This petrel, also known as the Dark-rumped Petrel, is about fifteen inches long from the tip of the bill to the tail, and is white beneath, with white forehead and cheeks. The back, upper wings and tail, and crown of the head, are dark. The birds nest in long horizontal burrows, at the end of which a single egg is laid. They can only shuffle about on land, for their legs are too weak to support fully the weight of the body. When moving in the burrows, the whole of the lower part of the leg rests on the floor of the burrow, and the folded wings

are also used to help move the bird along. The petrels feed at
sea on fish, squid and other marine animals during the day
and have a characteristic, lazy flight close to the water. After
sundown they return to tend the nest, and their strange calls,
rather like the barking of a small dog, can be heard as they
fly over the coast in the evening. On the Hawaiian island of
Maui, these birds nest in the great eroded crater of the volcano
Haleakala, and their calling can be heard for two hours or
more as they circle in search of their burrows after dusk. Adult
birds return to the ocean before sunrise, and on Sierra Negra,
Albemarle, are known as "los vaqueros" because of their activity
at about 4 A.M. when the cowmen are waking up. On Indefatigable, wild pigs are a menace to the petrel, for they destroy
its burrows by their rooting activities, and eat both adults and
young. Harris (1970) found that adults on Indefatigable were
preyed upon by the Short-eared Owl and feral dogs. Cats also
probably take a toll of the young petrels, but introduced black
rats appear to be the chief predators. Harris found that in 1966
and 1967, out of a minimum of sixty-seven eggs laid, only
four young fledged, and the species must be regarded as being
in great danger.

The Albatross

Five sea birds are endemic to the Galápagos, that is, they breed
nowhere else. They are the Waved Albatross, Galápagos Penguin,
Flightless Cormorant, and the two Galápagos gulls.

Albatrosses are related to petrels and shearwaters. The nostrils
of all these birds are in short tubes on the top of the bill. The
word albatross is thought to be derived from "alcatraz," the
name given by the Spaniards and Portuguese to all large sea
birds, particularly pelicans. The Waved Albatross, *Diomedea
irrorata* (PLATE 13) breeds only on Hood Island in the extreme
southeast of the archipelago. It weighs about eight pounds and
is the size of a large goose, but it has an eight-foot wingspan.
It is thought to stay at sea for two years, ranging from Panama

to Peru, before returning to Hood to breed every other year (Nelson, 1968a), or sometimes in succeeding years (Lévêque, 1963). The life span is probably at least twenty years.

Lévêque (1963, 1964) has estimated that there may be two to three thousand breeding pairs of albatrosses. On Hood there are two breeding areas, one at Punta Cevallos, and another near Punta Suarez at the other end of the island. Egg laying begins in April, and the last young leave the colony in January (Harris, 1969a). In 1965, the breeding colony was subjected to attacks by swarms of mosquitoes which severely curtailed breeding for that year, most of the eggs being abandoned (Peterson, 1967). Harris points out that this and other recorded "bad years" coincide with unusually heavy rainfall. This may be the result of increased sea temperature, which may also affect the birds' food supply, and unusually heavy rains may also result in unusually high populations of mosquitoes.

The albatross is interesting for its peculiar courtship ceremony, which has been described by Eibl-Eibesfeldt (1959).

The birds dance opposite each other, heads moving in time with side-stepping leg movements, the bill pointing downward touching the shoulder. They stop, facing each other, and with slight, rapid sidewise movements they rub and click their bills together. Suddenly one raises its beak to the sky with a low-pitched cry or opens and closes its bill, snapping the upper and lower mandibles together with a pronounced clicking sound. Then the two birds continue to strike their bills together or the dance begins again. From time to time both birds bow to each other, the neck stretched and the beak pointing to the ground or perhaps only one bird bows. Meanwhile they call a deep "go go go go" in rapid succession or they clatter with their mandibles. This appears to be a ritual pointing to the prospective nesting site. Often after these bowing movements both partners settle on the ground and may start rubbing their beaks or begin "social grooming," nibbling each other alternately on the neck or chin.

Unfortunately I have never observed this courtship, although on several occasions in May I have seen individual albatrosses, with occasional flaps of their great wings, sailing low over the water off the coast of Chatham. Albatrosses are, of course, the most famous of dynamic soarers. Wind speed over the sea is slowest near the surface, and increases up to about fifty feet above the surface. Albatrosses make use of this by gliding at speed against the wind. As they glide higher, their ground speed falls off but, because they are now gliding into wind of a higher speed, their air speed does not fall and they can continue the glide without stalling. At the top of the glide the birds turn and glide down the wind, increasing their speed until, near the surface of the waves, they swing back into the wind and soar up again under their own momentum. Albatrosses can glide for hours like this, and the stronger the wind, the better for dynamic soaring. The structure of their very long, slender wings, combining large span with low drag, makes normal wing-beating difficult. Once they have settled on a calm sea they find difficulty in taking off, flapping awkwardly and paddling with their legs for long distances; if full-fed they often lighten their load by disgorging food. In a slightly rough sea, however, they easily become air-borne by floating to the top of a wave and opening their wings into the wind. The same difficulties apply to taking off from flat land in calm weather.

The albatross colonies on Hood are not, as one might expect, near to the cliffs but, rather, some distance inland on flat land providing a runway for take-off and landing. Many accidents occur, particularly on landing, since the high aspect ratio of the long and narrow albatross wing gives it a high stalling speed, and it must come in to land at considerable speed on a "runway" strewn with large boulders and bushes. Nelson (1968a) noted evidence of many landing accidents.

The single egg weighs half a pound, and there is no nest whatsoever. The chick is covered with brown down and is brooded only for the first fortnight; after this it is left unguarded and shelters under bushes in company with others, in a hollow which it excavates by backward movements of the feet. The chick is fed on an oily secretion produced in the proventriculus, a part of the parent's stomach. This rich secretion is forcefully regurgitated by the parent and squirted into the chick, in response to the latter's begging behavior. The chick may be fed as much as four pounds of oil at one feeding, and visibly swells during the process (PLATE 14). After a big feed the chick can't even stand properly, but waddles about on its tarsi.

This method of feeding means that, unlike the parent booby for example, the parent albatross does not have to return quickly to the young to prevent digestion of the raw food, but can stay for days at sea, manufacturing "chick oil" which will not be digested or assimilated before it returns. Although some chicks may be fed every day for a week, others may go unfed for a week; most usually get a meal once every two or three days, and a parent bird may thus be out at sea feeding for almost a week without returning. The chick and the returning parent recognize one another by call, as is the case with sea lions.

D. Snow reports an albatross, ringed as a nestling on Hood, being shot off the coast of Ecuador three months later; another, which was also ringed as a nestling on Hood, was found dying on a beach in Esmeraldas, Ecuador, only a month later. Thus the young albatrosses set out to sea very soon after fledging. Other albatrosses do not return to be fed once they have ventured to sea, and probably the Waved Albatross juveniles also make a clean break with land. Since the death rate of chicks between hatching and fledging is apparently very low, and the adult death rate is also low, Nelson believes that this transition from the security of its parents' attentions to an independent life at sea is probably the most vulnerable stage in the life of the albatross, and that only a proportion must survive it. Those birds that do survive apparently do not return to Hood until their third year, and even then probably do not breed. A bird ringed as young in November 1961 was recaptured in December 1966, when its plumage suggested it had not bred in that year; the same bird was found incubating an egg in July 1967 (Harris,

1969a). This is the first Waved Albatross of known age to have been found breeding.

THE GALAPAGOS PENGUIN

The penguin of the Galápagos, *Spheniscus mendiculus* (PLATE 15), is closely related to the Magellan Penguin of southern Chile, the Falklands, and islands near Antarctica, and its presence is testimony to the effects of the cold Humboldt Current sweeping through this tropical archipelago. It is one of the smallest of the penguins, and also the one which occurs the farthest north, breeding as it does on the equator itself. Breeding appears to be restricted to the shoreline of Narborough and the coast of Albemarle opposite, in the cold waters of the Bolivar Strait, and also to the north coast of Albemarle. Ziswiler (1967) gives a population estimate of five thousand individuals, although Lévêque (1963) estimated their numbers as about fifteen hundred. At night their peculiar high-pitched barks can be heard from both sides of the Bolivar Strait.

The penguins nest in small groups. The nest, consisting of a few stones arranged in a circle, is made deep in cool, shaded caves near high-tide mark. For Galápagos animals, they are quite shy, diving rather clumsily into the water when approached to within a few yards. When swimming they often leap clear of the water in the manner of dolphins. Normally, two eggs are laid, during the cooler months of May to August. The young are covered with a fluffy brown down and make a strange contrast with the adults in their black and white "evening dress." Penguins swim quite slowly and rather clumsily on the surface, with short sharp strokes of the flipperlike wings. Submerged, they "fly" through the water at a surprising speed, using their feet as rudders. It is thought that penguins may have evolved from the same stock as the albatrosses. Both have beaks made up of a series of horny plates instead of a single continuous sheath.

THE FLIGHTLESS CORMORANT

The most peculiar bird of the Galápagos, and one of the strangest in the world, also occurs on the two shores of the Bolivar Channel. This is the Flightless Cormorant, *Nannopterum harrisi.* Cormorants, like boobies, frigate birds, and pelicans, and unlike other web-footed birds, have the back toe joined by a web to the other three. All these birds also have throat pouches, which are of course very large in the pelicans.

Although the largest of the cormorants, the Flightless Cormorant has only rudimentary wings (PLATE 16) and is quite incapable of flight. This is one of the few flightless birds in which loss of flying ability is not necessarily a disadvantage. Like the penguin, which is of course also flightless but whose wings have become modified into swimming flippers, it obtains its food underwater. Normal cormorants, when traveling fast underwater, keep their wings closed, and the body is propelled by simultaneous strokes of the bird's feet. Thus, unlike the penguin, the Flightless Cormorant does not use its wings for any sort of propulsion. The keel of the breastbone, to which the wing muscles are attached, and which is well developed in flying birds and in the penguin, is completely lacking in the Flightless Cormorant. When swimming at the surface, the cormorant sits deep in the water, often with only the head and neck above the surface.

The birds show no fear of man and can be observed at close range taking turns at shading the young in the shallow nest of seaweed and guano. They are somber, untidy-looking birds, with small green eyes and can be seen "panting," with open beaks and vibrating throat pouches, on warm sunny days, or spreading their stumpy wings to dry after returning from the water (PLATE 17). Clearly, wing drying was a form of behavior which was advantageous in the species' evolutionary past, when the wings were used for flight. Once its wings were dry the bird would be able to take off immediately if there was danger.

Although the wings are now useless for flight, the habit has persisted in the species, probably because it brings no disadvantage to the species in the present environment of the Galápagos, and may even serve a useful function, possibly in heat exchange.

Barbara Snow studied forty pairs of these birds between Caleta Black and Tagus Cove on the eastern shore of the Bolivar Channel in 1963 (B. K. Snow, 1966). Certain features of their behavior are of particular interest to the student of evolution.

Breeding takes place in small scattered groups of from two to about ten nests, from April to December, at a time when the Humboldt Current, bringing colder water to the archipelago with a stronger flow, causes increased eddies and upwellings with a resultant increase in plankton and marine organisms.

The Flightless Cormorant is unique among cormorants in that courtship begins in the sea. In the other cormorants, the early stages of courtship and mate selection take place on land. In the Flightless Cormorant, the swimming male and female go through a striking rhythmic display which Snow calls the "aquatic dance." Both birds swim around or back and forth past each other, bending their necks into a characteristic snakelike position and making a growling call by inhaling air. After a few such passes, first one and then the other of the pair raises itself half out of the water, pointing its head and beak upward, flapping its wings and shaking itself. Later, the male leads the way ashore with his tail cocked out of the water and periodically turning his head and "snake-necking." Snow noticed that although other birds frequently interfered with the completion of the aquatic dance by joining the pair and attempting to take part, at no time did a third bird interfere with a pair courting on land. She concluded that although courtship on land, chiefly at the nest site, is much more prolonged, and leads to a final securing of the pair-bond, the early and important stage of courtship, pair formation, takes place during the aquatic dance.

Seaweed for the nest is brought by the male from the seabed

and incorporated into the nest by the female. The nest is important for mating, for the male is unable to lower his tail and achieve contact with the female unless he is raised well above the surrounding rocks, and the final nest is cup-shaped and some eighteen inches in diameter. Three eggs are laid, (although usually only one chick survives to be fledged) and the parents take turns in brooding and guarding the chicks. After about ten days, chicks are able to climb up the outer rim of the nest by using their beak and wings, but Snow did not see any chicks doing wing exercises. Although juveniles were seen flapping their wings when begging from their parents, chicks were not observed to do this.

The young get extremely excited when the fishing bird returns, pushing the tip of their bills against the parent's throat and vibrating. However, the parent does not respond immediately, but delays the feeding for an hour or two. Then the parent bends over and regurgitates its food into the chick's open bill, which is pushed well up into the parent's throat. Snow suggests that the delayed response to the begging of a half-grown chick may be associated with the presence of piratical frigate birds; the return of the parent cormorant does not mean that a food exchange is about to begin, and is thus not a cue to the frigate.

Snow has discovered several other aspects of the bird's biology that are unique in the cormorant family and are related to the two most obviously unusual features of the bird—large size and flightlessness, themselves probably interrelated.

The birds apparently are bottom feeders, taking octopus, eels, and fish, and Snow suggests that an increase in overall size and in the size of the beak (which is unusually large and strong) may have been of survival value in enabling the cormorant to extricate octopus, and possibly also eels, from rock crevices on the bottom. An increase in size would also mean that a larger range of size of fish would become available as food, thus reducing competition with the only other underwater bird feeding on fish, the Galápagos Penguin.

The body plumage of the Flightless Cormorant is unusual in cormorants, being soft, dense and hairlike, in fact more like that of a penguin. Although the contour and wing feathers become waterlogged after only a brief submergence, water is unable to penetrate the minute air spaces between the dense body plumage. This method of waterproofing presumably had survival value in enabling the bird to remain submerged for longer periods. The Flightless Cormorant uses the preen gland in preening the wing and contour feathers, as do other cormorants, but Snow believes this behavior to be now functionless, since the body plumage no longer is suitable for waterproofing with oil, and in fact in the one bird examined no oil could be produced from the preen gland.

Thus underwater feeding efficiency was probably achieved at the expense of flying efficiency, because of the increased weight of water carried by the plumage and the increased size of the bird. Alternatively, if loss of flight occurred first, then selection for underwater efficiency by a change in the waterproofing mechanism and increased size would not be opposed by selection for efficiency of flight. Possibly both these processes occurred simultaneously, the balance of the two opposing selection pressures being tipped in favor of underwater efficiency because of the peculiar nature of the bird's environment. In the Galápagos, loss of flying ability was perhaps not as detrimental to survival as highly efficient underwater feeding was advantageous. The bird has a very restricted distribution, so that flight from one part of its range to another would not be of great importance. Frigate birds have occasionally been observed to rob the cormorants, and flight in the company of frigates would probably lead to greater food loss. Added to this, the absence of terrestrial predators would mean that there would be no selection for flight as a means of escape.

Barbara Snow has convincingly argued that the restricted distribution of this cormorant in the Galápagos is probably a consequence of the natural restriction of its optimal habitats. She suggests that its range is limited to coasts that have rich upwellings of relatively cold water, shallow seas with rocky bottoms, and easy landing places sheltered from wind and rough seas. These conditions are found on the west coast of Albemarle and both sides of the Bolivar Strait, and on few other Galápagos shores, although, as mentioned before, the birds have also been seen nesting on the northern point of Albemarle. Lévêque (1963) estimated that the total population consisted of at least a thousand individuals, and Snow does not believe that there is any good reason for regarding it as a disappearing species.

THE GULLS

The two gulls of the Galápagos are both interesting in a number of ways. The Lava Gull, *Larus fuliginosus*, is related to the Laughing Gull of the continent. It occurs throughout the archipelago, although it is never seen in large numbers, and the nests have only recently been discovered, in vegetation on low ground close to sheltered water (Snow and Snow, 1969). The species is not social, and each of the six nests so far discovered along a thirty-five-mile shoreline have been at least two miles from any other. Nesting adults are extremely wary; alarm behavior begins when the intruder is still half a mile from the nest, and if there are chicks (the usual clutch is two) an approach to within one hundred yards elicits repeated swooping, striking at the intruder with the feet, and soaring away again, to the accompaniment of an alarm call. The chicks are speckled, as are those of other gulls, but the adults are somber, dirty, sooty brown with black beak, legs, and feet. Although the adult has a brilliant white spot behind the eye (PLATE 18), and the inside of the beak and mouth is bright red, the adults, and particularly the juveniles, which have no white spot, are difficult to see as they stand motionless on the black lava shores. It has been suggested by J. P. Hailman (1963) that this gull's cryptic coloring has evolved not in response to pressure from predators, of which it seems to have none, but rather that the cryptic coloration gives it some protection from competing scavengers, such as frigates.

Like the Herring Gull, the Lava Gull is a scavenger. Often following the lead of frigate birds, it eats the afterbirth of sea lions and picks up fish remains from the sea after sea lions have been feeding. It is also a generalized predator, and feeds on newly hatched marine iguanas as well as the red Galápagos crabs, eggs, and fish. The Snows saw it probing the muddy sand of the lower shore for worms at low spring tides. Nelson (1968a) suggests that the Lava Gull is a somewhat inefficient gull in its feeding, but has been able to survive in the remote, arid parts of the Galápagos, safe from the competition of other species. The Galápagos, and therefore the world, population is estimated as three hundred to four hundred pairs.

The other gull, the Swallow-tailed Gull, *Creagrus furcatus* (PLATE 19), is perhaps the most handsome bird in the islands, and must be one of the most attractive gulls in the world. In flight the white forked tail and gray markings of the wings are seen to the best advantage, and on the nest site the pink feet, red ring around the eye, and black-and-white beak are very striking. But the interest in this gull is by no means limited to its appearance. It has a number of specialized characteristics not usually found in gulls. It is a nocturnal feeder, has an unusual cry, lays but a single egg, and is a cliff nester. Indeed, so unusual is it that it has been assigned to a genus all of its own.

Nesting Swallow-tailed Gulls display mostly at dawn or dusk, and fly out to sea to feed at night; their staple diet is small fish and squid, which are probably commonest at the sea's surface at night. Hailman (1964b) has suggested that this nocturnal habit may have evolved since it enables both adults to guard the nest from marauding frigates during the day and to feed unmolested during the night. However, at least on Tower, Nelson (1968a) found that Short-eared Owls take a heavy toll of chicks during the night. Certain possible nocturnal adaptations have been recognized by Hailman. The chick's plumage is speckled, but it has a white head (PLATE 20), whereas other gull chicks at this age are usually dark brown; presumably the white head makes the chick conspicuous at night when giving the begging call to the returning parent. Many gulls have on their bill a red or yellow mark at which the chick pecks; this behavior on the part of the chick acts as a releaser, causing the adult to give up its food to the chick. In the Swallow-tailed Gull, this peck mark at the end of the bill is elongated and grayish-white, and there is a tuft of pure white feathers at the base of the bill (PLATE 20). It is suggested that these two marks may be the only features visible in the dark and may thus serve to define the position of the adult's head for the chick. Hailman (1967) found that, although the releaser of the chick's begging response is the white tip of the parent's black beak, the chick is less responsive to the tip's movement than are chicks of other gull species. Hailman states (1968) that the pecten of the eye develops slowly in the chick; other nocturnal birds are known which have reduced pectens. (The pecten is a structure which is usually associated with sensitivity to a moving image.)

The gull's unique clicking call may possibly assist it at night in homing by echo-location to its cliffside nest, although it has been discovered that no very high-frequency waves are emitted.

The eye of the Swallow-tailed Gull is much larger than is usual for gulls, both absolutely and relative to the size of the bird. Moreover the eye, like that of nocturnal mammals, shines in the dark when illuminated. This is caused by the tapetum coating of the retina which lengthens its exposure to a dimly lit object by reflecting instead of absorbing light behind the retina.

Nelson noticed a possible adaptation to the cliffside nesting habit on Tower Island. He observed that in fights between males one would grasp the other's bill and twist it, forcing him off the edge. Most gulls fight by pecking downward or by pulling the other's bill; the only gull that fights in the manner of the Swallow-tailed Gull is the Kittiwake, which is especially adapted for nesting on cliffs (Cullen, 1957). The Swallow-tailed Gull resembles the Kittiwake and differs from other gulls in several other morphological and behavioral characteristics that can be associated with the cliff-nesting habit (Hailman, 1965). These characteristics presumably are related to the limited amount of nesting space and include the habit of allopreening by members of a pair and the dark neckband of the immature birds that is used in appeasement (found in chicks of the Kittiwake), both of which reduce hostility. Other such characteristics are the absence of chasing and moving displays, long-distance displays, and upright threat behavior. Certain cliff-nesting adaptations appear to be related to the danger of falling, such as the long period for which chicks stay in the nest, their immobility, even when attacked, and the fact that they face toward the cliffside.

In all these respects the Swallow-tailed Gull again resembles the cliff-nesting Kittiwake and differs from other gulls.

Barbara and D. W. Snow (1968) suggest that the presence of frigate birds may have influenced the evolution of colonial cliff nesting, as well as the nocturnal habits. Colonial breeding would mean that a more effective, concerted alarm call could be given on the approach of a frigate, and the cliffside habitat provides rocks and crevices under which the chick can hide. These authors also point out that the cliff-nesting habit is probably responsible for a striking aspect of the behavior of the Swallow-tailed Gull—the absence of a loud male advertising call. This is a characteristic feature of the behavior of many ground-nesting gulls, but is absent in the cliff-nesting Kittiwake, as well as the Swallow-tailed Gull. In both these species, the male does not mate until he is in possession of a nest site, and he proves his fitness as a mate simply by demonstrating the site he has acquired. Ground-nesting gull males advertise themselves only at a "club" gathering, and must thus use displays and loud calls.

The Galápagos shores do not offer good inshore feeding conditions for a typical gull. There are no estuaries or river mouths and relatively few beaches on which detritus could collect; most of the shores are made up of barren lava. The Snows believe this was possibly a factor in the evolution of the habit of feeding far out to sea. Such pelagic feeding could facilitate the adoption of colonial nesting. When long distances separate the feeding and breeding areas, the extra distance to be flown to a colonial nest as opposed to a single one is negligible, and if there were advantages to colonial nesting, the pelagic feeding habit would not counteract them.

Normally, gulls lay three eggs; the Swallow-tailed Gull, however, lays only one. Doctor M. Harris has pointed out in conversation with me some interesting implications of this peculiar fact. In most gulls, the three eggs are usually laid at two-day intervals, but actually four follicle cells of the ovary become large enough to produce eggs. Gulls do not begin to incubate with the first egg laid, so that this is often lost. If this happens, the fourth follicle continues to mature and a fourth egg is laid, so that the total clutch is still three. Similarly, if the first egg is taken away as soon as it is laid, the bird will lay the fourth egg. However, if the first egg is taken away after a day or two, the fourth egg will not be laid; the developmental gap between the fourth one and previous eggs would now be too large. If each of the eggs is taken away as soon as it is laid, some gulls can be made to lay up to fifteen eggs, as the follicles continue to mature.

In the Swallow-tailed Gull, only a single follicle matures, and if the egg is removed or lost, the gull cannot lay another for two or three weeks. Thus the ovaries are not capable of producing a clutch of two eggs. However, if a Swallow-tailed Gull is given two eggs, it is capable of incubating them both, for it retains two brood patches. Also, it can sometimes raise two chicks if it is provided with an additional one. There is more wastage of chicks when the birds have two, but the end result is that there is a greater total of raised chicks than if the birds had only one each. Thus the Swallow-tailed Gull *can* sometimes raise more offspring than its ovaries will allow. An evolutionary reduction in clutch size has been achieved by a reduction of ovarian production to a single egg, although the present food supply is such today that this does not seem advantageous; possibly food was less plentiful at some time in the gull's evolutionary history. Many island animals show such a reduction in the production of offspring, and it may be simply that a large number of offspring is no longer necessary to offset the losses due to predation, which is usually minimal on islands. Doctor Harris examined thousands of gulls on South Plaza islet and only once did he find an exceptional "throwback" where two eggs were laid; unfortunately only one hatched—the other was addled.

There is an interesting comparison here with razorbills. These have only one brood patch, and normally lay only one egg. If the bird is provided with an extra egg (or occasionally a bird may lay two), then it loses both, for the one brood patch is incapable of producing successful incubation of either egg. One brood patch too few is definitely highly disadvantageous. However, retention of an "extra" brood patch by the Swallow-tailed Gull is apparently no disadvantage. Possibly it is an additional area for heat loss, which would not be disadvantageous, however, in the tropics. Here, then, is an example of a bird whose internal organs (the ovaries) have evolved more rapidly than the external ones (brood patches).

CHAPTER FOUR

Plants and Insects

SEVERAL families of plants are entirely absent or poorly represented in the Galápagos, while others are disproportionately rich in species. Such a flora is said to be "disharmonic." There are no gymnosperms on the islands, and several monocotyledonous families are absent or poorly represented. On the other hand the ferns, composites, grasses, and sedges make up an unusually large part of the flora. If the flora were a mere segment of that of the mainland, it should be more balanced in its make-up. The disharmony is evidence in favor of the theory that the islands have always been separated from the mainland by sea. Groups that never succeeded in making the crossing and establishing themselves would be absent, while those that did succeed would have expanded to an unusual degree to fill the empty ecological niches available to them. The Galápagos flora has precisely the make-up one might expect if the islands were truly oceanic; the existing disharmony would be difficult to explain if the archipelago had been connected to the continent by dry land in the past.

Lichens were probably among the first plants to colonize the barren, sterile islands after their emergence from the sea and subsequent cooling. These plants do not require soil and rain for their sustenance, for they are capable of anchoring themselves to bare rock and absorbing moisture from the air. Many Galápagos lichens belong to groups that form fruiting propagules giving good dispersal and that do not have very well-marked preferences for particular kinds of substrate. These are just the kinds of lichens that might be expected to be successful in reaching and establishing themselves on oceanic islands. Also, in the Galápagos, conditions in the main are very dry, and the principal and most reliable moisture appears as mist. It is not surprising, therefore, that lichens are extremely well represented; they are particularly common in the arid and intermediate zones. Most of the rock-inhabiting species, especially in the coastal zone, show relationships to lichens on the coasts of Chile and Peru, while the bark-living forms are related to groups that are widespread in South America.

W. A. Weber (1966), who has studied the Galápagos lichens, has pointed out that for a number of reasons lichens are slow to form distinct races, and on archipelagos are thus relatively less likely to multiply their number of species. This is partly because of their predominantly vegetative method of reproduction and partly because any mutation that might occur in the fungus part of the lichen would have to be acceptable to the algal partner—the lichen's dual nature results in an extra "sieve" through which random mutations must pass before they can be subjected to the usual test of natural selection. In plants, selection pressure is often related to water requirements; this is relatively unimportant in lichens, which are extremely well adapted for withstanding unfavorable conditions, particularly conditions of aridity. Possibly this reduced selection pressure is also involved in the lichens' poor powers of species formation.

Ferns, whose very small spores are easily dispersed by air currents, make up the best-represented group of plants in the archipelago. Also, as might be expected for organisms with such very good powers of dispersal, this group has the fewest endemic species of any.

Another well-represented group, and in first position as far as flowering plants are concerned, is the Compositae, the family to which the daisy, sunflower, and dandelion belong. This again is a family well known for its small fruits and excellent dispersal mechanisms, and is also one that contains a very large number of species, so that it provides a large number of potential colonists. The composites are also "weedy," that is, easily establish themselves in pioneer situations that most other plants would not be able to tolerate. For these reasons the Compositae is the family of flowering plants which is most successful as a colonist, not only of the Galápagos, but of remote islands in general.

Other important families of flowering plants in the Galápagos are the grasses (also to some extent dispersed by wind), the Euphorbiaceae, Leguminosae, Amaranthaceae, and Cyperaceae (sedges). Together with the Compositae, these families make up almost half the flowering plant flora of the Galápagos. This is a much larger proportion than they would account for in a continental area of similar size, in which the make-up of flora would be more balanced or harmonic.

Within the archipelago—that is, comparing the flora of the various islands—Stewart (1911) found that the flora was harmonic. In other words, each island supports a flora with similar proportions of represented families and genera, and there are no obvious gaps in the floras of the various islands. Stewart thought that this "internal" harmony gave support to the theory that the individual islands were formed as a result of the subsidence of a once larger, although truly oceanic, land mass.

One of the genera that best demonstrates this internal harmony is the endemic composite genus *Scalesia*. The genus is represented on all the islands except the eastern outlying islands of Hood, Tower, and Bindloe, and the small island of Jervis, and, of the seventeen or so species, all but five are restricted to a single island. Four groups of species can be recognized: Pedunculata (trees, with small flowering heads), Dentatae (shrubs, with fairly large flowering heads and serrate leaves), Lobatae (shrubs, with deeply serrate or pinnatifid fernlike leaves), and

Foliosae (shrubs, with flower heads having leaflike bracts, and entire, spear-shaped leaves). The Pedunculata are represented on all the large central islands (FIGURE 5), with the species *microcephala* on Narborough and Albemarle, *cordata* on Albemarle, and *pedunculata* subspecies on each of James, Indefatigable, Charles, and Chatham. The Dentatae occur on the south-

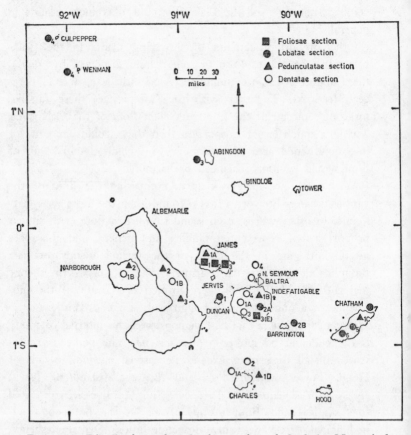

FIGURE 5. Distribution of endemic species of *Scalesia*. Numerical subscripts indicate different species, letter subscripts indicate different subspecies. (E)=extinct.

western group of islands, with *aspera* on Indefatigable, *crockeri* on Indefatigable, Baltra, and North Seymour, *villosa* on Charles, and *affinis* with three subspecies, one on Indefatigable, another on Charles, and a third on Narborough and Albemarle. Seven species make up the Lobatae group: *helleri* has a subspecies on each of Indefatigable and Barrington, *bauri* is restricted to Duncan, *divisa* and *incisa* to Chatham, *snodgrassi* is found on Culpepper and Wenman, and *hopkinsii* is found on Abingdon. James, which carries only a single species of those mentioned so

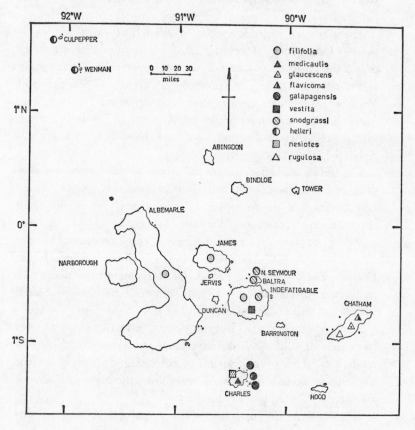

FIGURE 6. Distribution of species of the endemic plant genus *Alternanthera*.

far (the treelike *S. pedunculata*), has the three species of the Foliosae section all to itself.

A similar harmonic distribution is evident in the giant prickly pear opuntias of the Galápagos, although in this case the situation is complicated by their relationship to giant tortoises (see CHAPTER 6).

Although several other genera of flowering plants have given rise to endemic species complexes in the Galápagos, in only two of these, *Alternanthera* and *Mollugo*, have the systematics been worked out sufficiently reliably for an analysis of distribution patterns.

There are ten endemic species of *Alternanthera* on the archipelago. One group of seven related species has representatives on all the large central islands except, apparently, Narborough, while another species is present on distant Culpepper and Wenman, another on Charles, and yet another on Chatham. The genus has no endemic species on Abingdon, Bindloe, Tower, Narborough, Jervis, Duncan, or Hood, most of which are peripheral islands (FIGURE 6).

The seven endemic species of *Mollugo* are interesting because they include both annual and perennial species. Three annuals form a group which is represented on all the main islands except Culpepper, Wenman, Tower, and Hood. A loose grouping of four perennial species is represented on all the islands except Culpepper, Abingdon, Bindloe, Tower, Jervis, Duncan, Barrington, and Hood. Once again, what disharmony there is, is produced by a lack of representation on peripheral islands or small central ones (FIGURE 7).

Many of the endemic flowering plants have the characteristics of weeds or, like *Scalesia*, are related to groups with weedy tendencies. This of course is not surprising, for these are the plants most likely to succeed in establishing themselves on arrival; they are typically good colonizers.

Since soil is scarce, forest trees would be at a great disadvantage as colonizers. In any case, forest trees usually have large heavy seeds with a large food store enabling them to put

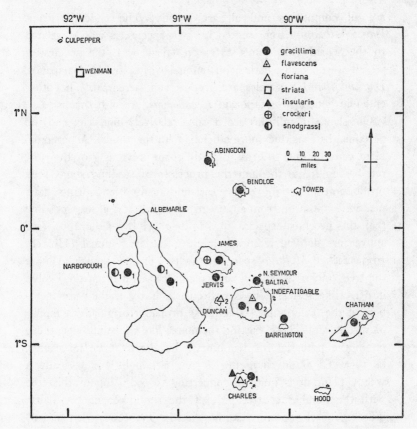

FIGURE 7. Distribution of endemic species of the plant genus *Mollugo*.

forth quickly a spread of leaves, and to manufacture maximum food in their shady surroundings. Their seeds are thus ill-fitted for long-distance dispersal and, in general, trees do not establish themselves on oceanic islands. Instead, many of the weedy plants have evolved shrubby or even tree forms, and in the Galápagos "forest" have been formed of *Scalesia*, some species of which are fair-sized trees.

The Compositae as a group have shrubby tendencies anyway, and the four endemic genera of Galápagos flowering plants

73

are all composites and all are woody. The endemic genus *Darwiniothamnus*, represented by two species, is closely related to the world-wide genus *Erigeron* (fleabanes), the species of which are normally herbaceous annual weeds. In the Galápagos, *Darwiniothamnus* species are woody and perennial. The other endemic genera, *Macraea* and *Lecocarpus*, are also shrubs.

On islands, conditions are usually relatively uniform, and the perennial habit is thus more efficient than the annual. A perennial plant can continue to grow directly from previous growth without having to go through the processes of seedling stage, seed production and dying each year, and many island plants have made the transition from annual to perennial. It is at least possible that the perennial species of *Mollugo* on the Galápagos (see above) are derived from an ancestor that was annual (Howell, 1933a), since *Mollugo* species elsewhere are all annuals. Where the tree "niche" is empty, such plants can, and often do, evolve into treelike forms. This is particularly likely if they are members of the Compositae, which was probably originally a family of shrubs, and whose existing members, like the sunflower, often retain the potential for woodiness. *Scalesia pedunculata* cannot be regarded as anything but a tree, although it is basically a weedy plant. It is quite disconcerting to see a log of this tree with the familiar central pith of the sunflower or the daisy. The recent chromosome studies of M. Ono (1967) led him to suggest that the genus *Scalesia* might have arisen by polyploidy.

Scalesia is also a very good example of another tendency of island organisms—the loss of dispersal ability. Once a plant has succeeded in establishing itself on an island, good dispersal ability, which of course was an advantage in enabling it to reach the island, now becomes a disadvantage. Very good powers of dispersal in island species lead to waste; if seeds are broadcast over a wide area, most of them will fall in a highly unsuitable environment—that is, sea water. Poor dispersal mechanisms, on the other hand, would result in most of the seeds falling near to the parent plant, on the island. Holdgate (1965) has made the observation that loss of dispersal ability in plants and flightlessness in animals may also evolve for negative reasons. Competition between species may be less severe on islands than on continental areas and, if so, the advantage of good dispersal would be reduced. Carlquist (1965) believes that this kind of reversed selection is taking place in *Scalesia*, which is in the process of losing its dispersal mechanisms.

Just over 40 per cent of the five hundred or so Galápagos species of vascular plants are endemic. Most of these possess small and inconspicuous flowers, a fact noted by Darwin. This condition is probably related to the very small number of pollinating insects that are on the islands; there has been very little selection for showy flowers that attract insect pollinators. Those groups of plants particularly well adapted for the visits of insects, such as orchids, Labiatae, and Scrophulariaceae, are poorly represented in the Galápagos. Rick (1966) believes that a dearth of pollinating insects would result in the flora evolving under selection for tolerance of self-pollination and for mechanisms ensuring automatic self-fertilization. Carlquist thinks that under these conditions there would instead be selection for mechanisms assuring cross-pollination, and though his argument is theoretically sound, for of course cross-pollination would ensure the necessary genetic variability of populations, the Galápagos flora is poor in such mechanisms.

Rick tested eighteen native species for self-pollination, and found that in thirteen the flowers automatically self-pollinated, while one other was self-compatible but did not automatically self-pollinate. In the absence of pollinating agents, a colonizing plant which was facultatively autogamous (capable of self-fertilization though not normally self-fertilizing) would be at an advantage, providing it was also able to tolerate the effects of the resultant inbreeding. Dioecious species, in which the individual plants bear flowers of only one sex, would clearly be at a disadvantage under these conditions unless they were wind-pollinated (see CHAPTER 11). In the Galápagos there is only one really successful dioecious species, the bush *Croton scouleri*, which is widespread over the archipelago and found over a wide range of habitat conditions. This plant is pollinated at twilight by a small moth, one of the few pollinating agents.

In the Faroe Islands, where there are also few insect pollinators, O. Hagerup (1950, 1951) found that water-pollinating mechanisms had been evolved in several species, as well as selfing mechanisms, both in open flowers and buds and as a result of the night closing and the withering of flowers.

Clearly, when self-fertilization is forced upon the founding populations by selection, this will greatly assist the rapid differentiation of local races and ultimately the multiplication of species.

INSECT POLLINATORS

Arid regions of the world usually support a number of solitary bees, and an area the size of Indefatigable might be expected to have about a hundred species were it part of a continent. In the Galápagos there is only one, the Galápagos carpenter bee, *Xylocopa darwini*. Although settlers speak of a "dwarf bee" on Charles, it has not yet been found. The Galápagos carpenter bee, the males of which are yellow and the females black, is thought to be a fairly recent arrival in the archipelago; it is related to the endemic carpenter bee of the Revillagigedo Islands off the Mexican coast. The bee nests in wood, and so may well have reached the archipelago in a drifting log, and has been on the archipelago long enough to have evolved into an endemic species. Nevertheless it is believed to have followed, not preceded, the endemic flowering plants, since it acts as a pollinating agent chiefly for the recently arrived non-endemic plants, several of which have colored flowers, often yellow, a color the bee appears to particularly favor (Linsley, Rick, and Stephens, 1966).

Other pollinating insects in the Galápagos are seven species of butterflies, only one of which is endemic, about a dozen hawk moths, a few syrphid flies and several beetles (Linsley, 1966).

Since the bee needs a supply of nectar as food, and nectar and pollen for its larvae, as well as wood in which to make a nest, it could not have established itself on the islands until plants were present which provided all these requirements. The butterflies and hawk moths need not only nectar but also the right food plants on which their larvae can feed. Their requirements are thus more specific than those of the carpenter bee, and for this and taxonomic reasons, Linsley and his co-workers suggest they are more recent arrivals. These entomologists sampled regions of the archipelago which are rich in endemic plant species, and noted which plants were visited by the bee. They found that 27 per cent of the plants visited were endemic species, although endemics make up 42 per cent of the flora. This difference in proportions is statistically significant, and they concluded that there is a preference for non-endemic plant species on the part of the bee. They suggested that although the bee probably played an important part in the establishment of immigrant plant species, the evolution of at least the older endemic plant groups could have taken place without the bee.

The bee is evidently short of attractive nectar-producing flowers in the Galápagos; it has been observed to extract nectar regularly from the flowers of *Clerodendron molle*, and *Periloba galapagensis*, both of which possess deep tubular corollas and are thus adapted for pollination by moths rather than bees. The bee's tongue is of course too short to reach this nectar in the normal way; instead, the bee rapidly bites through the corolla base and inserts its tongue into the bottom of the tube where the nectar lies, forming a slit in the base of the flower as a result.

DISTRIBUTION

Apart from the prickly pears, the other cacti of the Galápagos are cereoids, which flower in the early morning. These are the small *Brachycereus nesioticus*, and three species of the great candelabra-like *Jasminocereus* (PLATE 21). *Brachycereus* is the first colonizer of fresh lava flows (PLATE 22) and is an attractive, low-growing plant. It shows no evidence of island speciation and is thought to be a relatively recent arrival. It is confined to Abingdon, Tower, Narborough, Albemarle, and James.

The distribution of *Jasminocereus* species on the islands is rather intriguing. They are absent from the northern line of islands (Culpepper, Wenman, Abingdon, Bindloe, and Tower) and also, so far as is known, from Baltra, Jervis, Duncan, Barrington, and Hood (FIGURE 8). They thus occur only on the

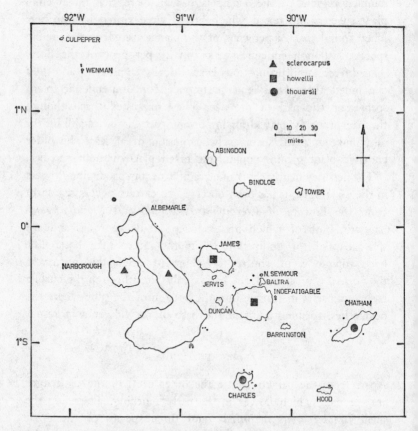

FIGURE 8. Distribution of species of the cereoid cactus genus *Jasminocereus*.

large high islands. One species, *sclerocarpus*, occurs on Albemarle and Narborough; another, *thouarsii*, on Charles and Chatham; and the third, *howellii*, on Indefatigable and James. According to E. Yale Dawson (1966) they are largely confined to areas near the shore, although we saw them at considerable heights both on Volcan Wolf and on Narborough. They seem to be absent from all the islands on which the low-growing type of prickly pears grow, being confined, in fact, to tortoise islands, though not occurring on all of these. *Jasminocereus* spines were found in tortoise droppings on Narborough, but on the other islands this plant does not appear to be a normal part of the diet of tortoises.

Many plants have a very restricted distribution on the archipelago. Two species of *Scalesia* and one of *Elvira* are found only in the vicinity of James Bay, and another species of *Scalesia* and one each of *Pectis*, *Mollugo*, and *Coldenia* occur only in the area around Sulivan Bay, at the other end of James. Some species are restricted to Duncan, and others to Charles,

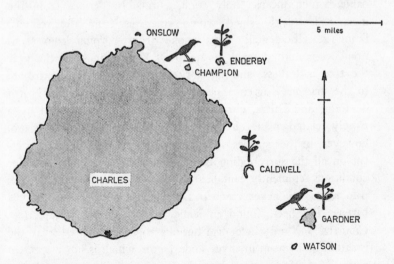

Figure 9. Distribution on islets adjacent to Charles of the Charles Island Mockingbird, *Nesomimus trifasciatus*, and the plant *Alternanthera galapagensis*.

the latter island having the only species of *Lecocarpus* in the world. One species, *Alternanthera galapagensis*, grows only on three small islets close to Charles—Gardner, Caldwell, and Enderby—but is absent from Charles itself (FIGURE 9). It has not been found on Champion, a fourth islet near Charles, which has a flora much more similar to that of Charles than have the other three islets. This may be a case similar to that of the Charles Island Mockingbird (see CHAPTER 7), which now only exists on Gardner and Champion. Small islets such as these, which are close to a larger island, may have an importance out of all proportion to their size. If the larger island has been colonized by man or his feral animals, the smaller islets may often provide a clue to the situation which existed on the larger island before the arrival of the disturbing influence.

There is one striking example of the reverse of the restricted distributions cited above. The "palo santo" tree, *Bursera graveolens*, is one of the commonest trees in the dry and transitional zones of the majority of the islands (FIGURE 10). The Spanish name, which means "holy stick," probably derives from the incense-like sickly smell which emanates from the resinous branches. (Incidentally, the smoke from burning palo santo branches is said to repel mosquitoes.) During most of the year the tree is leafless, and its stark, grayish branches contribute to the dry and barren appearance of the lowlands. On North Seymour and Baltra, close to Indefatigable, it is replaced by a closely related species, *Bursera malacophylla*. On Duncan Island, however, neither species occurs, although the palo santo is present on all the surrounding islands and Duncan appears to offer conditions eminently suitable for its growth. Presumably the palo santo has never reached Duncan. A similar distributional pattern has been found in some of the reptile groups (see CHAPTER 5), and these distributions together suggest that the isolation of Duncan involves some factor which is not at present clear. The suggestion of Van Denburgh and Slevin (1913) that Duncan is the central cone of the large submerged baylike crater of a once-united Albemarle-James-Indefatigable massif

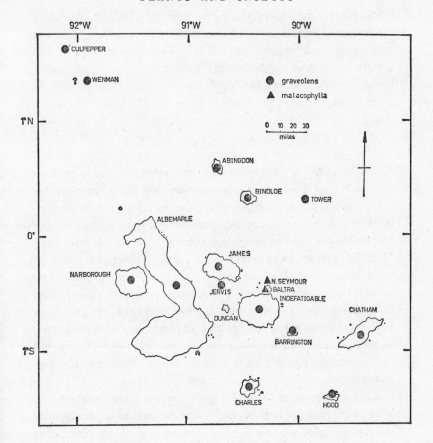

FIGURE 10. Distribution of the "palo santo" tree, (*Bursera* species).

would account for the peculiar biological isolation of Duncan, and this is discussed more fully in CHAPTER 12.

Within the archipelago, animals play a part in the dispersal of some plants. The Galápagos tomatoes' seeds have an increased power of germination after passing through the guts of tortoises and mockingbirds (Rick and Bowman, 1961), and the fruits of the prickly pear are eaten by tortoises (see CHAPTER 6), which thus assist its dispersal. The introduced guava, which has become a menace to the native flora on Chatham, is rapidly expanding in certain areas of Albemarle and is making alarming progress on Indefatigable and Charles. Feral pigs and wild cattle are probably responsible for the spread in this case, the seeds being disseminated on the pigs' feet or after passing through their guts.

INSECTS

Apart from the carpenter bee and the other few large pollinators, the insects of the Galápagos are for the most part inconspicuous, dull-colored, and retiring in their habits. Exceptions to this, however, are the short-horned grasshoppers, which are strikingly colored with red, orange, and black, and may often be seen in large numbers in exposed situations. Some of these have reduced wings and wing covers and are quite incapable of flight, while others are not unusual in this respect. Many of the beetles, of several families, also have reduced flight organs. This is a phenomenon parallel to the loss of flight power in several island birds (CHAPTER 13) and the loss of dispersal mechanisms in island plants, such as *Scalesia* (see above); presumably the explanation is the same in all these cases.

Another feature of the Galápagos insects is that several species, which are also present on the mainland, are of a smaller size on the Galápagos. This applies particularly to the butterflies and moths. A smaller size in insects is usually associated with a more rapid maturation, and it is possible that dwarfism in Galápagos insects is related to the very short rainy season of the islands. It may be, as Carlquist (1965) suggests, that insects that mature rapidly are at a selective advantage because they can then complete their life cycle during the short period when their food is available. However, it is also possible that the small size is a direct result of the limited duration of available food. Many insects, when food is in short supply, will pupate before the normal time and this advanced pupation results in a smaller-sized adult.

1. The *Santa Marianita*, a typical Galápagos fishing vessel, and its flat-bottomed "panga," off the islet of Bartholomew.

2. "Islands" of vegetation (kipukas) not covered by lava, in the caldera of Bindloe.

3. The caldera of Volcan Wolf, Albemarle, is approximately 5400 feet above sea level.

4. A pair of Blue-footed Boobies on Hood. The female (left) is larger than the male, and the eye appears to have a larger pupil.

5. The brown phase of the Red-footed Booby and chick, on Tower. This is the only booby to make an actual nest and live in trees.

6. The white phase of the Red-footed Booby on Wenman. On this island the white phase seems to be unusually common for the Galápagos.

7. A pair of Masked Boobies, Wenman.

In general, the Galápagos insects do not show anything like the same degree of archipelago differentiation as do the insects of Hawaii. There is a much smaller proportion of endemic species, and there are fewer cases of the evolution of endemic species complexes, that is, of groups of species derived from a common ancestor and found only on the archipelago, usually with each species restricted to a single island.

A few of the Galápagos insect groups, however, do show

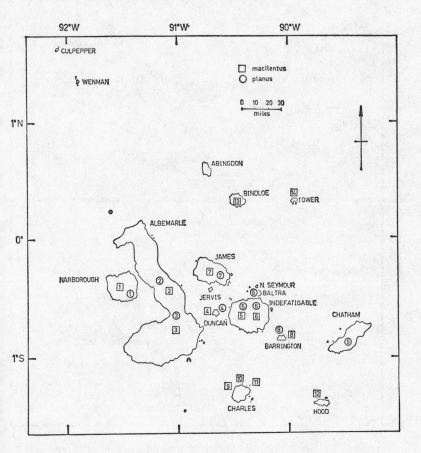

FIGURE 11. Distribution of ants of the genus *Camponotus*. Numbers indicate different varieties.

the beginnings of this process. Two endemic species of ants of the genus *Camponotus* occupy similar and overlapping ranges in the archipelago, including most of the central islands (FIGURE 11). However, in the case of each species, the populations on the various individual islands are distinct, and were recognized as varieties by W. M. Wheeler (1919, 1924, 1933).

There are four species of flightless grasshoppers of the endemic genus *Halmenus* (Dirsh, 1969). One of them, *robustus*,

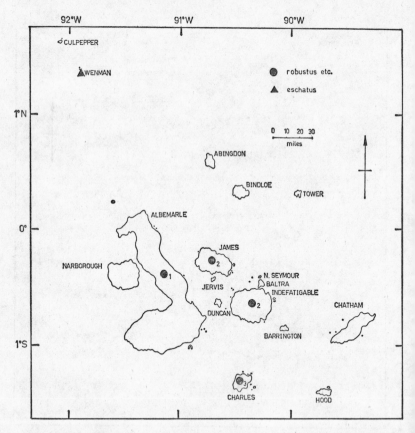

FIGURE 12. Distribution of flightless grasshoppers of the endemic genus *Halmenus*. Numerical subscripts indicate three closely related species of the *robustus* group.

occurs on the central islands of James and Indefatigable, and similar species occur on Albemarle (*cuspidatus*) and Charles (*chloristopterus*). M. Hebard (1920) regarded these three populations as subspecies of the single species *robustus*. The fourth species, *eschatus*, is known only from a single individual taken from the stomach of a mockingbird on Wenman Island, but the specimen was nevertheless in excellent condition. This species is clearly derived from the same stock as the other three, but the differentiation on this remote island has been greater than that on the central islands, and Hebard assigned this specimen to a separate full species (FIGURE 12).

In the winged grasshopper species of *Schistocerca*, a genus related to *Halmenus*, there are two species (FIGURE 13), and the ranges overlap slightly. The species *melanocera* occurs almost throughout the archipelago, but has not been found on Wenman or Hood. The second species, *literosa*, is found only on the southeastern islands of Tower, Chatham, Charles, and Hood. Evidence of distinct island populations of *literosa*, put forward by Scudder in 1843, is discounted by Dirsh.

There are other cases of such complexes in various beetle families, and in many of these cases the most distinct forms are found on outer, more isolated islands. The Cerambycidae is a family of long-horned beetles whose larvae tunnel into the wood of trees, and on the Galápagos one of them, *Estola insularis*, is associated with the shrubby composite *Scalesia affinis* which has a subspecies on Narborough and Albemarle, one on Indefatigable, and a third on Charles. In parallel with its host plant, this species of beetle has also diverged (Linsley and Chemsak, 1966), producing separate subspecies on Albemarle, Indefatigable, and Charles. Too few specimens were collected from Narborough for the status of this population to be decided.

N. Leleup (1965a and b) has recently studied the cryptozoic arthropods of the Galápagos. The distributions of such animals as these, which are adapted to specialized but relatively uniform and stable habitats, hidden beneath stones, in caves, ground litter, cracks, crevices, and the like, presumably are good indicators

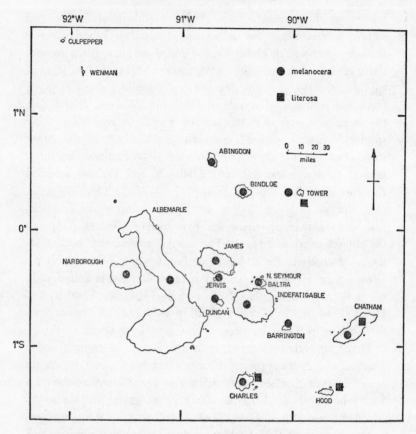

FIGURE 13. Distribution of two species of winged grasshoppers (*Schistocerca*).

of former changes in the distribution of land masses. Leleup found that many families of such insects, which are well represented in Ecuador, are absent altogether or represented by very few species in the Galápagos. This basic poverty in the Galápagos cryptozoic fauna, and in particular the absence of certain families associated with high humidities and usually found in such habitats in extraordinary variety, supports the view that the archipelago is truly oceanic. Had the Galápagos been formerly connected with the continent, even for a short period of time, Leleup believes that at least some representatives of these families would have made the passage to the Galápagos. Colonization by chance rafting or aerial transport would prevent forms with narrow tolerances of temperature or humidity, or those requiring a moist or dark atmosphere, from ever reaching the archipelago.

From the relatively high percentage of the Galápagos cryptozoic insects that have reduced pigmentation, are blind, or have reduced eyes, and that represent the ends of lineages in which regressive evolution has taken place, Leleup considers that at least some of the islands, such as Indefatigable, have been above water for at least a million years and probably for more. The internal harmony of this fauna within the archipelago itself, leads Leleup to believe that the segregation of populations has been recent, and that the isolation of individual islands by subsidence cannot have occurred before the Pleistocene (a million years ago).

Although Leleup's studies support the theory of an oceanic origin for the archipelago, and its subsequent isolation, the basic poverty of the cryptozoic fauna is not so great as it is in other oceanic faunas. This lends some support to the theory of Vinton (CHAPTER 2) that only a narrow stretch of sea originally separated the primitive Galápagos land mass from tropical continental America.

CHAPTER FIVE

Reptiles

THE Galápagos Islands have often been described as a land
where prehistoric reptiles roam, taking one back in time to the
geological past. Such, of course, is not the case. The similarity
with past eras is simply that the dominant land quadrupeds are
the reptiles; the mammalian fauna is scant, and amphibians are
completely absent. The reptiles are represented by iguanas,
snakes, lava lizards, geckos, and, of course, tortoises. All these
show evidence of relationship to South American forms, and
in many cases, certainly in the case of the *Phyllodactylus* geckos,
the small iguanid lava lizards (*Tropidurus*), the harmless snakes
(*Dromicus*), and the giant tortoises (*Geochelone*), there is evidence of a clear differentiation between the populations of different islands.

LAVA LIZARDS

The lava lizards are practically ubiquitous on the rocky regions
of the archipelago and, being quite strikingly colored, sun-
loving, active during the day, and without fear of man, are
quite a conspicuous feature of the environment. They may even
be seen on sea lions and marine iguanas, hunting for flies. They
occur on all the islands except the small outliers, Wenman,

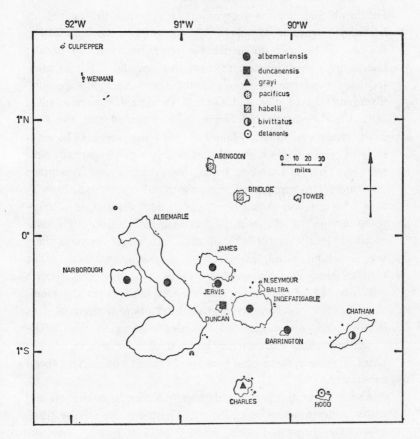

FIGURE 14. Distribution of lava lizards (*Tropidurus* species).

Culpepper, and Tower, and on each island only a single species is present (FIGURE 14). However, although Abingdon, Bindloe, Duncan, Barrington, Chatham, Charles, and Hood each have a distinct island species, the populations on Narborough, Albemarle, James, Jervis, Indefatigable, and Baltra are all considered to belong to the same species. This distributional pattern has been used by Eibl-Eibesfeldt (1961) as evidence of the geological history of the archipelago. This author follows Van

Denburgh and Slevin's suggestion (1913) that the mass Narborough-Albemarle-James-Jervis-Indefatigable-Barrington was the last to be split up, hence the populations on the present islands have had insufficient time for specific differentiation. Certainly the forms on Hood, Chatham, and Abingdon are quite divergent. On Charles and Duncan the lizards are now quite rare. Van Denburgh and Slevin have suggested that the mass Narborough - Albemarle - James - Jervis - Indefatigable - Barrington was once a single huge volcano, which has been partially submerged. The sea between James, Indefatigable, and Albemarle was thought to represent a vast submerged crater, with Duncan as a central crater cone. This hypothetical situation is a large-scale version of the situation existing on Narborough until recently. In the crater lake of the Narborough volcano there was a central island, in which there was another lake. The bathymetrical data provides no evidence against this theory, which would, of course, provide some explanation for the anomalous position of Duncan in the distribution pattern of lava lizards: although surrounded by islands carrying the species *T. albemarlensis*, Duncan has its own peculiar species of lava lizard. However, there is no geological evidence of such a general subsidence.

The sexes of the lava lizards usually differ in coloration and pattern, sometimes quite strikingly. The males are usually black around the throat and chest, while females of many species are usually marked with red or orange around the face, throat, and chest; the females are also usually smaller than the males and often half the weight.

Stebbins and his colleagues (1967), who studied these lizards on Indefatigable intensively for a month in 1964, found that they become active at sunrise and that activity continues until sunset, although on clear sunny days many lizards take shelter around midday beneath objects or under the ground. At sunset, the lizards retire to quite well-defined "beds," accumulations of soil and leaf litter in depressions of the lava, into which they dive headfirst, and completely bury themselves by alternate kicks of the hind legs and side to side movements of the head. The same bed is often used by the same lizard on successive nights, and even when an animal changes beds it tends to sleep in the same general area. The lizards are territorial, and both males and females are aggressive toward members of the same sex but not to adults of the opposite sex. Normally, each male is associated with two or three females, but larger harems do occur. When mating, a male may seize the female by her leg, back, or apparently even by the tail, carry her in his jaws for some distance, then shift his grip to the back of her neck before copulation, which lasts for less than half a minute. The female digs one or more shallow nest burrows, in which from one to four, usually two, eggs are laid.

A characteristic behavior pattern of iguanid lizards in general is their aggressive display. The lizard stands high on both front and hind legs, and then successively straightens and bends its front legs, resulting in the head and shoulder region moving up and down—very like the "pushup" exercises of humans in keep-fit classes. The Galápagos lava lizards are no exception to this, and such displays are most marked during a "challenge" between two males. The challenging males stand sideways to each other, usually facing in opposite directions, extend the flaps of skin under their jaws, and the mid-dorsal crest of large scales, flatten the body sideways making it appear larger, and go into the pushup routine.

Carpenter (1966a) has recently made a most interesting analysis of these pushup movements for populations of lizards from the twelve principal islands on which they occur. He recorded the amplitude of the raising movement, and the timing between successive groups of movements. His results (FIGURE 15) show that the pattern of these display movements differs for each of the island populations except those of Narborough and Albemarle, in which the pattern is identical. Moreover, the patterns for those populations of *T. albemarlensis* on other islands are all island-specific, although the patterns on Indefatigable and Barrington, and James and Jervis, show certain similarities. The pattern of the Duncan population is very similar to

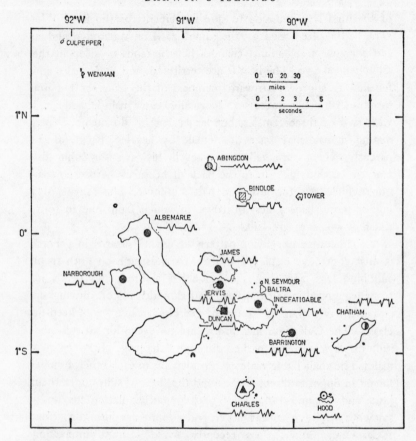

FIGURE 15. Graphical representation of display-behavior patterns of male lava lizards of various island populations. Data from Carpenter, 1966. Horizontal scale of pattern graphs indicates time, vertical scale shows extent of vertical movement (see text, page 91). Only two cycles of movements are shown. Species symbols as in FIG. 14.

those of the James and Jervis populations, although the Duncan lizards are regarded as a distinct species. The patterns of the separate species on Bindloe and Chatham also show certain similarities, while those on Hood, Charles, and Abingdon are quite clearly differentiated. (The lizards on these last three islands are also each very distinct forms. The Hood lizards are the largest on the archipelago and possess an unusual stumpy tail; those on Charles are the smallest; and those on Abingdon have unusually small scales and a characteristic light color.)

These behavior studies have refined our knowledge of the island populations. They have confirmed the specific status of six of the species, and they have revealed most interesting relationships between the populations on six of the islands which, on morphological grounds, were believed to possess the same species. The display pattern of the Narborough and Albemarle populations differs markedly from those of the lizards on Indefatigable and Barrington, which are the farthest away, but is less different from those of the populations on James and Jervis, which are nearer. The Duncan lizards have a display pattern which is closest to those of the James and Jervis populations.

Taxonomic problems have thus been raised concerning these lizards, but whatever the taxonomic decision, one interesting conclusion has been made by Carpenter. There is reason to believe that such display-action patterns in other iguanids, where they have also been found to be characteristic for each species, may function, as a result of selection, as a means whereby lizards recognize members of their own species when another species is living in the same area. They act as behavioral isolation mechanisms. A modified form of the aggressive display, the "assertion display," is an early part of the courtship ceremony of male lava lizards. The sequence and pattern of up-and-down movements is the same as in the aggressive display, but the hindquarters and tail are not lifted from the ground, and there is less flattening of the trunk and extension of the dewlap. In courtship, the assertion display is followed by "courtship nodding" when the male is within a foot of the female. The head is lowered and nodded weakly. In some island populations these head nods follow the same species pattern as the assertion display, while in others they do not. The morphological differences between the Galápagos island forms could of course have evolved by selection as adaptations to the different island environments. However, it is very difficult to believe that the behavior patterns have arisen by selection as behavioral isolating mechanisms, in spite of their use in court-ship, since only one species occurs on each island, and there is absolutely no reason to believe that more than one form ever occurred on any one island. The behavioral differences are thus thought by Carpenter to have arisen without selection. Each island's original lizard population was presumably small, and carried with it only a fraction, not the whole range, of the genes of the parent population. Thus the original island populations would have similar, though slightly differing, gene pools, and in time, with the isolation of populations provided by the islands themselves, these would diverge even further, resulting in the differing behavior patterns observed at the present day.

SNAKES

The Galápagos snakes, which are not poisonous but are constrictors, are all fairly similar in appearance. They are slender, about two or three feet long, brown, and spotted or bearing two or three yellowish stripes along the back. The distribution of the snakes is quite similar to that of the lizards, on which they feed along with grasshoppers and other small prey. The snakes, however, evidently never reached any of the northern line of islands, for they are absent from Culpepper, Wenman, Abingdon, Bindloe, and Tower. Three species are recognized by Mertens (1960): *Dromicus biserialis*, which has a separate subspecies on each of Charles, Hood, and Chatham—the south-eastern group of islands; *D. slevini*, which has one subspecies on Narborough, Albemarle, and Duncan, and another on James, Jervis, Indefatigable, Baltra, and Barrington—the central group of islands; and *D. dorsalis*, which has three subspecies, one on all five central islands, James, Jervis, Indefatigable, Baltra, and Barrington, another on Narborough, and a third on Albemarle.

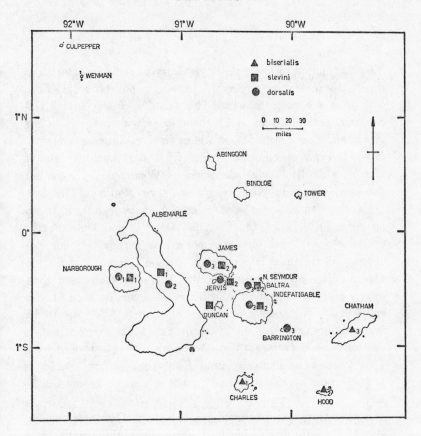

FIGURE 16. Distribution of Galápagos snakes (*Dromicus* species). Numerical subscripts indicate different subspecies.

D. dorsalis is thus distributed over the central group of islands, but with the notable exception, once again, of Duncan (FIGURE 16). Thus the distributions of both snakes and lava lizards support the theory of a former close connection between the islands of the central group, but in both cases Duncan is an exceptional island.

GECKOS

The distribution of the little *Phyllodactylus* geckos supports this theory to some extent. Six species occur on the archipelago, five of which occur nowhere else (that is, are endemic) and the sixth, which occurs on Chatham, has a wide range including North and South America, and is of little evolutionary interest. *Phyllodactylus* species are absent from the northern line of islands, with the notable exception of Wenman, and have not yet been found on Narborough or Jervis (FIGURE 17).

Of the five endemic species, one, *P. galapagensis*, is found on Albemarle, James, Indefatigable, Daphne, and Duncan (the central group), and three subspecies are recognized, one occurring on the three larger islands, one on Daphne, and one on Duncan. Barrington, Chatham, and Wenman each have their own distinct species, and the fifth species occurs on both Charles and Hood. The species occurring on remote Wenman is the most distinct, and that on Chatham, also a peripheral island, is the next most distinct (Van Denburgh, 1912b). Hendrickson (1965) came to the conclusion that the Wenman species is preyed upon by the nocturnal foot-long centipedes of that island.

A seventh gecko, unrelated to the others, *Gonatodes collari*, associated with man's dwellings throughout the tropics, is a recent introduction and is so far confined to Chatham.

LAND IGUANAS

The iguanas are the Galápagos animals which have chiefly inspired the "antediluvian" and "mesozoic" epithets for the archipelago. These large reptiles are represented on the islands by two types, the land and the marine iguanas. Land iguanas occur in continental America and in the West Indies, and although the Galápagos land iguanas are endemic, they differ little from the continental iguanas, except that they are much less fright-

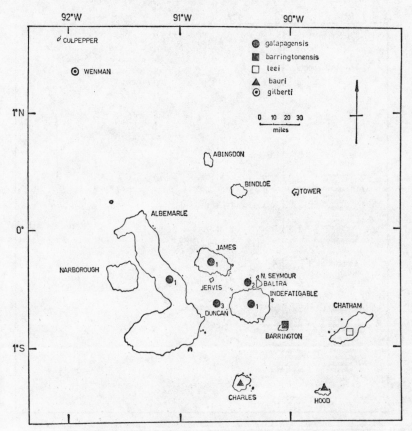

FIGURE 17. Distribution of gecko species (*Phyllodactylus*) endemic to the Galápagos. Numerical subscripts indicate different subspecies.

ened of man. The Galápagos land iguanas are found only on the central group of islands, and two species have been recognized: *Conolophus subcristatus*, which occurs on Indefatigable, Narborough, and Albemarle, and formerly was present also on Baltra and James, and *Conolophus pallidus*, which is restricted to Barrington (FIGURE 18).

C. *subcristatus* is a large lizard, some three or four feet long (PLATE 23). It feeds on almost any kind of vegetable matter,

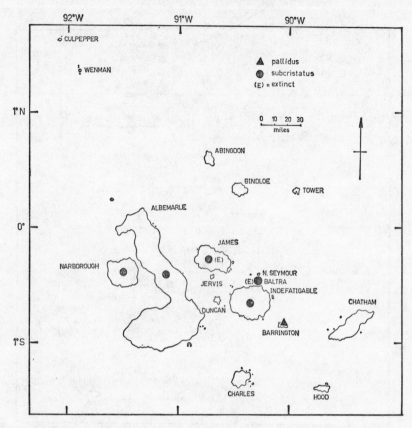

FIGURE 18. Distribution of the two species of Galápagos land iguana (*Conolophus*).

ranging from grasses and sedges to flowers and the pads and fruits of the prickly-pear cactus, the spines of which pass through the mouth and alimentary canal of the animal unchanged and apparently without any ill effect. Pinchot (1931) seems to be the only person to have seen a land iguana "preparing" a fallen cactus pad for eating by brushing off the spines with its front feet. The reptiles occasionally climb into the branches of trees to feed on the leaves, and have even been observed on South Plaza eating the remains of a crab. Pinchot saw one chase a mockingbird that had a grasshopper in its beak until it dropped the insect, which the iguana then ate; he then fed the animal by hand with grasshoppers. They may also be fed by hand on the fruits of prickly pear; this tameness is in direct contrast to the shyness of continental iguanas.

Each individual digs a shallow burrow, and the burrows of the male and female are usually fairly close together. Darwin, always ready to experiment, pulled the tail of a burrowing land iguana: "At this it was greatly astonished, and soon shuffled up to see what was the matter; and then stared me in the face, as much as to say, 'What made you pull my tail?'" (Darwin 1845).

Darwin wrote that the land iguanas of James were in such high density in 1835 that "we could not for some time find a spot free from their burrows on which to pitch a single tent." The California Academy of Sciences expedition to that island found nothing but a few bones, and none has been found on James since. Wild pigs, which occur on James, probably destroyed their burrows. According to William Beebe, there were many land iguanas on Baltra in 1923, when he called Baltra the "Eden of land iguanas"; none was found in 1954. The culprits in this instance were the United States servicemen who were stationed on the island during the war and senselessly exterminated the population. However, a thriving population exists on South Plaza islet, close to Indefatigable. This islet is less than a quarter of a mile long, and the western half is covered with prickly pears. On this part of the islet the iguanas dig burrows both in the open and under the low shrubs. Other populations occur at various places on Indefatigable itself, and the beasts may be seen wandering around the research station at Academy Bay, and will even walk into the rooms of visiting scientists. They do not appear to be common on Albemarle, the southern volcanoes of which support feral animals, but in May 1967 I saw three individuals in an hour and numerous burrows on the rim of the caldera of Volcan Wolf, Albemarle's northernmost volcano. On Narborough we saw land iguanas in very good numbers amongst the thick *Scalesia* forest around the rim of the crater, as well as down the crater sides to the lake 2000 feet below. In the late afternoons, landslides often occurred on the precipitous eastern sides of the crater, when the sun had fallen quite low and the crater walls became shadowed. These slides may have been caused by rocks cooling and contracting, but iguanas, renewing their activity at this time of the day, may also have been responsible. Land iguanas also occur on North Seymour, though in small numbers, and on Hood. On both these islands they have been recently introduced by man.

Conolophus pallidus, which is restricted to Barrington, differs from the other land iguana in having a more distinct row of spines along the back of the animal; it is also more predominantly yellowish-orange in color, like the lichen-covered lava rocks of this island. On Barrington the iguanas compete with feral goats for the succulent pads of the tree-like prickly-pear cacti, the growing branches of which eventually droop down under their own weight and either fall off or drop to within reach of the animals. However, although recent reports have suggested a decline in iguana numbers, they appeared to be quite common in the spring of 1967 and were distributed all over the island. Although few small individuals were seen, a dozen adults were seen in a day, and the characteristic trails, with a sinuous line left by the tail of the iguana, were indicators of their lairs, which were often beneath lava blocks.

Like most gregarious animals, including sea lions, lava lizards and marine iguanas, land iguanas are territorial. A male will regard a certain piece of ground as his territory and will defend it against other males by threatening postures and behavior. The loser usually retreats tailfirst, without an actual fight taking place. At mating time, however, fights between males occasionally develop, and the animals are capable of damaging one another quite severely. In the field, they have to be handled with care, in spite of their apparent tameness. An adult iguana has been filmed successfully defending itself from attack by a Galápagos hawk.

The iguanas, at least of Volcan Wolf and Narborough, are parasitized by small ticks. After spending four days on the Narborough volcano, sleeping on the ground and sometimes walking through thick vegetation, we found that we had inadvertently collected their ticks, and had to spend about half an hour in removing them from our skin after returning to the boat. Beebe (1924) refers to land iguanas being deticked by mockingbirds. Mosquitoes, which were very numerous on the islet in the crater lake of Narborough, possibly also feed on iguanas.

MARINE IGUANAS

Distributed along the rocky shores of the archipelago, and in places existing in very high densities indeed, is the marine iguana, *Amblyrhynchus cristatus*. Packed hordes of these large somber reptiles, which usually grow to three feet in length and are completely unconcerned by the presence of man, may be seen at various places in the archipelago (PLATE 24). These are the only lizards in the world that regularly feed in the sea, and almost certainly they evolved from the land iguanas.

One of the earliest references to marine iguanas feeding in the sea was by Captain Colnett (1798) who thought they went "to sea in herds a-fishing." Darwin, however, rightly suggested that the iguanas made forays to the seabed for seaweed. In his journal he says, "I have reason to believe it grows at the bottom of the sea, at some little distance from the coast. If such be the case, the object of these animals occasionally going out to sea is explained." Although Beebe (1924) discounted this possibility, believing that feeding was limited to seaweed exposed at low tide near the shore, it has since been amply proved (Eibl-Eibesfeldt, 1963; Hobson, 1965; Carpenter, 1966b). Marine iguanas feed on many different types of seaweed, both the weed exposed at low tide and that on the seabed, under water.

In comparison with the land iguana, the marine reptile shows certain morphological adaptations for this unique mode of life. The tail is laterally compressed, and is thus well adapted to its function as the swimming organ. Although Darwin noted that all four feet are partly webbed, the animal does not use them at all in swimming. When swimming, either on the surface or under the water, the legs are held close along the sides of the body and the tail is moved laterally in a sinuous fashion, resulting in quite rapid movement through the water. When swimming on the surface, the head is held up with the eyes clear of the water. The claws are long, sharp, and very strongly curved, serving perfectly to anchor the reptile to lava boulders in heavy seas, so that it is not swept away from its feeding grounds by the swell. The claws probably also function in retaining the reptile on the seabed when feeding on the bottom. The snout is much shorter and blunter than that of the land iguana and allows the animal to get its jaws into very close contact with the rock when cropping the seaweed. The teeth, which have three cusps, are in a single row and are flattened laterally, forming a very efficient serrated rasp. When feeding, the lizard clings firmly to the rock, turns its head sideways, brings the jaw across the rock in a tearing movement, and then, with a twist, jerks its head away.

These iguanas also certainly possess physiological adaptations to their marine existence. They drink sea water, and Schmidt-Nielsen and Fange (1958) have shown that, like other terrestrial animals that do this, they possess a pair of salt glands that get rid of the excess salt thus obtained. The salt glands of the marine iguana are located beneath the skin between the eye and the nostril on each side of the head, and open into the nostrils. The highly saline secretion of these glands, almost twice as salty as sea water, is periodically ejected forcibly from the nostrils as a jet of fine spray which may be expelled for a distance of a foot or more, complementing their already drag-on-like appearance. When suddenly startled, a group of lizards may eject spray together, and it is possible that this behavior may have some survival value in startling possible predators, although these are few today, and there was probably none for much of the iguana's evolutionary past.

The iguanas have been observed feeding at depths of thirty-five feet, and they are apparently able to control their buoyancy in some way, for they have been seen to hover in the water like submarines at fifteen feet (Hobson, 1965). Some observers have seen them swallowing stones (Eibl-Eibesfeldt, 1966) which possibly serve as ballast; and pieces of coral have been found in the feces (Mackay, 1964). Hobson reported that iguanas stayed submerged for thirty minutes, and Bartholomew (1966a) showed that they could stay under for fifty minutes and then not begin to breathe immediately on surfacing. The record observation, however, is still that of an experimentally minded sailor on Darwin's *Beagle*, who sank a marine iguana with a heavy stone attached to it. When the lizard was pulled up an hour later it was found to be none the worse for its experience.

Unlike the land iguanas, marine iguanas do not live in burrows, but sleep at night either exposed on the lava, hanging by their claws in vertical crevices or under vegetation. Some even climb mangroves and spend the night in the branches. The body temperatures of the animals fall to that of their surroundings within two or three hours after sunset. Marine iguanas do construct burrows for the purpose of egg laying, and the greatest concentrations of marine iguanas in the Galápagos occur in areas where there are lava reefs providing feeding grounds and also areas of ground suitable for nest building. Mating and egg laying occur in the first part of the calendar year, which includes the hottest months on the coast.

At this time, while juveniles usually keep to themselves in small isolated groups, adult males begin to show territorial behavior, establishing areas that they regard as their property. Carpenter (1966b) saw a territorial male challenge and display at boobies that had alighted within his territory, but such behavior is usually directed at rival male iguanas. An adult male will take up a stance in a prominent raised position within this area, and will challenge other approaching males by taking up a threatening posture, usually with his side facing the intruder. The mid-dorsal crest of scales is erected, the body inflated, and the throat region bloated. The lizard stands stiff-legged, tail down, head lowered with mouth half open—exposing the red color inside—and bobs his head up and down two or three times. Usually such encounters do not result in contact; when they do, the defending animal quickly changes position and moves head first toward his opponent and butts him with the top of his head, which is equipped with large conical scales (PLATE 24) not found in other iguanas. The intruding male may also lower his head, and the butting and pushing contest may go on for as long as five hours, with interruptions for rest, before one male, usually the intruder, gives in and retires. The loser normally takes up a submissive attitude by prostrating himself on his belly before the victor (Eibl-Eibesfeldt, 1955). These butting fights, which result in one male becoming dominant without serious damage to either, do not occur in other iguanas. The territorial males have been observed to stay in their ground for as much as seven days without going to sea to feed. At this time of year (the early months) the males have an abundance of subcutaneous fat, which possibly allows them to go for long periods without feeding.

Many of the territorial males have harems of females, which are allowed to enter the territory and stay there, where the male frequently courts and mates with them. The courtship consists of nodding, which differs from the territorial nodding display in that it is more rapid and without any definite pattern. After mating, the males gradually lose their territorial behavior and again assemble in large groups with little mutual antagonism.

The females, now inseminated, form aggregations near the nesting areas and become aggressive and quarrelsome. They display toward other females and butt them as they dig their shallow nest burrows. Females have been observed to become trapped when a half-completed burrow has caved in on them, and several deaths occur in this way. On Hood, burrows occur on the top of cliffs from sixty to one hundred feet high, which the females climb from the shore to reach the nesting areas. Once the burrow is completed, the female turns round in it and lays usually two white, large, soft, bluntly rounded eggs about three inches long, then closes the entrance to the burrow, packing it tight with legs and head. Development of the embryos probably takes place at 83–86° F. (Bartholomew, 1966b). After more than two months the eggs hatch, and the young dig their way out through the roof of the egg chamber. At this time, they are particularly vulnerable to predators, and Miguel Castro has seen gulls and herons feeding on such newly emerged young.

The Galápagos Hawk feeds largely on marine iguanas where these are abundant, and Carpenter records that they scatter at the flight of a hawk over the beach. Snakes also take young marine iguanas, and mockingbirds have been seen pecking at freshly laid marine iguana eggs. Iguana carcasses are eaten by the bright red Galápagos crabs, *Grapsus grapsus*, as well as by hawks. Ticks infest marine iguanas, and the small Galápagos finches *Geospiza difficilis* (on Narborough) and *G. fuliginosa* (on Hood) move freely among the reptiles, hopping onto their backs and feeding on ticks from the neck, groin, and axillae. Mockingbirds and crabs have also been observed deticking marine iguanas.

A reptile, of course, is ectothermic—its body temperature does not remain at a constant independent level, but varies with, and is largely dependent on, the conditions of its external surroundings. The daytime temperature of the environment of the marine iguana varies from a maximum of over 122° F. on the bare surface of a lava flow at noon in the sun, to a minimum of from 72 to 81° in the sea, depending on the season.

Mackay (1964) measured the body temperature of a free iguana at Academy Bay by means of a thermistor inserted into the abdominal cavity. This was connected to a small radio transmitter, of neutral buoyancy, which was fixed to the base of the iguana's tail. A small loop antenna was strapped across the animal's back, and pulse signals from the transmitter, indicating the body temperature of the animal, were received on a pocket transistor radio. Mackay released the animal at about 4:00 P.M., when its body temperature was 83°. By midnight its temperature had dropped to 80° and at 8:00 A.M. the next morning it was 78°. Its temperature then rose, to 92° at noon, when it entered the sea, the temperature of which was 79°. After about an hour the animal's temperature had fallen to that of the sea, and the signal was then lost. The animal was located again at 8:30 A.M. the next morning, basking in the sun; its temperature was then 100°.

The behavior of marine iguanas appears to be remarkably independent of their body temperature. Bartholomew (1966b) has observed that the marine iguanas of Narborough are as alert, their movement as rapid, and their nesting and egg-laying activities as persistent and efficient at body temperatures of 77°F. as they are at body temperatures of 99°. Carpenter (1966b) has recorded marine iguanas feeding under water, the temperature of which was 73° and too cold for prolonged observation by the skin diver. The activity temperatures of other iguanid lizards are generally around 95°. Marine iguanas thus carry out their most strenuous activity at a body temperature which is unusually low.

Although marine iguanas feed at a low temperature in the sea, they do have a preferred body temperature on land of between 95° and 99°F. This preferred temperature is some 18 to 21°F. above that at which they carry out their feeding activities.

Reptiles, being ectothermic, must regulate their body temperatures largely by behavioral means. Most of them rely on movement between cooler and hotter regions of their environment, but many also supplement this method by changes in posture. Marine iguanas are unusual in relying almost completely on postural changes, and do not move between sunlight and shade to regulate their temperatures. Apart from the single feeding excursion they make each day, they remain on bare lava, completely exposed to the sun, which at noon in the Galápagos is directly overhead. While ashore during the day, by changes in posture only, they are able to achieve body temperatures that are higher or lower than the environmental temperature and that approach the preferred range of body temperature. Bartholomew (1966b), in a most interesting study of these reptiles at Punta Espinosa, Narborough, has shown how this is done.

In the early morning, or at any time when the sky is overcast, or when the iguanas have just returned from the sea, they assume a prostrate posture. They lie quite flat on their bellies, with their legs splayed out at right angles and the head and neck resting on the substratum. In hot weather, I have seen a boxer dog assume a similar posture on a cool tiled floor. But whereas the dog will do this to cool off, bringing a maximum of body surface into contact with the cool floor, the marine iguana assumes the posture when its body temperature is lower than 95° F. and it needs to obtain as much heat from the environment as possible. The sprawling prostrate posture is taken up with the body at right angles to the sun's rays. In the early morning the reptiles assume the posture on the east-facing slopes of the smooth convex lava flows at Punta Espinosa, thus exposing as much of their bodies as possible to the warming rays of the rising sun.

On clear sunny days, when the iguanas' body temperatures are likely to rise above the preferred limits, the lizards change their position, assuming an elevated posture with the fore part of the body held clear of the substratum on extended front legs. Except around noon, all animals face one direction—toward the sun. This posture and orientation exposes a minimum of body surface to the sun's rays, and the elevated posture increases exposure of the body surface to the cooling breezes, which seldom exceed 86° F. Moreover, conduction of heat from the hot laval substrate to the body of the animal is minimized, and some heat is probably lost by radiation from the underside of the animal to the small area beneath it, which is in the shade of the fore part of the body. This posture and orientation is so effective in keeping down body temperature that although the temperature of the lava and of a black-bulb thermometer may be over 122°F. the body temperatures of the iguanas never exceed 104°F. Bartholomew tethered some iguanas, so that they were prevented from assuming the elevated posture and could not point themselves at the sun. They soon overheated, their body temperatures quickly rising above air temperature to approach the temperature of the lava. One such experimental animal died when its body temperature rose to 115°F.

Bartholomew has shown that, depending on body size, the body temperature of an iguana can fall from 104° to that of sea water (81°F.) within from ten to sixty minutes after immersion. However, the rate of cooling appears to be under physiological control, at least to some extent. Bartholomew and other workers have shown that lizards of three other families have some physiological capacity for regulating their rates of heating and cooling, their cooling rates being 64 to 95 per cent of their heating rates. The marine iguana, which experiences an unusually large range of body temperatures, has the greatest control of the rate of its temperature change so far observed in any lizard. In both air and water its cooling rate is about half its heating rate.

Bartholomew and Lasiewski (1965) suggest that in the marine iguana, as in lizards of two other families, this control is probably effected by adjustments of the blood circulation. The heart rate is much slower during cooling than during heating at any given body temperature, and this difference in heart rate is much greater in water than in air. Like other aquatic reptiles, such as alligators, grass snakes, and turtles, the marine iguana's heartbeat slows down and becomes irregular when the animal is submerged. During experimental submergence, simulating a dive, the heart rate fell off, until within from ten to twenty minutes after submergence it had dropped to 16 to

45 per cent of the rate before submergence. This is about the same as the minimum heart rate in air, which, however, takes hours to develop. On emergence, the heart rate immediately rises, often with a slight overshoot. The rapidity of this restoration of heart rate suggests that it may be under nervous control.

By reducing its rate of cooling in this way when in the sea, the marine iguana is able to extend the time during which its body temperature is near the preferred range, and yet it is able to warm up again very quickly once it has left the sea.

Thus, on land the marine iguana maintains its body temperature at a level close to its preferred range by changes in posture rather than by movement, and on submergence its rate of cooling is evidently under physiological control. It is capable of quite normal and vigorous activity at an unusually low body temperature, although by behavioral and physiological means the duration of such low body temperatures is kept to a minimum.

Bartholomew suggests that the maintenance of an elevated body temperature might be advantageous because in social encounters a warm animal would have an advantage over a cold one. However, this is difficult to accept in view of his observations on the unimpaired activity of animals at low body temperatures. He also points out that a high body temperature would facilitate the digestion of seaweed.

There is some evidence of island differentiation in the marine iguana, although it is a swimming marine animal, which, theoretically at least, can move freely between islands (Eibl-Eibesfeldt, 1956, 1962). However, the island populations are usually all referred to a single species. The most differentiated population is that on Hood, in the extreme southeast. Reproductive adults of this population, particularly males, take on an extremely bright and characteristic color pattern, being largely mottled red, orange, and black, with green front legs and a green crest from the back of the head to the tail. Moreover, the Hood form seems to be unique in defending its egg-laying sites after laying (Eibl-Eibesfeldt, 1965). The form on Tower, in the extreme northeast, is small and dark and has even been referred to a separate species, although this is not generally accepted. Dowling (1962) recognizes seven forms, on eight islands, and although his map shows marine iguanas to be absent from Charles, Barrington, Duncan, Jervis, Bindloe, Culpepper, and Wenman, I have seen them on all these islands. There is a population at Punta Albermarle, the northernmost point of Albemarle, which appeared to me to show differences from the others. The individuals were much larger, over four feet in length (as big as the fur seals that also occur there) and of a striking black-and-buff coloration. The greatest concentration of marine iguanas on the archipelago is undoubtedly at Punta Espinosa on Narborough, although dense populations also occur on Jensen, Isla Pitt near north Chatham, and on a rocky islet south of the western tip of Hood.

Eibl-Eibesfeldt (1955) discovered that on land, marine iguanas have some "homing" ability. He moved individuals as much as 400 yards, and they returned to their original area of ground. Many observers, including Eibl-Eibesfeldt, have noticed that marine iguanas frequently lick the ground with their tongue, as though testing it, and this behavior could possible provide the animal with information about the detailed geography of its basking site.

Swimming iguanas have been seen as much as 850 yards offshore, but such long-range forays are dangerous in the shark-infested waters of the Galápagos, and the lizards' swimming powers would be no match for the strong currents which sweep through Galápagos waters. Darwin, who referred to these animals as "imps of darkness," noticed that even when alarmed, iguanas were reluctant to take to the water and that an iguana cast into the sea would invariably return to the nearest piece of land—that is, to the thrower. He observed: "Perhaps this singular piece of apparent stupidity may be accounted for by the circumstances that this reptile has no enemy whatever on shore, whereas it must fall prey to sharks. Hence probably urged by the hereditary instinct that the shore is its place of safety, it there takes refuge." As mentioned above, today at least the marine iguana has enemies ashore too, in the hawk and the snake; however, it is not known how long the Galápagos hawk has been on the archipelago, and it is likely that it is a more recent arrival than the marine iguana.

Bartholomew noted that only iguanas that had been basking in the sun were reluctant to enter the water. He found it very difficult to obtain body temperatures of animals that had been at sea feeding: as he approached them when they emerged from the water, they immediately returned to the sea and swam away. Bartholomew suggests that marine iguanas normally maintain their body temperature above 95° F. while ashore during the day, and that basking iguanas will only enter the water, and thus lower their body temperature by from 18 to 21° F., for the purpose of feeding. An iguana returning from the sea would already have a low body temperature, which would not be decreased by an immediate return to the sea. Feeding activity was probably more vital to the life of the iguana in its evolutionary history than was escape from predators.

Although iguanas feed mainly on seaweed, their stomach contents occasionally include the remains of crabs and shrimps. The iguanas around the research station sometimes enter the dining room during meals, when they will quickly pick up any scraps of meat or other kind of food thrown to them. Karl Angermeyer, who lives in a cliffside home at Academy Bay, regularly feeds his marine iguana neighbors by hand with table scraps of all kinds. Nevertheless, they are said to be very difficult to feed in the captive conditions of zoos.

CHAPTER SIX

Giant Tortoises

In the days of the early Spanish visitors, these huge, grotesque reptiles, the males of which may grow to five or six feet in length, weigh as much as six hundred pounds and be capable of carrying a man on their backs, were so common on the archipelago that the islands were named "Islas Galápagos,"—tortoise islands.

J. Van Denburgh (1914) quotes one of the earliest descriptions of the tortoises, that of the buccaneer Woodes Rogers: "The creatures are the ugliest in Nature, the shell not unlike the top of an old hackney-coach, as black as jet; and so is the outside skin, but shriveled and very rough . . . and look very old and bleak. . . . Two of our men affirm they saw vast large ones of this sort, about four feet high. They mounted two men on the back of one of them, which, with its usual slow pace, carried them and never regarded the weight. They supposed this could not weigh less than 700 pounds." On another occasion he comments: "I saw no sort of beast, but there were guanos [iguanas] in abundance, and land-turtles almost on every island. It is strange how the latter got there, because they cannot come of themselves, and none of that sort are found on the main."

Amasa Delano described his first encounter with these reptiles in 1817 as follows (from Van Denburgh):

I was put in the same kind of fear that is felt at the sight or near approach of a snake at the first one I saw, which was very large. I was alone at the time, and he stretched himself as high as he could, opened his mouth, and advanced toward me. His body was raised more than a foot from the ground, his head turned forward in the manner of a snake in the act of biting, and raised two feet and a half above his body. I had a musket in my hand at the time, and when he advanced near enough to reach him with it, I held the muzzle out so that he hit his neck against it, at the touch of which he dropped himself upon the ground and instantly secured all his limbs within his shell. They are perfectly harmless, as much so as any animal I know of, notwithstanding their threatening appearance. They have no teeth, and of course cannot bite very hard. They take their food into their mouths by the assistance of the sharp edge of the upper and under jaw, which shut together one a little within the other, so as to nip grass, or any flowers, berries, or shrubbery, the only food they eat.

This author also credited them with a certain learning ability.

They are very prudent in taking care of themselves and their eggs, and in their manner of securing them in their nests; and I have observed on board my own ship, as well as on others, that they can easily be taught to go to any place on the deck which may be fixed for them to be constantly kept in. The method to effect this is by whipping them with a small line when they are out of place, and to take them up and carry them to the place arranged for them, which being repeated a few times will bring them into the practice of going themselves.

Giant tortoises are present today only on Narborough, Albemarle, Duncan, James, Indefatigable, Hood, and Chatham. They are now extinct on Jervis, Abingdon, Charles, and Barrington, and apparently have never populated Culpepper, Wenman, Bindloe, or Tower. Brosset (1963) stated that a few individuals remained on Marchena (Bindloe) and mentioned the severity of tortoise-hunting on that island. This is surely an error; there is absolutely no evidence that there were ever tortoises on Bindloe, and there is no reference to this island in whalers' logs. Possibly Brosset mixed up the island with Pinta (Abingdon), where tortoise skeletons were recently found in fissures in the lava.

Although Hendrickson (1966) regards them all as belonging to the single species *Geochelone elephantopus*, first described by Harlan in 1827 under the genus *Testudo*, he recognizes no less than fifteen subspecies, ten of which occur or have been known to occur on ten separate islands. Of the remaining five, each is restricted roughly to one of the five major volcanoes of the large island of Albemarle (FIGURE 19). Van Denburgh has suggested that the five Albemarle subspecies evolved each on

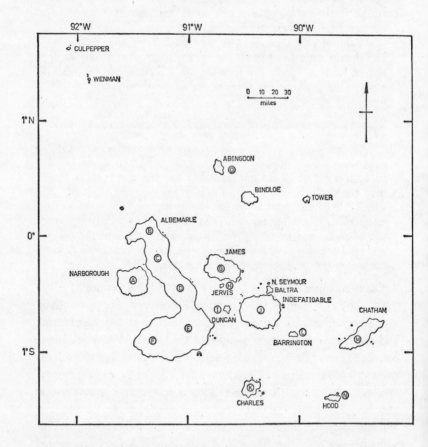

FIGURE 19. Distribution of subspecies of the Galápagos tortoise *Geochelone elephantopus*. Letters indicate different subspecies.

separate islands which were later united into a single large island in the geological past.

Darwin (1845) made a number of observations on the habits of tortoises, many of which have not yet been improved upon; he even timed them, finding that they moved 360 yards in an hour, or four miles in a day "allowing a little time for it to eat on the road."

> The tortoise is very fond of water, drinking large quantities, and wallowing in the mud. The larger islands alone possess springs, and these are always situated towards the central parts, and at a considerable height. Therefore the tortoises which frequent the lower districts are obliged to travel from a long distance when thirsty. Hence, broad and well-beaten paths branch off in every direction from the well down to the sea coasts; and the Spaniards, by following them up, first discovered the watering places. When I landed at Chatham Island, I could not imagine what animal travelled so methodically along well-chosen tracks. Near the springs it was a curious spectacle to behold many of these huge creatures, one set eagerly travelling onwards with outstretched necks, and another set returning after having drunk their fill. When the tortoise arrives at the spring, quite regardless of any spectator, he buries his head in the water above his eyes, and greedily swallows great mouthfuls, at the rate of about ten in a minute.

The dome-shelled tortoises of Indefatigable spend much of their time half-submerged in such pools, or in semiliquid mud wallows which they actively form by churning up grass and mud with their legs. On Duncan, there are rocky hollows in the crater area which collect water in the wet season, and in these places the rocks have been polished smooth by the undersides of tortoises. According to Carpenter (1963), Moncayo has seen as many as 280 tortoises on Indefatigable in an area fifty yards square where there was standing water. Three weeks previously only twenty were present in this area, and when it became dry there was none.

In contrast to mammals, reptiles lack a muscular diaphragm. Breathing is usually accomplished by increasing the thoracic volume simply by an outward movement of the ribs. However, in tortoises the ribs are fused together to form a bony shell and are immovable. There has been some controversy over the way in which tortoises do breathe. Some workers, for example Hendrickson (1965), believe that tortoises normally force air into their lungs under pressure by a sort of pumping-swallowing mechanism, periodically allowing the air to escape in a long hissing sigh. Hendrickson believes that the habit of wallowing in pools may assist in lung ventilation, since when a tortoise is partially submerged its shoulder blades do not have to act in supporting the animal's weight and can then be used in breathing. The shoulder blades lie within the ribs and against the lungs, and Hendrickson thinks that rhythmic pressure on the lungs by the shoulder blades results in efficient lung ventilation by a sort of bellows action. He has observed this type of breathing on Indefatigable in a male which had become exhausted after chasing another and used a deep pond in this way after a presumed oxygen lack. D. W. Snow (1966a and b) suggests that for this reason the availability of water holes and ponds may be a factor limiting the size of some of the Galápagos races. Those races on dry islands such as Hood and Duncan never attain the great size of, for example, the dome-shelled forms of Indefatigable or Volcan Alcedo. As Snow points out, however, food supply must also be an important factor.

Gaymer, who has studied the giant tortoises of Aldabra Atoll in the Indian Ocean, thinks that this explanation of the wallowing behavior is most improbable. He points out that on land the legs of a tortoise can be relaxed when its weight is taken by the underpart of its bony shell, the rigid plastron. Gaymer believes that inspiration of air would be more difficult when the animal was partially submerged in water than it would be when the animal was resting on its plastron on land, for the external pressure would be greater in water (Gaymer, 1968).

The studies of Gans and Hughes (1967, also Hughes and Gans, 1966) on *Testudo graeca*, the common pet tortoise of Europe which is fairly closely related to the Galápagos tortoises, have shown that the swallowing mechanism is unimportant in lung ventilation, but movements of the forelimbs are important, even when the animal is not submerged in water.

The lungs are very large and occupy the dorsal part of the body cavity. Their walls are closely attached, above and to the sides, to the inner sides of the rigid carapace, and below to a non-muscular diaphragm of connective tissue, which lies above the peritoneal cavity in which lie the remaining viscera. Thus the only way the volume of the lungs can change is by a deflection of the diaphragm. Although this is non-muscular, it is kept stretched downward by the weight of the liver and alimentary canal which are firmly attached to it but do not have other firm connections. The viscera are surrounded by fluid and, although their cavity is enclosed by rigid skeletal structures to the sides and below, the anterior and posterior boundaries of the visceral cavity are not rigid. Outward rotation of the shoulder girdles extends the anterior limit of the cavity, and their inward rotation reduces it. The posterior boundary is a cup-shaped layer of muscle and connective tissue, and changes in the convexity of this layer are possible. A flattening of the layer tends to reduce the volume of the cavity and a deepening of the cup shape tends to increase it. By changes at both anterior and posterior boundaries a hydrostatic pressure in this cavity can be built up, resulting in the upward deflection of the diaphragm and thus a reduction in the volume of the lung cavity.

Gans and Hughes recorded the pressures both within the lungs and within the visceral cavities of living tortoises. They also measured the extent of forelimb movement and the electrical activity in the muscles associated with the anterior and posterior boundaries of the visceral cavity and the opening and closing of the glottis. From these records they were able to show that both increase and decrease in pressure in the lungs is synchronized with muscular activity at each end of the visceral cavity and movement of the forelimbs. The tortoise opens its glottis and expels air from the lungs by flattening the curvature of the posterior boundary of the visceral cavity and moving the forelimbs inward. It then inspires by increasing the convexity of the posterior boundary of the visceral cavity and moving the forelimbs outward. The glottis is then closed, and the posterior border of the visceral cavity slightly drawn in, recompressing the lungs to slightly above the pressure at the beginning of the breathing cycle. Another cycle of activity occurs after a pause varying from four seconds to twenty-three minutes, during which the tortoise does not breathe at all. During this pause the lung pressure gradually falls to the original level, which is above atmospheric pressure.

Thus both inspiration and expiration were shown to be active processes, powered by an unusual hydrostatic mechanism. Gans and Hughes observed that after fright or exercise, the tortoise's limb movements increased in amplitude and frequency, and the head and neck came into play, pumping in and out in time with the limbs. From these studies it is clear that this species of *Testudo* can actively ventilate its lungs on land by limb movements and that partial submergence in water would not facilitate this process.

TEMPERATURE REGULATION

Gaymer has suggested that on Aldabra the mud wallows may assist in temperature regulation. On the Galápagos, it is the bulkier, dome-shelled forms that inhabit moist areas, while the smaller forms with more flared carapaces generally occur in arid environments. The former types have the smaller surface area to volume ratio, and if they become overheated it is more difficult for them to lose heat from the body surface.

Mackay (1964) studied temperature regulation in Galápagos tortoises by telemetry. Small radio transmitters the size of marbles were fed to the animals, which were then free to roam in natural surroundings. The transmitters were introduced by turning the tortoise on its back, tickling its foot to elicit a hiss, and then dropping the transmitter into its open mouth. The transmitter would then be swallowed. Alternatively, the transmitter was secreted in a banana which was then fed to the animal. The transmitters indicated temperature by the rate of pulses transmitted, and the signals were picked up on an ordinary pocket transistor radio receiver. The transmitter did not move much within the body of the animal, until passed after a few weeks, and continuous transmission of signals was possible during this time.

Mackay showed that when the animal had freedom of movement its deep body temperature varied by only a few degrees, and the cyclic fluctuations followed much more pronounced fluctuations in shell temperature, but with a lag of about five hours. Both air temperature and ground temperature also showed much greater fluctuations than the deep body temperature. The results indicated that waves of heating and cooling were not simply diffusing through the animal's body, but that heat was flowing through the high thermal resistance of the animal's shell and into the body tissues where it was rapidly and evenly distributed by the blood circulation. This thermal mechanism allowed the animal to regulate its body temperature within quite narrow limits by heating up and cooling the shell through movements into and out of the sun.

BEHAVIOR

The tortoises of the arid regions feed chiefly on the prickly pears and grass, and also eat low herbage, such as the leaves of the *Croton* bush and *Castela galapageia*. They seem to ignore the salt bush, *Cryptocarpus*, which is common in the dry lowlands. In the moist and transitional zones they are recorded as eating grasses, *Scalesia* leaves, the acid berries of the "guayavita" (*Psidium galapageium*), and the green tresses of filamentous lichens (*Ramalina* and *Usnea* species), which hang from the branches of trees. The reptiles are particularly fond of the poisonous, applelike fruits of the "mancanillo" (*Hippomane mancinella*), which pass through their guts unchanged except in color and cause a swelling of the intestine. Moncayo is reported to have seen them on three occasions eating the dried skin of a goat and once feeding on a rotting goat carcass. Loveridge (1945) states that a captive Galápagos tortoise was observed to capture and eat two live rats and a live pigeon, and was suspected of killing and eating a macaw and an agouti, which shared its cage. This tortoise readily ate raw meat. Evidently the tortoises are rather opportunistic in their feeding, and their choice of food depends to some extent on what is readily available.

At dusk the tortoises push their way into thick grass or vegetation, and by side-to-side movements make a snug "form" in which they lie up during the night.

Old males are in general larger than females and have relatively longer tails. When mating begins, the males become quarrelsome and large males indulge in ritual combat. Heller (1903) writes that each stands as high as possible, and with jaws widely gaping, attempts to strike down on the top of the other's head. Carpenter says Moncayo witnessed males fighting by repeatedly charging each other from six feet away and withdrawing the head just before impact. The animals also often extended their necks and waved their heads from side to side, sometimes banging their heads together.

At this time the sexual drive is so intense that males will attempt to mate with large rocks. Mating occurs, according to most reports, in about February in the transitional and moist zones on the islands where these are present, and continues through March and April. There are reports that during courtship the male circles the female, stops—facing the side of her shell—then raises himself as high as possible and drops his heavy plastron onto her carapace with a loud thud. Carpenter has reported Moncayo's description of copulation, which usually occurs during the day. The male smells the female's tail, and mounts her carapace, stretching his neck so that his head lies beside that of the female, which is partially retracted. The male moves forward rhythmically, sliding back each time, while the female moves up and down. The male is often so much larger than the female that all four of his legs may remain on the ground during copulation. Following each thrust, the male makes a loud grunting roar, which Moncayo says can be heard a mile away. Many other field workers, including Darwin, have remarked on the ability of mating males to produce loud grunts. Beck wrote: "Love affairs were in full progress during our stay, and the amorous exclamations of the males could be heard at a distance exceeding 300 yards, even in the thick forest." Moncayo watched one pair which kept up these copulatory movements from 7 A.M. to 1 P.M., when the male twisted his tail round that of the female. The female then began circling around, breaking sticks and fallen branches in the process, and this continued for a further three hours, after which the pair separated. Hendrickson (1966) states that in Bermuda successful copulation in captive Galápagos tortoises lasts for only up to thirty minutes, and that the female stands passively throughout the process.

Most observers have noticed that the animals appear to be deaf, ignoring loud noises, even gunfire, and only withdrawing with a hiss into their shells when they see the intruder. Darwin, Porter (quoted in Slevin), Slevin (1935), and Hendrickson (1966) have all remarked upon this, although an interesting note is provided by Heller of the 1899 Stanford expedition: "No amount of noise seemed to frighten them and the Ecuadorians assert that they are deaf. A small one, however, taken at Iguana Cove, Albemarle, learned to recognize the voice of its keeper in a few months, and would come to the gate of its pen when called though the keeper was hidden from its sight."

NESTING

The natural history of these great reptiles is now being thoroughly and systematically studied by Miguel Castro and his colleagues at the Darwin Research Station, but certain aspects of the egg-laying behavior have already been discovered by Hendrickson, who studied the Indefatigable populations.

Toward the end of the wet season, in April or May, the

female, with her bladder and body cavity full of stored water, moves down to certain quite well-defined nesting sites in the arid lowlands. These are flat depressions covered with fine, dense soil. Here, she urinates on a patch of soil in an open sunny spot and by rotating and pressing her hind foot on the resulting muddy area she forms a hole about seven inches in diameter and from eight to ten inches deep. In this hole she lays about seven, but occasionally as many as twenty, white, hard-shelled, spherical eggs about the size of billiard balls. She then lowers herself over the opening and by sliding her underside about on the surrounding raised mud forms a smooth cap almost flush with the surrounding soil. This dries and hardens in the sun to the consistency of baked clay, and the surprising thing is that, although the underside of this cap is irregular, according to Hendrickson there is almost no extraneous soil in the cavity with the eggs. The peculiar method of producing the cap, which appears to be so inefficient, nevertheless seems to have been carried out in some way without fragments falling onto the eggs.

Beck gives rather a different description of the nests of the Sierra Negra, Albemarle, form: "The holes were about 15 inches in depth, and nearly a foot in diameter. The eggs were placed in layers of 3 to 6, the first layer being on the soft soil on the bottom, separated from the rest by an inch or so of dirt, and the second layer separated from the third in the same manner. The dirt surrounding the eggs was loose, but the top of the hole was covered to a depth of 3 to 4 inches with a very hard crust that had probably been formed by the tortoise lying on it and working from side to side in the same manner that we frequently noticed them working down a form to lie in."

Moncayo says that sometimes a female will push a stone over the completed nest. This field worker once followed a female for half a day and watched her make five nests. He examined the first and last, and found five eggs in each. Moncayo states that nesting and egg laying occur in April or May, although

Hendrickson quotes reports in the literature indicating a nesting season from September to November.

Shaw (1967) states that breeding in the San Diego Zoo was only successful after a fairly yielding surface was provided which facilitated copulation. Wetting the surface with a sprinkler also helped to induce females to lay. At San Diego, eggs were broken and cracked by females arranging the eggs in the nest with their feet, and also during the laying process, when eggs dropped on others already in the nest. Shaw also believes that the females' habit of covering the eggs with earth and forcibly stamping it down also resulted in the further cracking of eggs. From two to twenty-two eggs were laid in a clutch, with an average of twelve, and the period from laying to the emergence of young tortoises onto the sand varied from 161 to 246 days. In the Galápagos, Moncayo built an enclosure round a nest in which he had observed egg laying, and the young tortoises began digging their way out thirteen months later. He believes hatching takes place at the time the females are again laying. Shaw has observed that just before hatching, the eggshell becomes friable and the outer layer is easily broken by the movements of the young tortoise within. The inner membrane is then ruptured by the claws and by the prominent egg tooth at the top of the snout. At San Diego, females sometimes laid more than a single clutch a year, but fertility was very low (10 per cent of all eggs laid). In the Galápagos, Moncayo has found nests in which the eggs were infertile or rotting.

Hendrickson suggests that in the wild the hatchling tortoises spend long periods sealed in the egg chamber and are only able to dig their way out if heavy rainfall causes water to collect over the nest sites and soften the hard walls and lid. He found many nest cavities which had not received such rainfall, and which contained dead, sometimes mummified, hatchling tortoises. The function of this careful nest-sealing behavior is difficult to understand; many nests must never be softened, particularly on the low, dry islands, and the mortality of young must thus be very high. The tortoises live to a very great age, however, and their reproductive life is probably well over fifty years, so that an occasional successful hatch—say one year in ten —would be enough to replace individuals that died of old age (before the advent of man, these old tortoises had no real enemies).

There are no reliable records of tortoises living more than 100 years, although greater ages have been claimed; Slevin mentions individuals for which there is some evidence of ages of 152 and over 300. The annual growth rings on the plates of the carapace are good indicators only for the first score of years or so; after that the carapace becomes worn and the rings are obscured. In 1902 Beck noted that on Sierra Negra, Albemarle, the carapaces of older tortoises near the summit were scarred as though with falling ash and lava, while those of the younger ones were smooth and unspoiled, as were those of old individuals living near the foot of the mountain. He suggested that the scarring was in fact due to an eruption, although from features of the terrain this must have happened a very long time previously, testifying to the tortoises' great age. Large individuals are not necessarily very old; a large size is reached after about twenty years, after which growth continues, although more slowly. On hatching, tortoises weigh under ¼ pound, and may reach 1¼ pounds after one year. Heller records that a 29-pound Albemarle tortoise, captured probably in its fourth year, gained 101 pounds in the following three years. After seven years in captivity this animal weighed 350 pounds, and when it died eight years later it weighed 415 pounds.

Tortoises are one of the few animals upon which lichens grow (Gressitt reported in 1966 that lichens also grow on the backs of weevils in the high mountains of New Guinea). The lichens on tortoises grow only on the crescent-shaped area on the upper rear of the carapace; the underside, sides, front, and top being continually scraped as the animal forces its way through the undergrowth. Moreover, the lichens only grow on males. This is probably because the rear part of the carapace of females is subjected to scraping by the underside of males during copulatory activity.

Roger Perry has informed me that mosquitoes, as well as ticks, attack the giant tortoises and can be seen in the early evening lining up along the sutures on the plates of the tortoises' carapaces where they feed. Tortoises in the moist areas often spend the night almost totally immersed in pools, a habit that presumably reduces mosquito attack.

THE ORIGIN OF THE TORTOISE POPULATIONS

The various islands' tortoise populations are all recognizably distinct. In fact, the vice-governor of the islands at the time of Darwin's visit claimed to be able to tell from which island a tortoise came, just by looking at it, a fact that greatly interested Darwin. However, all the island forms clearly seem to be derived from a common stock. Loveridge and Williams (1957) classify them, along with living and Pleistocene fossil South American species, into a subgenus, *Chelonoidis*, of *Geochelone*. The related Pleistocene fossil West Indian species are placed in a second subgenus, and the living species from the Aldabra Islands of the Indian Ocean in a third. The question is, how could tortoises from South America have reached the Galápagos, which are now some six hundred miles away and separated by open ocean? There seems to be general agreement that whether the present islands were formed by the emergence of separate volcanoes or by the subsidence of a large land mass, they have never been directly linked to the continent by land (see CHAPTER 2). Although all the authorities agree that the intervening water gap was probably not always of the same extent that it now is, there are some who argue that the water gap was much smaller in the past, and others who claim it was even more extensive. The conclusion seems unavoidable, however, that the ancestors of the present Galápagos fauna must, in the past, have crossed a stretch of open ocean of at least a few hundred miles. The present ocean currents would carry a floating object from the South American coast to the Galápagos in about two weeks (see CHAPTERS 2 and 10).

It is perhaps more difficult to imagine giant tortoises—the adult males sometimes weighing five hundred to six hundred pounds and having five or six foot shells—crossing such a gap, than, for example, the ancestors of the lava lizards. However, it must be borne in mind that the tortoises' ancestors may not have been of such gigantic proportions as those of today, and also that it need not necessarily have been adults that made the first successful colonizing crossing.

Simpson (1942) provides some evidence of the ability of tortoises to cross stretches of ocean over long periods of time. A fossil giant tortoise named *Testudo gringorum* (the name *Geochelone* had not then been used, as it is now, for the larger part of the old genus *Testudo*) was discovered in Argentina. This was found in deposits formed some 10 to 25 million years ago in the Miocene epoch, at a time before the Galápagos Islands are thought to have been built up. The genus first occurred 40 to 60 million years ago in the Eocene, an earlier epoch near the beginning of the Tertiary era, and it was later widespread over the northern continents, before the late Tertiary land bridge, the Panama Isthmus, existed. After this it became world wide, and survives to the present, having now mainly a southern distribution. Simpson concludes that the most likely explanation of a *Testudo* occurring in South America *before* the existence of the Panama land bridge is that it made the journey by a partly marine route, probably from North America, possibly from Africa, its migration being facilitated by islands.

Simpson states that this genus "floats readily and can survive long periods of involuntary immersion in the sea. Once within sight of land it can and does purposefully swim to it if tide and currents permit." William Beebe filmed a Galápagos tortoise that swam well and was able to direct its course toward an objective, although the animal died a week later. Moncayo says that although tortoises do not enter the sea, if thrown overboard from a vessel, they get to shore.

Van Denburgh (1914) gives a graphic account of the perils and discomforts of tortoise collecting near Iguana Cove in 1906, which has some relevance to this problem. He describes how two male tortoises were driven down to the shore.

> They were too large to get them into the boat. We failed to get them in while the boat was on the beach. Then we towed one out and tried to get him in; but as the boat was in the breakers and half full of water it sank when we got the tortoise aboard, and he floated off while we struggled in the water. Luckily, King was on the beach, for he cannot swim. Williams struck out for shore, while Beck and I tried to turn the boat over, for by this time the swells had rolled it bottom up. The current was too strong for Williams to make the beach, so he came back to the boat. With his assistance we righted it, and getting two oars that were stuck under the seats, Beck sculled and I pulled till we got near the rocks. Then I swam ashore with the painter and pulled the boat in, so Beck and Williams got ashore. We tried to pull the boat along the rocks to the beach, but the swell was so heavy that it was smashed into a thousand pieces. All that was saved was the painter and two oars . . . By this time it was five o'clock, so we put on what clothes we had left, and made back along the coast, while our tortoises were drifting away out to sea. [His field notes for the following day continue:] Still anchored at the Cove. We sighted the two tortoises drifting down the coast and, putting out the boat, rescued both of them. One was badly battered up, and evidently had been knocked up against the rocks by the surf. We also picked up several pieces of our skiff. The tortoises had been in the water about eighteen hours, and seemed none the worse for it. They would stick their heads out of the water ocasionally and look around while they floated along like corks, nearly all the carapace being out of the water.

Captain Porter (later Admiral Porter) of the U.S. frigate *Essex* stated in 1815 that two vessels captured by him had large tortoises on board, many of which were "upwards of three hundred-weight [336 pounds]." His account, quoted by Van Denburgh, contains the following pertinent passage: "Numbers of them had been thrown overboard by the crews of the vessels before their capture, to clear them for action. A few days afterwards, at daylight in the morning, we were so fortunate as to find ourselves surrounded by about fifty of them, which were picked up and brought on board, as they had been lying in the same place where they had been thrown over, incapable of any exertion in that element, except that of stretching out their long necks." Whether or not the tortoises were incapable of "any exertion," this account is certainly evidence that large tortoises can float in the sea without ill effect for "a few days."

However, it is also possible that tortoises may have reached the islands by means of natural rafts. Masses of vegetation can be seen floating down the Guayas River at Guayaquil during the early part of the year; some of these are quite large and could probably support a small animal. Agassiz (1892) reported currents off Panama carrying large quantities of drift toward Cocos Island and the Galápagos, sometimes moving seventy-five miles in a day; he mentions too that the Albatross Expedition found the ocean floor covered with decaying vegetable matter far out to sea. Possibly this is the foundered waterlogged vegetation of the floating mats seen near the coast.

There is thus considerable circumstantial evidence to support Simpson's conclusion that the distribution of giant tortoises is not dependent on and not primarily the result of land connections. The presence of giant tortoises in South America in the Miocene (10 to 25 million years ago), as a possible ancestral stock of the Galápagos tortoises, means that the accidental crossing from the continent could have occurred at any time since the Galápagos first were formed, and the chances of such an event happening over this long period of time cannot be ignored. It also means that a very long period of time may have been available for the differentiation of distinct island forms of tortoise in the Galapagos.

One of the enigmas of the distribution of the Galápagos tortoises is the problem of their colonization of the different islands. Bearing in mind their powers of endurance without food or water, we can conceive how tortoises could have reached the archipelago from the mainland, either floating from river mouths or on natural rafts of vegetation. It is much more difficult, however, to explain how the original colonists moved from their first island landfall to the other islands, for there are no rivers on the islands, and only one permanent stream, on Chatham. It is very unlikely that tortoises would wander into the sea, for they do not normally inhabit the shore zone. Tortoises do, however, inhabit the coastal arid zone of some islands, and certainly did in the past, when they were more numerous. Also, the remains of tortoises that fell into lava caves and fissures and could not get out have been found on Abingdon and Albemarle. Occasionally, living tortoises are seen that have damaged carapaces, caused by falls when negotiating rocky inclines. So it is at least possible that tortoises very occasionally could have fallen over low cliffs directly into the sea. On most of the tortoise islands there are places where such cliffs abut directly on the sea, without a true shore zone.

The "subsidence" theory would account for the distribution quite well, if one assumed that tortoises had populated a continuous primitive Galápagos land mass before it subsided and was thus subdivided into different islands. Tortoise populations would then be left on the new-formed islands (the five Albemarle volcanoes would be separate islands), and these populations, now effectively cut off from one another, would go their own evolutionary ways, subject to their own particular selection pressures. One might assume that the northern line of islands was cut off from the central group before the arrival of the tortoises and thus received no tortoises, except for the fact that Abingdon, a member of the northern line, is a tortoise island. One would also have to assume a later rising of Albermarle to effect the junction of its five volcanoes into the present island. Van Denburgh points out that the geologist of the Academy Expedition found that at Tagus Cove on Albemarle "a series of terraces, still containing the characteristic cavities of sea urchins, are now several hundred feet above the present sea level."

TYPES OF TORTOISE

The tortoises of the various islands differ chiefly in their carapaces, different island forms having consistently higher or lower domes on their shells, and developing distinctive, flared margins at the front and back. The tortoises on different islands also grow to different sizes, have longer or shorter necks and legs, and differ in the color and thickness of the carapace.

Two main types can be distinguished. One type, with a really dome-shaped carapace and short neck (PLATE 25), is represented by the forms on James, Indefatigable, Chatham, Charles (this form is now extinct), and southern Albemarle—areas of the Galápagos where vegetation is lush in the hills, and the tortoises can feed on grass and low herbage. The other type has a characteristic carapace resembling a Spanish saddle in shape, narrow and flared outward and upward in front (PLATE 26), and has a long neck and legs. The most extreme examples of this type are the forms from Narborough, Duncan, Abingdon, Volcan Wolf, and Hood. Subspecies of the saddleback type inhabit arid areas, where the tortoises must feed on the drooping branches of the giant prickly-pear cactus and on the sparse foliage of shrubs, a situation in which the ability to feed higher up the shrub or prickly pear would be advantageous. On Duncan, the saddleback subspecies has been seen eating the highest leaves of the epiphytic *Tillandsia*. Thus it is supposed that the longer necks and legs and upwardly flared anterior end of the carapace, allowing greater upward movement of the neck, evolved in these forms. The longer legs of the saddleback type have also been associated with the more difficult terrain of its arid habitats. It has also been suggested that the shape of the carapace might affect the ability of the tortoise to lose heat and that selection for this ability may have been involved in the evolution of carapace shape. All young tortoises, of whatever race, are very much alike; the saddle-shaped characteristics only appear as the tortoise grows older and are more pronounced in males than females.

D. W. Snow (1966b) has pointed out an interesting problem involving the tortoises of Indefatigable. In an area to the northwest of the island, which is fairly well isolated from the rest of the island by lava, the Angermeyer brothers, residents of Academy Bay, discovered a large male of the saddleback type, along with several young ones, the largest of which was beginning to develop the saddle shape. No adult female has yet been found in this area. The large tortoise population of Indefatigable is otherwise a typically dome-shelled race, and the male in question cannot be ascribed to this race at all, resembling much more the Abingdon, Duncan, or northern Albemarle subspecies. It is possible, though unlikely, that two distinct subspecies occur on Indefatigable. It is also possible that the male was introduced, perhaps from Abingdon or northern Albemarle, by some fisherman. If the latter, it is evidently breeding with a female of some kind, and producing young of the saddleback type. If the female (or females) with which this male is breeding is eventually discovered, it would be of great interest, particularly if the female in question is found to be of the dome-shelled type. This would mean that the subspecies can interbreed in nature and produce viable offspring, although in the normal course of events they would get no opportunity to do so. They would thus be correctly regarded as belonging to the same species. The fact that the offspring of the cross are developing the saddleback type of carapace would be of genetical interest if it could be established that the female was of a dome-shelled type. However, unfortunately, this small population is in danger of extinction because they must compete for food with the numerous goats in the area.

TORTOISES AND PRICKLY PEARS

An interesting mutual relationship between the giant tortoises and the prickly-pear cacti of the Galápagos has been pointed out by Dawson (1964, 1965, 1966). The prickly pears of the islands show evidence of a considerable evolution, and six species are recognized. On the northern islands, on which tortoises have never occurred—that is, on Culpepper, Wenman, Bindloe, and Tower—the only prickly pear found is *Opuntia helleri* (PLATE 27). This has soft, flexible spines, and is a low-growing, spreading species. Moreover, *O. helleri* occurs nowhere else in the archipelago. *Opuntia zacana*, which is also a low-growing, decumbent form, is found only on the island of North Seymour, also an island without tortoises.

On the tortoise islands, however, the prickly pears have sharp stiff spines and are large treelike forms with an erect growth habit and a straight thick trunk which lacks branches (PLATE 28); such an extreme treelike habit is found in prickly pears nowhere else in the world. This group includes *Opuntia galapageia* on Abingdon, James, Jervis, and Duncan, *O. saxicola* on Narborough and Albemarle, *O. megasperma* on Charles, Chatham, and Hood, and *O. echios* on Albermarle, Indefatigable, Daphne Major, Baltra, and Barrington (FIGURE 20).

Dawson suggests that the treelike habit was evolved as a result of selection pressures produced by the feeding of tortoises, and that *helleri* on the northern non-tortoise islands is close to the ancestral form of *galapageia*, *saxicola*, and *megasperma*, while *zacana* represents the ancestral stock of the various *echios* varieties. Recent morphological and chemical analyses of Galápagos prickly pears by Anderson and Walkington (1968) support Dawson's classification and proposed lines of evolution among the Galápagos opuntias, but provide no support for the hypothesis that they originated from opuntias in coastal Ecuador. On two islands, Jervis and Daphne, there is some

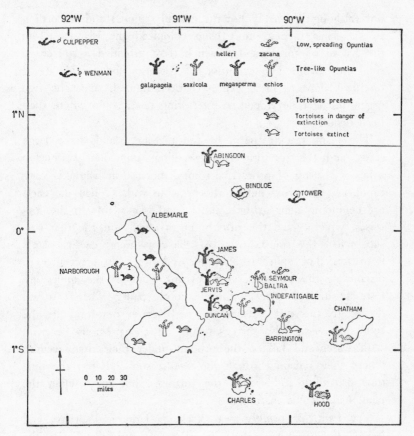

FIGURE 20. Relationship between tortoise distribution and growth habit of prickly-pear species.

evidence of a regression to the low-growing, bushy habit of the presumed ancestral stock, and Dawson believes that this may be related to the absence of tortoises and goats. On these islands regeneration from fallen pads results in low, spreading plants, although existing seedlings tend to retain the treelike form.

The prickly pears of the Galápagos are thus probably derived from a single stock originating on the mainland of Ecuador (although probably not the coastal regions) and, according to Dawson's theory, must have colonized the islands before the arrival of tortoises, for which they provided a source of food and drink. The evolution of tortoises and prickly pears on the Galápagos may well have been mutual, since the two organisms have developed an interesting relationship where they both occur.

The giant prickly pears of the tortoise islands have large seeds, and the resulting large seedlings immediately develop a heavy coating of protective spines. Increase in height is very rapid, as pads grow out of the previous pads. When the cacti are beginning their growth, other food is available to the tortoises, which graze the prickly pears chiefly in the dry season, when the spiny armor of the developing cactus plants is mature. This spiny basal armor and the rapid erect growth discourage the tortoises; as the trunk thickens the spines are lost, but in their place a thick, smooth, papery "bark" is laid down. In the wet season, the pads grow out, and in the following season the shriveled pads of the previous year fill with water and fall to the ground under their own weight, where they remain through the wet season and into the dry, thus providing fodder for the tortoises, but only when the plant has become mature.

The fruit, or prickly pear itself, is large and fleshy, and falls to the ground on maturity. It is soft and palatable to the tortoise, and the contained seeds pass unharmed through the gut of the reptile, whose feces provide nutriment for the growth of the seedling during the early critical stages. The tortoise, in its wanderings, also ensures that the seedlings are well distributed. Studies on the Galápagos tomatoes have shown that passage through the guts of either tortoises or mockingbirds increases the germinating power of their seeds. It would be interesting to find out whether passage through the tortoise gut has a similar beneficial effect on the germinating seeds of the prickly pear, for it has been observed to have a low percentage germination in several of the present forests.

On several islands the goat has now replaced the tortoise as a browser on prickly pear, and will even gnaw through the thick trunk and cut it down.

PREDATION BY MAN

Although Darwin found tortoises to be numerous on the islands in 1835, they were already extinct on Charles by 1876, and they were very rare on Chatham. On Hood, James, and Indefatigable they were no longer present in numbers sufficient to warrant hunting (see CHAPTER 1).

Vast numbers were taken first by the Spanish, and the buccaneers and pirates of the seventeenth century who used the archipelago as a safe refuge and provisioning station, and later by the whalers and fur sealers in the nineteenth century. The pirate-naturalist William Dampier describes how Captain Davies of the *Bachelor's Delight* in 1684, took sixty jars of oil from the Galápagos tortoise, to be used "instead of Butter to eat with Doughboys or Dumplins in his return out of these Seas" (Shipman, 1962). Townsend (1925) reports that over 5000 are recorded as being removed between 1811 and 1844 in the logbooks of American whalers. Added to this must be an unknown number removed by British whalers, whose logs were not available to Townsend. The fur sealers also took their toll; one such, Captain Benjamin Morrell, in describing his visits of 1823 and 1825 states that he saw "some that would weigh from six to eight hundred pounds." He is quoted by Van Denburgh:

> I have known whale-ships to take from six to nine hundred of the smallest size of these tortoises on board when about leaving the islands for their cruising grounds; thus providing themselves with provision for six or eight months, and securing the men against the scurvy. I have had these animals on board my own vessels from five to six months without their once taking food or water; and on killing them I have found more than a quart of fresh water in the receptacle which nature has furnished them for that purpose, while their flesh was in as good con-

dition as when I first took them on board. They have been known to live on board of some of our whale-ships for fourteen months under similar circumstances, without any apparent diminution of health or weight.

Morrell took 187 tortoises from Indefatigable in a fortnight in 1825.

War vessels also used tortoises as a source of meat, water, and oil. Captain Porter of the U.S. frigate *Essex* writes (1815) that when the Americans captured two English vessels from James, they "found on Board them eight hundred tortoises of a very large size, and sufficient to furnish all the ships with fresh provisions for one month." Of one of his own visits to James he writes:

> In four days we had as many on board as would weigh about fourteen tons, which was as much as we could conveniently stow. They were piled up on the quarter-deck for a few days, with an awning spread over to shield them from the sun, which renders them very restless, in order that they might have time to discharge the contents of their stomachs; after which they were stowed away below, as you would stow any other provisions, and used as occasion required. No description of stock is so convenient for ships to take to sea as the tortoises of these islands. They require no provision or water for a year, nor is any further attention to them necessary than that their shells should be preserved unbroken.

The early settlers used tortoises encountered in the bush as a source of water. Darwin believed that the bladder acted as a reservoir of water, its contents being quite limpid, and having, according to him, "only a very slightly bitter taste." He states that the inhabitants, however, would for first preference drink the water in the pericardial sac. In the nineteenth century, settlers hunted tortoises for their oil, the fat from a full-grown animal yielding about three gallons of clear oil. Darwin describes how captured tortoises were cut to expose the fat under the dorsal plate; if this was thick, the tortoise was killed, if not, it was released, and apparently quickly recovered from the incision made near the tail.

In the late nineteenth and the early part of the present century the plunder went on, but this time in the name of "science." In the expedition reports quoted by Van Denburgh (1914) about 500 tortoises are mentioned as being removed. The total number must be a good deal greater than this. The New York Zoological Society took away another 180 specimens in 1928 (see below). On many expeditions, embryo tortoises were pickled and eggs were blown whenever they were discovered. Time and time again, scientists, after collecting on an island, declared the tortoises of that island to be extinct, only for some later expedition to discover survivors, which were promptly skinned and carried away as precious specimens of a "dying" race. These "last survivors" were collected from Duncan by four different expeditions in 1897, 1898, 1900, and 1901, and yet the Academy Expedition of 1905–6 discovered eighty-six tortoises on that island, which they killed and removed for study; over sixty of these were females.

In comparison with the thousands removed as provisions in the previous two or three centuries, these numbers admittedly are small; but it must be remembered that the populations from which they were taken were already drastically reduced and struggling for their very survival. Indeed, the paradox is that this was the very reason given for their removal!

Such thoughtless, overenthusiastic collecting happily is not possible today. Scientists must first obtain permission from the Ecuadorian government, which is advised by the Director of the Charles Darwin Station. He must be satisfied by watertight scientific arguments before a single specimen can be removed from the islands. Such government permission is extremely difficult to obtain, and rightly so. Scientists wishing to study the tortoises are encouraged to use the facilities of the station and study them alive, in their natural habitat—the Galápagos Islands.

Today, wild pigs uproot tortoise nests and eat eggs and young, rats prey on eggs and small hatchlings, and wild donkeys and cattle roll and step on nests. Donkeys appear to be the least damaging in this respect. On Volcan Alcedo, where there are many wild donkeys, there is a thriving tortoise population. Wild dogs and cats feed on young tortoises, and even today, man is still an occasional predator.

POPULATIONS TODAY

On Narborough, only a single specimen has ever been found. This was seen by that energetic naturalist, Beck, during the 1905–6 Academy Expedition. He climbed the 4900-foot-high Narborough volcano by the very difficult southern route from Punta Mangle on the coast, found tortoise droppings half-way up the mountain, continued to the crater rim, where he was the first man to see the great crater lake of Narborough, returned to the tortoise droppings, searched for and found a large male, skinned it by moonlight, and then carried the heavy shell and skin to the shore, all in the space of three days. No tortoise has since been seen on Narborough, in spite of several expeditions with the particular aim of searching for it. Surely, though, tortoises still exist on Narborough. Hendrickson (1965) found recent droppings and a partly eaten cactus pad, although no tortoises were seen. There are no feral predators on Narborough, and the island is sufficiently uninviting and difficult of terrain to discourage any would-be hunters, and there are no records of tortoises being removed by whalers. There is the possibility, however, that volcanic action may have reduced the population to a very low level; and there was an eruption as recently as 1968.

Of the five Albemarle subspecies, that on Volcan Wolf still appears to exist in fair numbers, D. W. Snow (1966b) reporting many hundreds on the northern slopes. There is a fair-sized colony behind Punta Albemarle, although we saw none on the rim of the crater in 1967. The only feral animals on this mountain are cats.

On the adjacent Volcan Darwin, 64 individuals have been marked by Miguel Castro, Conservation Officer of the Research

Station, and its seems likely that a fair population survives on this volcano, on which we saw no feral animals at all.

The research workers of the Darwin Research Station mark the tortoises so that their movements, ages, and growth rates may be more easily studied. The method of marking tortoises is rather interesting. Fairly large individuals over two years old are marked by sawing notches in the margins of the carapace. At the front and hind margins there are eight large plates, which are coded in the following way: the anterior left plate nearest the mid-line is allocated the value 1, the next one laterally 2, the next 4, and the next 7. Thus by no more than two notches any number from 1 to 9 may be recorded. On the right front side these plates are coded as 10, 20, 40, and 70, while the rear plates are coded in hundreds on one side and in thousands on the other. In this way up to 15,000 individuals can be numbered without repeating any number, and using at the most, ten notches (FIGURE 21). Growing tortoises, which have the notches renewed, are sometimes marked with paint instead.

Wild dogs, cattle and possibly goats are said to live on Volcan Alcedo, although I saw only wild donkeys during my visit. Castro has marked 174 tortoises on this volcano, where they may be found on the rim of the crater and on the huge circular crater floor itself, as well as on the slopes. Castro has expressed the opinion to me that Alcedo probably carries the largest population in the Galápagos. During my own short climb of this mountain I encountered 19 individuals above 1200 feet, 5 of which were marked. A rough computation would thus suggest that about 700 individuals must be present, although it is likely that free movement of individuals is hampered since their range includes the crater floor, and thus this estimate must be only very approximate. A pair of adult hawks was seen at 1400 feet; Darwin stated that "young tortoises, as soon as they are hatched, fall a prey in great numbers to carrion-feeding buzzards."

The population on Sierra Negra is not in such a healthy

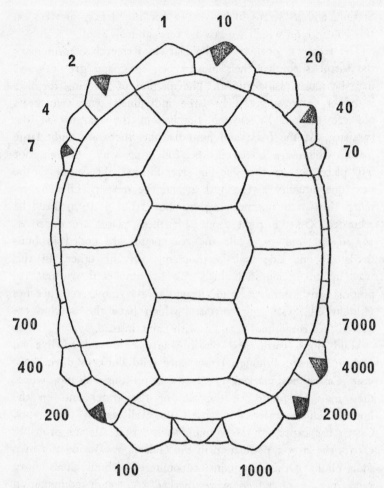

FIGURE 21. Method of marking tortoises by sawing notches in the carapace scutes (see text). The individual represented is marked number 6259.

state and only 12 individuals have been marked. This mountain has wild dogs, cattle, cats, goats, pigs, and horses, and in 1928 the New York Zoological Society Expedition removed 180 tortoises of various sizes from the mountains of southern Albemarle.

A single individual has been marked on Cerro Azul; wild cattle and packs of wild dogs roam the southern slopes and the summit plateau. Doctor Eliasson and I were attacked by a small pack of wild dogs on this mountain in April 1967.

Tortoises still occur on James in the east-central part of the island. Two were seen in 1963 near James Bay, and Castro has marked 26 on the island. The situation on the small neighboring island of Jervis is puzzling. Although tracks were seen in 1897, only one specimen has ever been found there, and this was removed by the Academy Expedition in 1905. Whalers' logs make no mention of Jervis as a source of tortoises although the island has a good anchorage. Search parties from the *Zena's Coffin* found none in 1850. The actual locality from which the type specimen of the Jervis subspecies, *wallacei,* was collected is unknown, and it was only referred to that island by Van Denburgh because it was like the specimen removed by the Academy Expedition. This latter, however, could easily have been an accidental escape. Jervis still has, near the anchorage, the remains of a tortoise enclosure in which tortoises, possibly from other islands, were coralled by whalers before their departure from the archipelago. It is thus quite possible that Jervis never had a tortoise of its own at all. Van Denburgh states that there was a rumor that the tortoises on Jervis were introduced there by Doctor Baur, who visited Jervis in 1891, and continues, "I confess it is with a certain lack of confidence that I have concluded to use the name *T. wallacei* for this Jervis Island tortoise."

In 1906 the Abingdon tortoise was already rare, and the Academy Expedition was only able to find three specimens, which were removed to the United States. A survey expedition in 1957 was not successful in discovering any, although in 1964 Castro found the remains of 27 individuals at the bottom of deep overgrown fissures in the lava. These tortoises presumably had met an accidental death, and seemed to have been dead at least for several years. In 1957 there were no goats on Abingdon, but in 1963 a few which had been released there were in the early stages of expansion, and they were numerous by 1964. Today, the southern slopes are literally overrun by goats. The tortoises, however, were clearly rare before the advent of goats, which cannot be blamed in this instance for their decline.

The Academy Expedition in 1906 found only three Hood Island tortoises, which they removed. Twenty-three years later, the Pinchot Expedition found two individuals, which were removed, since the race was "believed to be extinct." Goats have been present on Hood for the last fifty years and here constitute important and dangerous competitors of the tortoise. Castro has so far marked five individuals on Hood, and in 1963 he observed one chewing a fallen *Opuntia* pad in the company of no less than fifteen goats. The pad was soon finished, and the animals then started on the trunk. Probably the population on this island is very low.

In 1964 a family of colonists on Chatham were found to have as pets two young tortoises, less than five years old, which they said had been found in the neighborhood. Castro's subsequent search in 1965 resulted in the marking of four individuals and two years later he discovered eight more tortoises and a recent nest containing four eggs which had been trampled by wild donkeys. In June 1969, a third expedition was made to northeast Chatham and 69 individuals were marked. Thus Castro has shown that the Chatham population is certainly not yet extinct, as had been supposed (Castro, 1970).

Despite the ravages in the "interests of science," chiefly by the Academy Expedition, which removed 86 Duncan tortoises, over sixty of which were females, this island race has survived. However, it is now in danger from the introduced rats, *Rattus rattus*, which eat its eggs and young. Snow estimated that about 140 tortoises occurred on Duncan, all adults. Castro has now marked 98 individuals on the island. The Research Station has begun a program of removing eggs from the wild and hatching them in the laboratory. The resulting offspring are carefully fed and reared for some months, and then liberated on the island when they are big enough to fend for themselves. In 1967 more than 70 young were being reared in this way, and when we visited the tortoise area of Duncan several adults were seen and Castro brought back another batch of eggs as the result of our visit. This program shows much promise, and it is possible that the Duncan population will thereby be saved.

The best-studied population in the islands is that on Indefatigable, where over a thousand individuals have been marked. They occur in the southwest and western regions of the island, in the coastal and transitional zones, and are successfully propagating in spite of the depradations of wild pigs which force open the shells of young individuals and also root up nests.

In 1928 the New York Zoological Society, believing the tortoises of the Galápagos to be nearing extinction, removed 180 specimens from the islands as a breeding stock, and sent them to zoos and scientific organizations in various parts of the world. The success of this venture has been very limited. Shaw states that most of the animals in collections are the larger, more display-worthy males, and that, since the distribution to zoos was made, only 34 tortoises have successfully hatched in captivity. At the San Diego Zoo, where there is the largest collection, only 10 per cent of eggs laid were fertile, and only 7 per cent hatched. In Honolulu, Bermuda, and Miami, fertility has been equally low. By 1960 only 122 Galápagos tortoises survived in zoos (Honegger, 1960), and often it is not known from which island population these have arisen.

The situation on the islands is not as desperate as was believed in 1928, although it is serious. On Albemarle it is likely that the population on Alcedo will survive, and with careful conservation those on the Darwin and Wolf volcanoes may also be saved. The Indefatigable population, lying as it does under the watchful eye of the Research Station, would seem to have a future, and the Chatham and Duncan tortoises have good chances of survival. On James and Hood the outlook is less hopeful, while the status of the Narborough tortoise is still a mystery.

Contrary to the statements of Street (1961a, b), not all the Galápagos Islands are overrun with predators, and the place to save the Galápagos tortoise is in the Galápagos Islands themselves. With the whole archipelago now declared a national park and nature reserve, and the presence of the Darwin Research Station to ensure conservation and protective measures, the outlook for the Galápagos tortoises is brighter than it has been for two hundred years. Man has finally awakened to the fact that by his actions he has partly destroyed an irreplaceable assemblage of living creatures intimately associated with the discovery of the greatest and most all-embracing process that affects living things. Whether this awakening has come in time for him to salvage at least some of the unique forms involved remains to be seen.

CHAPTER SEVEN

Land Birds

THE land birds of the Galápagos, taken as a whole, show a very wide range of differentiation from continental forms and of divergence among themselves within the archipelago. Wallace (1880), in drawing attention to this, suggested that the degree of divergence might be an indication of the length of time the various groups had been present on the archipelago, those reaching it earlier having had more time in which divergence and differentiation could proceed. However, we know that evolution proceeds at different rates in different organisms, the rate depending on several factors, both genetic and environmental, so that time is unlikely to be the only factor involved in these different degrees of divergence. For example, birds that are habitually wide-ranging will be less likely to produce locally distinct forms than birds that are weaker flyers or relatively sedentary in their habits. This is because in a wide-ranging species there will be a continuous flow of genes between populations, preventing any local accumulations of particular assortments of genes from resulting in the appearance of distinct local forms. The pressure exerted on the local populations by selective forces is also an important factor determining the rate of evolution, and this will surely be different for different organisms. Of course, time is also a factor, but it is by no means the only one, and it is necessary to bear this in mind before drawing conclusions concerning past events from the present situation.

Some Galápagos birds are identical with mainland species, such as the cuckoo, moorhen, and American Egret. Others have diverged only slightly from continental forms, producing races or subspecies peculiar to the Galápagos, such as two of the herons, the pintail duck, flamingo, yellow warbler, martin, and the owls. The hawk has differentiated to the extent of becoming a distinct species peculiar to the archipelago, but it has not evolved further into endemic island forms. The vermilion flycatchers, however, do show the beginnings of divergence within the archipelago. The doves and mockingbirds are sufficiently distinct on the Galápagos to be regarded as endemic genera, and among the mockingbirds there has been a considerable evolution of distinct island forms. Finally, there is the remarkable assemblage of finches, which constitutes a subfamily peculiar to the Galápagos and Cocos; adaptive radiation and divergence into particular and often unusual habitats has resulted in an array of forms with a range of structure and habits as great as that of continental birds from different families.

The cuckoo, *Coccyzus melacoryphus*, is said to be identical with the South American species (Lack, 1947) and the moorhen, *Gallinula chloropus*, which breeds on Indefatigable and near Villamil, Albemarle, is the same species as the European moorhen. The moorhen is found on all continents except Australia, and has colonized many oceanic islands. The subspecies *cachinnans*, which occurs in the Galápagos, is the same as that on the American continent. Three egrets occur in the Galápagos: the Snowy Egret, *Egretta thula*, a migrant visitor; the Cattle Egret, *Ardeola ibis*, also a migrant, which has recently extended its range to the New World and has now reached the Falkland Islands as well as the Galápagos; and the American Egret, *Egretta alba*, which breeds on the archipelago. None of the three Galápagos egrets differs from the continental form. The turnstone, *Arenaria interpres*, is found in the

Galápagos, although it breeds as far away as the Arctic. In general, the remarkable tameness of Galápagos land birds is confined to the residents; the migrants show normal fear at the approach of man.

Swarth (1931) considers the Black-necked Stilt, *Himantopus mexicanus*, to be an example of a Galápagos form in an early stage of differentiation from the ancestral mainland stock. He found that the Galápagos birds were shorter legged than those in California, although he was unable to compare them with South American specimens, and so did not designate the Galápagos population as a separate subspecies.

Swarth (1931) and Palmer (1962) regard the Yellow-Crowned Night Heron of Cocos and the Galápagos (*Nyctanassa violacea*) as a distinct subspecies (*pauper*) of the Mexican mainland form, and Swarth believes there is the beginning of divergence between the Cocos and Galápagos populations. This heron (PLATE 29) is a common shore bird of the islands, although it does not seem to occur on Culpepper or Wenman. On Hood, I found this bird nesting about half a mile from shore; there were two eggs in the nest together with a stone of about the same size and shape as the eggs. The Great Blue Heron, *Ardea herodias*, is less common, and has not yet been reported from any of the northern line of islands. The Galápagos subspecies, *cognata*, is rather paler than the mainland form, whose nearest breeding place is in Mexico (Voous, 1960; Palmer, 1962).

Endemic forms have also evolved in two other water birds. The flamingo, *Phoenicopterus ruber*, is like the West Indian Flamingo but with some of the characteristics of the South American species. The Galápagos birds are quite pink, with black markings on the wings, and are fairly shy, taking off if approached nearer than about fifty yards. This is the Galápagos bird most in danger of extinction; Lévêque (1964) estimated that only about 100–150 individuals remained. They are usually found in shallow salt-water lagoons and build their exposed, raised, mud nests near James Bay (north James), Tortuga Bay (Indefatigable), on Bainbridge, and on Charles. They can also sometimes be seen on southern Albemarle and in the Jervis lagoon.

The Galápagos pintail is a subspecies of *Anas bahamensis*, the Bahamas Pintail. In contrast to the flamingo it is still fairly plentiful, although it is fairly tame. It can be found in the salty crater lakes on Tower and near James Bay; in the Jervis lagoon; on bodies of both fresh and saline water on Indefatigable; in the fresh-water crater lake of "El Junco" on Chatham where we saw about fifty individuals; and on the warm sulphurous lake of the great Narborough crater, where we saw hundreds of birds in 1967 and where the population was estimated as about 2000 in February 1968 (before the June eruption and crater collapse).

The Galápagos martin is also an endemic subspecies of the continental martin, *Progne modesta*. It occurs in small numbers on the main group of islands, although it has not yet been seen on Narborough or on any of the northern islands (Culpepper, Wenman, Abingdon, Bindloe, or Tower).

Ridgway (1919) has described the Galápagos oyster catcher, *Haematopus palliatus*, as an endemic subspecies, *H. palliatus galapagensis*. Swarth pointed out that this is more closely related to the Lower California form than it is to the Atlantic form, which crosses to the Pacific in the Panama region.

Two owls occur in the archipelago—the Barn Owl, *Tyto alba*, and the Short-eared Owl, *Asio flammeus*. Both are endemic Galápagos subspecies of wide-ranging species that are well known in Europe, for example. The Short-eared Owl is present on all the islands except Wenman, whereas the Barn Owl only occurs on the large central islands of Narborough, Albemarle, Indefatigable and James, and possibly also on Chatham and Abingdon. The Barn Owl is truly nocturnal but the Short-eared Owl hunts partly in daylight. These Galápagos forms are fearless and inquisitive, often coming to the campfire at night and perching a yard or two away, staring at the unusual activity. A study of the ecology of the owls is now in progress at the Darwin Research Station.

Brosset (1963) remarks upon the habit of Short-eared Owls and Galápagos Hawks of "lodging" for periods of several days in the midst of breeding colonies of sea birds, from which they take nestlings. He cites the examples of a hawk staying among Swallow-tailed Gulls for five days and nights, and a pair of Short-eared Owls taking up residence in the middle of a colony of Blue-footed Boobies, on Hood. These two birds of prey, unlike the Barn Owl, do not appear to have fixed home ranges, but move about in an opportunistic way to wherever food is abundant, probably staying until the supply is exhausted—for example, when the breeding cycle of the sea birds is completed. The sea birds, having young, do not flee from the predator, but stay at their nest sites throughout the predator's sojourn among them. (A similar phenomenon has been observed by Ian Spellerberg (personal communication) in the Antarctic, where groups of juvenile skuas visit breeding colonies of penguins in almost the same way.)

The Yellow Warbler of the Galápagos, one of the only two brightly colored birds on the islands, although very similar to the Yellow Warbler of Ecuador, *Dendroica petechia*, is regarded as a distinct race, *aureola*, and is confined to the Galápagos and Cocos Island. It is found on all the islands of the archipelago, and is particularly common in mangroves and thick vegetation. Gifford (1919) says that "of all the Galápagos land birds, this warbler is met with most frequently away from the land." Of course, this would account not only for its wide occurrence in the Galápagos and Cocos, but also for the lack of distinctive island forms either on Cocos or within the Galápagos.

According to Gilliard (1958), the Green Heron, *Butorides sundevalli* (PLATE 30), is a separate species confined to the Galápagos. Swarth found some evidence of slight differentiation in the Chatham population. This bird is quite common, and is found practically throughout the archipelago. It is very tame, and is often seen at night feeding on insects about the village at Academy Bay, Indefatigable.

THE GALÁPAGOS HAWK

The Galápagos Hawk, *Buteo galapagoensis*, which is restricted to the archipelago, is related most closely to *Buteo swainsoni* of North America. Brosset (1963) believes that the whole Galápagos population now consists of not more than two hundred individuals. Hawks are now extinct on Baltra, which has lost most of its indigenous fauna, and they apparently no longer occur on Tower, where Beebe saw a dozen in 1924. After human settlement of the archipelago the hawks took to chicken stealing, and have been hunted by settlers to such a degree that on Charles, Chatham, and Indefatigable they are now absent or very rare. They have never been recorded from the outlying islands of Wenman and Culpepper. On the small island of Duncan, which is infested by the black rat, the hawk is particularly common.

For some reason, one does not expect tameness in a hawk; yet the Galápagos Hawk is very tame. These birds have the habit of following a man and coming down to investigate any ususual activity. On Duncan I slung my shirt on a stick to dry, and within a few minutes six hawks were visiting me, some settling within a yard or two. If sudden movements are avoided, these hawks can be touched by the hand without their taking flight. However, if there is any interference with their young, their behavior is not so amenable. When Doctor DeVries was ringing young hawks on Barrington, I had to defend him from their diving attacks as they came winging out of the sun, one after the other, striking at his head with their talons and swinging away to circle and dive again. He wears a sun helmet as protection from these attacks, and on one occasion a hawk knocked the helmet off his head. They also knocked the piece of cloth, which I was waving as protection, out of my hand. Later in the day we were fortunate enough to witness the mating display. The male flew above and behind the female, making mock attacks on her, and she then descended and landed, followed by the male. Copulation was carried out to the accompaniment of peculiar clucking noises. Afterward the male moved off with a low, slow flight, to sit and rest on the top of a cactus tree.

A bird of prey such as the hawk has no natural predators. It is at the top of a "food chain," and this of course applies to the hawks and eagles of continental areas as well as those of the Galápagos. Yet the hawks of the Galápagos are quite unusually tame and approachable in normal circumstances. Here is a clue to the reason for the remarkable tameness of the Galápagos animals. It is not that the animals have lacked natural predators in the past, but, as Darwin correctly observed, simply a matter of lack of selection for behavior that would be advantageous in circumstances where man is a "predator." Galápagos birds with a behavior pattern that would lead to their avoidance of man had no particular advantage over their fellows in the past, since man never came into contact with them; so this behavior was not selected for in the evolutionary history of the species and thus is not present today.

The juvenile hawks are pale-breasted and spotted liberally with dark brown flecks (PLATE 31), but the adults are very dark and, with their yellow bill and mouth and barred tail, are strikingly handsome birds. Their prey varies from island to island, and also with availability and the season. The main prey consists of lava lizards, rats, doves, centipedes, Audubon's Shearwaters, and marine iguanas, with some mockingbirds, Swallowtailed Gulls, finches, young land iguanas, young goats, boobies, flycatchers, and grasshoppers (DeVries, *in litt.*). There are occasional records of finches being taken, but they do not seem to be a regular feature of the diet, and they make up a very low percentage of the hawk's food spectrum. Finches have a good alarm system, and most species seem to forage more within bushes than around them. The inclusion of centipedes is rather surprising, for these creatures are seldom seen during the day.

The hawks are also scavengers of the islands. Except for the carcasses of seals, sea lions, and marine iguanas, they will feed upon any dead animal, including fish. They often follow goat hunters and investigate fishing boats, usually obtaining an easy meal of scraps for their trouble.

Brosset has pointed out several behavioral and ecological features in which he believes the Galápagos Hawk to be unusual among the family of buteonids. The Galápagos Hawks live in family groups of two or three, which roost, fly, and hunt together. Like vultures and the Galápagos Mockingbirds (see below), the members of a group of hawks co-operate in the surveillance of a large area, hawking within sight of one another. If any individual finds a large food source, all members of the group, and often other groups, quickly arrive to share the food. This social behavior differs somewhat from that seen in mockingbirds; a group of mockingbirds surveys a combined but well-defined territory, and groups are antagonistic toward one another, performing aggressive displays at the territorial borders. Brosset noted that some hawks at large sources of food, such as a goat carcass, were physically prevented from feeding by others, which knocked them over. In watching this behavior on several occasions, Brosset never saw retaliation; intimidated individuals, "emitting plaintive cries," simply waited their turn to feed. There was no evidence that hunger, age, or size played any part in determining which was the dominant individual. Brosset's observations were not sufficiently extensive to show whether the same individual persisted in being dominant in these encounters or not, nor was he able to make any distinction between encounters involving members of the same or of different roosting groups.

The Flycatchers and the Rail

Other birds that, like the hawk, have evolved into distinct Galápagos species during their isolation on the archipelago, but have not diverged into a number of forms on the archipelago itself, are the Galápagos Tyrant Flycatcher, *Myiarchus magni-rostris*, and the endemic rail, *Laterallus spilonotus*. In common with many other rails of oceanic islands, the Galápagos Rail may be in the process of losing the power of flight. This dark, medium-sized bird, with a somewhat laterally compressed body, is found in the thick vegetation of the moist zone, where it skulks and probes about the ground litter under the thick undergrowth. It occurs on the central islands of Narborough, Albemarle, James, Indefatigable, and also on Abingdon. On Abingdon we watched one for about an hour, and it never showed any sign of taking to flight. Even when challenged and chased away from the territory of a male lava lizard, it ran, scuttling away through the undergrowth. However, rails even on continents are notoriously reluctant fliers, a fact which has probably contributed to the ease with which their power of flight is lost on islands, and further studies should be made on this Galápagos rail to determine the extent of flight, if any.

The beginning of differentiation within the Galápagos can be seen in the Vermilion Flycatcher. The genus *Pyrocephalus* is represented on the mainland, and has been reported from all the Galápagos Islands except Culpepper, Tower, and Hood, all peripheral islands. The population on Chatham, also a peripheral island, is regarded as a distinct species, while those on the other islands are all placed in a second species. There is, however, sufficient difference between the population on Indefatigable and those on the remaining islands for the Indefatigable form to be regarded as a distinct subspecies by Swarth (FIGURE 22). In this group then, it seems that species multiplication on the islands is just beginning; three outlying islands have not yet been colonized, and a distinct species has arisen on a fourth. This demonstrates very nicely that, although isolated islands of an archipelago are less likely to receive immigrants, when they do there is much more likelihood of endemic forms arising. Immigrants to isolated islands are so very rare that there is very little or no intermixing of genes. Thus a new assortment of genes can be selected on the outlying island without con-

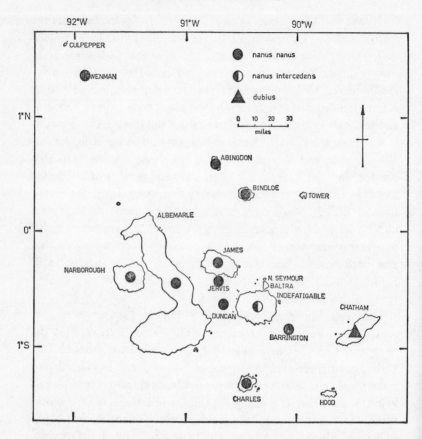

FIGURE 22. Distribution of Vermilion Flycatchers (*Pyrocephalus* species).

stant contamination and dilution from genes of the parental population. Although both the species are restricted to the Galápagos, they are quite similar to the mainland form. The male is bright red and black, and is the second of the two brightly colored Galápagos birds. Like most other Galápagos birds they show no fear of man; they are common in the hills, less so in dry country.

8. The female Magnificent Frigate Bird differs from the female Great Frigate in breast markings and eye ring.

9. A pair of Great Frigate Birds on the nest, Tower. The male's red gular pouch is inflated.

10. Immature Brown Pelicans, Cerro Brujo, Chatham.
11. Mature Brown Pelicans, Indefatigable. Photo U. Eliasson.

12. Galápagos Storm Petrel, Isla Pitt, North Chatham.

13. Waved Albatrosses, Hood. These birds are performing the "sway walk," a part of the courtship ritual. The head and neck of the retreating bird can be seen to be swung far over to the left as the right foot is raised; the bird in the foreground is following, with the same exaggerated walk. Photo Inga Eliasson.

14. The young of the Waved Albatross can ingest as much as four pounds of "chick oil" at one meal. Photo U. Eliasson.

15. A group of Galápagos Penguins on the lava rocks of Narborough. The Galápagos shore crab, seen in the foreground, is bright red. Photo U. Eliasson.

16. The wings of the Flightless Cormorant, photographed here on Narborough, are not used either in flight or in swimming, and the breastbone lacks a keel completely. Photo U. Eliasson.

17. The cormorants often spread their wings after swimming. Is this behavior a relic of the evolutionary past, when the immediate drying of functioning wings would have had survival value, or is it related in some way to temperature regulation?

18. The Lava Gull is well camouflaged as it stands on the lava shores. Its beak and legs are black, and the plumage is sooty gray; the white eye mark is only developed in adult birds. Photo M. Harris.

19. A Swallow-tailed Gull on the cliffs of North Seymour, with its single egg. At night, when stimulating the parent to regurgitate its food, the chick pecks at the tuft of pure white feathers at the base of the bill.

20. The white plumage of the immature Swallow-tailed Gull's head may be another adaptation to night feeding by its parent. This immature bird is in the typically hunched, submissive posture.

21. This tall, jointed, candelabralike cactus, *Jasmino-cereus thouarsii*, on Charles, bears the nest of a Darwin's finch. Photo U. Eliasson.

22. A large colony of *Brachycereus nesioticus* on Albermarle. This small cactus is one of the first colonizers of fresh lava flows. Photo by George Holton, Photo Researchers.

23. The land iguana *Conolophus subcristatus* on South Plaza islet, off Indefatigable. Photo U. Eliasson.

24. Marine iguanas at Punta Espinosa, Narborough.

25. A dome-shelled race, *vandeburghi*, of the giant tortoise, *Geochelone elephantopus*, on the crater floor of Volcan Alcedo, Albemarle. Dome-shelled races usually occur in localities where the vegetation is lush, and the reptiles can feed on grass and low herbage. Photo U. Eliasson.

26. A male tortoise of the saddleback race *hoodensis* from Hood. The flared carapace allows greater vertical movement of the long neck, and saddleback races are generally found in more arid environments where the tortoises must feed on the foliage of shrubs and the drooping branches of prickly pears.

27. The prickly pear on Bindloe, which has never supported a tortoise population, is the decumbent, soft-spined *Opuntia helleri*. Photo U. Eliasson.

28. *Opuntia echios* is treelike, and grows on Indefatigable which is a tortoise island. The undergrowth is chiefly *Croton scouleri*. Photo U. Eliasson.

29. The Galápagos subspecies of the Yellow-crowned Night Heron, photographed here on Bindloe, is a common shore bird of the islands, and occurs also on Cocos Island. Photo U. Eliasson.

30. The Green Heron of the Galápagos is regarded as a distinct species. Photo by H. F. Flanders, Photo Researchers.

The Galápagos Dove

This is also an extremely attractive bird. It is extremely common in some places and rare in others, although it is found on all the islands. Swarth regards the Wenman and Culpepper populations as together constituting a separate species, though other authorities would classify them only as a separate subspecies. In any case, here again is an example of differentiation proceeding on isolated, outlying islands. The Galápagos Dove, unlike the Vermilion Flycatcher, is classified in a distinct genus (*Nesopelia*) that is restricted to the Galápagos; it has thus diverged considerably more from its mainland stock. Unlike other doves and pigeons, the bill is rather curved. The eye is ringed with blue, and on either side of the neck there is a patch of bronze iridescent feathers. The doves are very tame, except near settlements, and were even tamer a century ago, when they were recorded as settling in clusters on the shoulders and headgear of buccaneers. These birds have thus suffered very severely from hunters; Peterson (1967) reports that as recently as 1965 ten men on James ate a total of nine thousand doves in three months. Early writers on the Galápagos invariably remarked how easily these birds were killed with sticks, and thousands upon thousands were killed for either food or "sport." The buccaneer William Dampier, who visited the islands in 1684, found the doves "so tame, that a Man may kill five or six dozens in a forenoon with a stick" (Shipman, 1962). They were somewhat less tame when Darwin visited the islands a century and a half later. However, in spite of their fatal tameness the birds have survived on all the islands except Baltra, where the toll taken by U.S. servicemen during the war was too much for the population to survive. On Tower and Hood they are particularly common, though on the inhabited islands of Charles, Chatham, and Indefatigable they are now rare.

The doves are ground nesters and usually lay a pair of fairly large white eggs. On Hood we disturbed a dove with a pair of chicks and the bird went into the conspicuous fluttering behavior of feigning a broken wing to distract our attention from the nest. Why should this endemic dove possess this distracting behavior if it has no ground predators? Although today on the inhabited islands this ground nester probably suffers severely from the attacks of cats and possibly also dogs, this situation is a very recent one, and in any case Hood is uninhabited and there are no wild cats or dogs on the island. Perhaps this is a behavioral relic of the species' previous evolutionary history which has survived because it is not actually disadvantageous and has thus escaped the pruning effect of selection.

THE MOCKINGBIRDS

Although the mockingbirds of the Galápagos are clearly derived from continental mockingbirds (genus *Mimus*), they nevertheless differ from them sufficiently to be placed by all authorities in a quite distinct Galápagos genus, *Nesomimus*. They are moderately large birds, about the size of thrushes, often with black markings about the sides of the head, gray-brown above and whitish cream below, with a fairly long tail and a curved, moderately long bill. Their behavior differs from that of their mainland relatives; the predatory habit is exaggerated, and they behave rather like jays (which are not present on the islands). They kill and eat young finches, small lava lizards, centipedes, and insects, and also feed on the eggs of other birds. Their legs and beak are longer than those of their mainland relatives, and they are highly cursorial, frequently sprinting along with wings held out to the sides, rather than flying.

There is an interesting social structure. A group of mockingbirds will feed in a communal territory, and within the group a peck order is developed, similar to that found in domestic hens. When any member of the group finds food, others come running to the find, and in doing so attract other birds even farther afield. Thus the territory is thoroughly and efficiently exploited, and the stronger birds of the community are able to benefit from food found by any one of the group. If food is in short supply, it will be the weakest, most expendable members of the group that go without.

The mockingbirds are extremely inquisitive, bold, and quite fearless of man, although they are said to show normal fear of cats. Curio (1966) states that mockingbirds show normal fear of snakes and birds of prey, but Doctor DeVries has seen one sitting on the head of a Galápagos Hawk and pecking at its feathers.

Speciation has proceeded further in the mockingbirds than in any other group of Galápagos birds except the finches. There are four species, and, in contrast to the finches, no two species occur on any one island (FIGURE 23). One species is restricted to Hood, another to Chatham, and a third to two small islets close to Charles, where it has possibly become extinct. The fourth species, *Nesomimus parvulus*, occurs on all the other islands of the archipelago except Baltra, where it was exterminated during the war by U.S. servicemen. In this widespread species seven subspecies are recognized, one each being present on Tower, Abingdon, Wenman, Culpepper, and Barrington, one on Bindloe, James, and Jervis, and one on Narborough, Indefatigable, Albemarle, Daphne, and (formerly) Baltra.

Hatch (1965) claims that the Hood species, *N. macdonaldi* (PLATE 32), is unique in that it feeds on eggs. Certainly the species on Hood is the most divergent, having an unusually large and heavy bill, well suited for breaking the large eggs of sea birds. Several colonies of sea birds occur on Hood, including the Waved Albatross, which is restricted to that island. The Hood Island birds have been seen to attack the eggs of many birds, including the Waved Albatross, Masked and Blue-footed Boobies, Swallow-tailed Gull, oyster catcher, and Galápagos Dove, as well as the eggs of the lava lizard and the marine iguana. However, Harris (1968) thinks it unlikely that the eggs of sea birds are normally available as a primary source of food. They have also been seen pecking at bleeding wounds on the feet of albatrosses, and pecking at blood on the

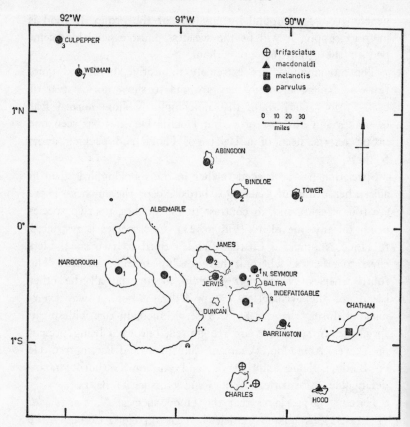

FIGURE 23. Distribution of Galápagos Mockingbirds (*Nesomimus* species). Numerical subscripts indicate different subspecies.

edge of the cloaca of a Blue-footed Booby, actually lacerating the cloacal rim itself and tearing off pieces of tissue. Nelson (1968) also saw them surrounding albatrosses that were feeding young, and picking up any of the oily regurgitate accidentally squirted on to the ground. They will also eat the contents of putrid albatross eggs, sea lion feces, fruit, and butter, and will drink almost any liquid available, including vinegar and even warm antiseptic! Many observers on Hood have remarked on their fearless and inquisitive nature, which seems to be even more marked than that of the populations on other islands. Hatch suggests that in this population a unique, exploratory type of behavior, like that of the finches of Wenman Island, has evolved. He also believes that, as in the Wenman finches (see next chapter), a unique feeding habit (in this case egg eating) has arisen, which has been prevented from spreading to the other islands by the isolation of Hood.

Harris has pointed out that this conclusion does not appear to be fully justified, for the subspecies of *N. parvulus* on Tower will also eat eggs. It has been seen eating eggs of Red-footed Boobies and frigate birds that had been broken by other frigates or lava gulls. Harris has also seen the Tower Mockingbirds pecking at unattended eggs of the frigate bird and trying to eject them from the nest, a habit which is paralleled by the Wenman population of the Sharp-beaked Ground Finch (see next chapter). This mockingbird also eats eggs of the Galápagos Storm Petrel, *Oceanodroma tethys*, that have been ejected from the nest site by the petrels as a result of competition within the species for nest sites. The mockingbird will even go several feet underground to get at the undisturbed eggs of this storm petrel. Harris also believes that broken eggs of the Galápagos Dove on Tower were the result of predation by mockingbirds, and Beck (1904) mentions the Tower Mockingbird picking at the eggs of a Yellow-crowned Night Heron that the photographer had temporarily disturbed on its nest.

The Charles Island Mockingbird, *N. trifasciatus*, confined to two small islets off Charles, is also suspected by Harris of eating the eggs and newly hatched young of the Blue-footed Booby.

Thus the egg-eating habit does not appear to be confined to the Hood species. Interestingly enough, those forms observed to eat eggs, or suspected of doing so, are those having the largest beaks. Swarth measured about three hundred individuals and found that the Hood species had the longest beak, the

Charles species the next longest. The subspecies of *N. parvulus* with the longest beak was the one occurring on Tower.

There is some evidence that the habit of eating the large foot-long Galápagos centipede *Scolopendra galapagoensis* is particulary well developed in the Culpepper subspecies of *N. parvulus*. This centipede seems to be unusually common on Culpepper (Fosberg, 1965).

There is a good deal of mystery surrounding the Charles Island Mockingbird. Darwin stated that the Charles species "was shot by myself and several other parties on board." The species is now believed to be extinct on Charles. The Academy Expedition did not discover a single bird in thirty-three days of collecting, and since Darwin's visit, no mockingbirds have ever been seen on Charles. The species does exist, however, on the islets of Gardner and Champion (FIGURE 9), which are adjacent to Charles, although a recent estimate by Harris and DeVries puts their numbers at not more than 150 individuals. It has been concluded that the species was formerly present on Charles, but was exterminated there by introduced cats and dogs, which ran wild after the island was settled. However, cats and dogs occur on Indefatigable and Chatham, where mockingbirds still exist. Moreover, at the time of Slevin's visit at the turn of the century, the northern coast of Charles, opposite Champion, was not inhabited by dogs or cats. If disease were responsible for the extinction of the Charles population, why did the disease not also spread to Champion which is separated from Charles by less than three-quarters of a mile of sea? Swarth pointed out that although it has been assumed without question that Darwin's specimens came from Charles, there is no positive evidence for this in his writings. Gardner-by-Charles was also visited by the *Beagle* expedition. Thus there remain the possibilities that the mockingbird was never established on Charles, or became extinct there long ago for some unknown reason. But whatever the truth may be about the bird's absence from Charles, it is extremely strange that no birds have been able to re-establish themselves on the island from neighboring Champion. Possibly mockingbirds are extremely sedentary in their habits, and do not fly very far afield from their home territories.

Such sedentary habits might also explain why in the mockingbirds, unlike the finches, there has not been a succession of reinvasions resulting in a number of species on each island. Nor has there been any adaptive radiation such as has occurred in the evolution of the finches. The mockingbirds, in fact, are at an evolutionary stage much more similar to that of the reptiles than to that of the finches. Most observers believe that the mockingbirds were much later arrivals than the finches, and are thus now at an earlier stage of differentiation in the Galápagos.

CHAPTER EIGHT

Darwin's Finches

THE most conspicuous land birds of the Galápagos, strangely enough, are inconspicuous in themselves. Sparrow-sized or a little larger, they are dull-colored with stubby tails (PLATE 33) and are noticeable because they occur in almost all parts of the islands, often in quite large numbers. Their song is not particularly attractive; they are noisy, active little birds. These are the animals that together with the giant tortoises and mockingbirds, interested Darwin so much, and have been appropriately referred to as "Darwin's finches" (Lowe, 1936). They belong to the finch family, but constitute a separate subfamily, the Geospizinae, which is found only in the Galápagos and on Cocos Island farther north, and which surely must be one of the most famous groups of birds in the whole of the history of biology.

Darwin noticed that the Galápagos finches consisted of many different species, each of which was quite clearly related to the others, but each species differed from the others in several respects, notably in the shape and size of the beak. It was only after his return to England, and after analyzing his collections of finches, that Darwin began to amass the formidable evidence that successfully challenged the then-existing belief that all animal species had been separately created and were then fixed for all time. If the "Special Creation" theory were true, Darwin reasoned, then it must have been a very strange coincidence that thirteen very similar species of these finches had been created on the Galápagos Islands, and nowhere else. This was a coincidence that Darwin was not prepared to accept. Instead, he postulated that the thirteen species were all descended from an original species, and that it was because they shared a common ancestor that they all had many features in common and thus looked very much alike. He also noticed that, apart from the finches, there were very few species of land birds on the islands, so that many environmental habitats would be unoccupied when the original colonists established themselves.

As early as 1845 Darwin was able to summarize his thinking, albeit rather cautiously: "Seeing this gradation and diversity of structure in one small, intimately related group of birds, one might really fancy that from an original paucity of birds in this archipelago, one species had been taken and modified for different ends."

If the population of the ancestral species were split up into smaller units that did not mix—as they generally could not on the different islands of an archipelago—then natural selection would work on each of these smaller populations slightly differently. In the environment of one such population, for example, it might be advantageous for a finch to be able to crack hard seeds, and, if so, any finch whose beak, by some accident of heredity, was larger and stronger than the others' would be more successful in contributing offspring to the next generation. In this way, large strong beaks would evolve in this population. The environment of another population, however, would be slightly different. In this environment there might well be a premium on ability to catch insects as food; in this case, selection would favor any individuals possessing more slender beaks, better suited to this type of feeding, and in this population an "insect-catching" type of beak would be evolved.

Today, Darwin's finches have been well investigated. Darwin's original collection was studied by Gould (1837, 1841, 1843,

1844). Later Gifford (1919) and Swarth (1929, 1931) revised the group systematically, and Lack (1940, 1945, 1947, 1953, 1969) treated the whole problem from an evolutionary and ecological point of view. Recently Bowman (1961, 1963) has made a further ecological and anatomical study, in which many of Lack's earlier conclusions are disputed.

The finches can be grouped into a number of genera (groups of species) according to their characteristic beak shapes and feeding habits. The six species of ground finch (*Geospiza*) are finchlike, feeding mainly on the ground in the arid and transitional zones and taking mainly seeds, but also some insects. The different species have bills of different strengths and sizes, enabling them to feed on seeds of different sizes and degrees of hardness. One species, the Cactus Ground Finch, *Geospiza scandens*, has gone its own way and, having taken up an arboreal existence, probes the yellow flowers of the prickly-pear tree cacti and feeds on the young ovules. It has a long, somewhat curved bill, and a split tongue, but its beak is thicker than most other flower-feeding birds, possibly because it is not completely restricted to flowers for food, but also feeds on seeds and some insects, like the other ground finches. It also occasionally feeds on the soft pulp of the cactus and builds its nest only in these cacti, usually between two terminal cactus pads. Sammalisto (1966) reports that this finch is also unusual in having a song-flight.

The three tree finches (*Camarhynchus* species) have somewhat parrotlike beaks and habits. They feed largely in trees, in the transitional and moist zones, excavating with their beaks into twigs and branches for concealed insects, but also taking a few seeds.

One species, the Warbler Finch (*Certhidea olivacea*), is placed in a genus of its own. This bird has the habits of a warbler, feeding exclusively on insects, which it takes with its slender, pointed bill from the surface of leaves or lichen clusters, or occasionally on the wing. It feeds in trees and bushes from the arid zone to the high moist zone.

In contrast, the Vegetarian Tree Finch, *Platyspiza crassirostris*, the largest of the Galápagos finches, feeds almost exclusively on plants, taking fleshy fruits and soft to moderately hard seeds, young leaves, buds, and flowers with its short, thick, and slightly curved beak. Like many other bud-eating and fruit-eating birds it is rather sluggish and leisurely in its activities. This species is also placed in a genus by itself.

Two other species, the Woodpecker Finch (*Cactospiza pallidus*) and the Mangrove Finch (*Cactospiza heliobates*) have straight stout beaks and take the place of woodpeckers. However, they lack the long, barbed, protrusible tongue and long, sharply pointed beak of the woodpecker. Instead they make use of small twigs or cactus spines as tools, to probe for insects deep in holes or cracks in the branches and trunks of trees. These two species feed chiefly on insects, although the Woodpecker Finch occasionally feeds on soft fruits. This is a remarkably agile species; it climbs up and down vertical trunks and branches, and often hangs upside down from a perch while searching for food. Whereas the Mangrove Finch, as its name implies, is restricted to the shore zone, the Woodpecker Finch occurs from the arid zone to the moist zone.

This wide range of feeding adaptations is just what one would expect if, in the course of their evolution, the finch species had exploited various ways of life that were open to them because of the absence of other competing birds with similar feeding habits.

A similar "adaptive radiation" has occurred in another bird family, the honey creepers (Drepaniidae) of the Hawaiian Islands, although in this case the divergence between species is so great, and so many species have become extinct, that the similarities between those species still surviving have been obscured. In fact it has been said that if Darwin had visited the Hawaiian Archipelago instead of the Galápagos, he might never have arrived at his important conclusions concerning evolution.

THEORIES OF DIVERGENCE

Within the ground finch group of species (*Geospiza*), each species of which is thought to be adapted to a different range of foods, all gradations in beak size and shape are found, so that it is often difficult, for example, to decide whether a particular bird is a Large Ground Finch (*G. magnirostris*) with a small bill, or a Medium Ground Finch (*G. fortis*) with a large one. A part of the reason for this state of affairs is that, unlike the situation in the snakes, lava lizards, tortoises, geckos, and mockingbirds, each species of finch is *not* restricted to a single island of the archipelago. The finch complement of each island is composed of representatives of several groups of finches, rather than several representatives of a single group. For example, there are twelve islands that each have seven or more of the thirteen species of finches, and of the thirteen finch species eight occur on ten or more islands. Only one species is restricted to a single island, and only one species is restricted to two islands. The different species probably arose in geographical isolation and developed barriers to interbreeding with one another, but since then they have come together by reinvading other islands of the archipelago. Sammalisto considers that some of the divergence may have occurred on single islands as a result of topographical isolation. The interesting feature of this situation is that where a species now occurs on several islands, small differences can be observed between the various island populations of the same species, and these populations are thus regarded as subspecies.

It is in the explanation of these slight differences between the various island populations of the same species that controversy exists among students of the Galápagos finches.

Lack (1947) first believed that although some of these differences were adaptations to the different island environments, some at least may just be the result of chance. Mutations arising in one island population would be unlikely to be the same as those arising in another. Thus, even if the environments of the two islands were identical, selection would be operating on slightly different material in the two populations. The result would be populations that differed slightly from each other. Moreover, if the colonizing group of birds was small, it might not be an average sample of the population of the parent species, but might instead consist of birds that were atypical in some particular features. In other words, the full range of the species characteristics might not be represented in the colonizing group. Thus, again, selection would operate in the new environment on material differing in its scope and range from the parent population and, even if the new environment were identical with the old, some divergence would result.

Bowman, however, believes that probably all of the differences in these island populations are adaptations to the differing conditions on the various islands. He has been able to correlate differences in skull and bill structure, and the associated musculature, with differences in the feeding habits of the species populations on the different islands. In a recent paper, Lack (1969) comes to agree with Bowman, and points out that the differences between the island environments (both vegetational and in the presence of other finch species) are correlated with isolation.

Lack believes that some of the differences between island populations may be adaptations to the biotic environment, that is, they may depend upon what other finch species are present as possible competitors. Bowman again disputes this, and maintains that all interisland differences between species populations are adaptations to the availability and diversity of food, and that significant competition between different species, where they occur together, does not exist.

The evidence both for and against the occurrence of such competition is unconvincing. However, should competition have occurred, it might be expected to have resulted in an accentuation of the differences between species where they occur together, so that competition would be reduced and both species would be able to persist in the area. There is some evidence of such "character displacement," but since most species do not exist singly on any islands, there are very few bases from which to measure any possible secondary divergence. One such case, reported by Lack, concerns the small Crossman Islets. Here the Small Ground Finch, *Geospiza fuliginosa*, is present, and the closely related, rather heavier-billed, Medium Ground Finch, *G. fortis*, is absent. On Daphne, another very small island, it is the other way round and only the Medium Ground Finch occurs. Both species occur together on many of the larger islands, and on these islands the bills of the Small Ground Finches are smaller than they are on Crossman, and the bills of the Medium Ground Finches are larger than they are on Daphne. Thus, where the two species coexist, they take rather different sizes of seeds, and competition between them for food is probably reduced. Nevertheless, it is likely that competition was initially responsible for the divergence in bill size and in food habits.

The predominantly dark, dull coloring of the finches has been variously explained. Swarth thought that the dark plumage was a general characteristic of the subfamily, as is the habit of using the feet to assist the beak in foraging, and was not associated primarily with the Galápagos environment. Lack also suggested that black plumage was ancestral, and that it is now gradually disappearing since it has no survival value, there being no really significant predators of the finches on the Galápagos. Bowman again takes issue with Lack, asserting that the dark coloration makes the finches less conspicuous against the predominantly dark laval backgrounds of the islands. He believes the dark plumage to be adaptive, cryptic coloration, and that the selective force is provided by natural predators, which he believes to be important in the Galápagos. He reasons that it is difficult for humans to detect finches against their natural backgrounds, that many other Galápagos animals are dark-colored, that the darkest populations of several finches are restricted to what he believes to be the "darkest" islands or habitats, and that the finches do have important predators on the islands. His first and third points are essentially subjective, and his second, which is rather overstated (he lists the tortoises as being dark-colored, although they are not particularly dark taken as a group), provides no case for the *finches'* coloration being adaptive. Concerning Bowman's last point—the significance of finch predators—there is a division of opinion; Lack, for example, believes that predation has not been a significant selective force in the evolution of the finches.

Predation as a Selective Force

As an adaptation against predation, cryptic coloration is usually evolved in association with a particular behavior pattern. This behavior almost always involves immobility; however well-camouflaged an animal may be, if it moves, much of the advantage of its camouflage is lost. Observations on the behavior of finches in the presence of hawks and owls provide no evidence of any such immobility. Indeed, their reactions to these birds of prey are very similar to those of songbirds which are clearly not cryptically colored.

The Short-eared Owl of the Galápagos, *Asio flammeus*, feeds largely during the day and is not a truly nocturnal owl. Bowman suggests from this that the owl may therefore intensify the daytime "predation pressure" on the finches. However, the evidence that the Short-eared Owl actually takes finches in numbers is, at present, slight. Abs *et al.* (1965) made brief surveys on four islands, Indefatigable, Tower, Hood, and Champion, and concluded that the owl preys chiefly on birds. On Tower and Hood the prey recorded consisted almost wholly of storm petrels, and on Champion yellow warblers and black rats formed the major part of its diet. There was evidence of significant predation on finches on Indefatigable, although 35 per cent of prey items were black rats and house mice. The owl also takes native rats, lava lizards, grasshoppers, and crabs. In general, the prey spectrum on any particular island seems to reflect the relative abundance of the prey species on that island. The Barn Owl, *Tyto alba*, is nocturnal; its prey is chiefly introduced mice and rats, and it has never been suggested as a possible predator of finches. There are a few reports of the Galápagos Hawk, *Buteo galapagoensis,* taking finches, but there is no evidence at all at present to suggest that they form a major part of its diet. Doctor T. DeVries, of the Charles Darwin Research Station, is currently making an ecological study of Galápagos birds of prey, including an investigation of their food, and the results of this work will be of great interest with regard to the problem of the adaptive nature of finch plumage in particular, and the question of predation on finches in general. The Galápagos snakes (*Dromicus* species) are possible predators, although actual quantitative evidence is conspicuous by its absence.

The finches build their nests at the ends of branches, and this might suggest that the choice of this inaccessible nest site is a behavioral adaptation on the part of the finches to resist nest predators. However, Lack has shown that the nest plays an important part in courtship; males build several nests at which they perform courtship displays. This involvement of the nest in courtship is usually only found in birds that have no nest enemies.

Bowman (1961) suggests that the construction of the finch nest, which has a domed roof and a single side entrance, is an adaptation against predators. However, Lack (1947) pointed out that such nests "are common in tropical weavers and in Central American finches, but are rare in such birds outside the hot regions." Lack believes that the domed roof may serve to shade the eggs and incubating bird from the intense heat of the equatorial sun.

It has been suggested that if selection has involved predation by fast-flying birds of prey, good flying ability would have had selective value for the finches, and any tendency toward inefficiency in flight would have been checked at the outset. Indeed, some improvement in flying ability might have resulted. However, compared to other songbirds, Darwin's finches are weak and clumsy fliers, and this has been cited as evidence that such predation has not been a significant selective force in their evolution.

There is thus disagreement among the authorities on the significance of predation on finches. On the existing evidence, Bowman's contention that "the presence of avian and reptilian predators" is one of "the most important (factors) in shaping the evolutionary pattern of Galápagos finches" can only be regarded as unsubstantiated.

Curio (1964, 1965, 1966) has recently conducted a number of field tests to find out the reaction of finches to predators. These provide some slight but confusing evidence of the significance of predation, at least in the evolution of the island subspecies. For the test, four islands were used: Wenman, where no possible predators occur; Tower, where only the Short-eared Owl occurs; Abingdon, where the owl and the hawk are present; and Indefatigable, where owls, hawks, and snakes are found.

Models of snakes were presented to finches on Abingdon and Tower, which are both islands on which snakes do not occur, and to finches on Indefatigable, where snakes do occur. The Abingdon and Tower finches showed less fear of the snake model, as measured by the frequency and extent of their reactive behavior, than did those on Indefatigable. Moreover, the responses of all species of finches on a particular island were more similar to one another than they were to populations of the same species on the other islands. These findings suggest that the island subspecies have become adapted to the predator situation on their particular islands. The Abingdon and Tower finches reacted to living snakes in just the same way as did those on Indefatigable, showing that their reduced response to the snake models was not simply because they had not learned to fear snakes. In fact, the Abingdon and Tower finches do fear snakes, but the response to a snakelike form is less easily elicited than it is on Indefatigable, where snakes occur. Curio suggests from this that the finches on the two snake-free islands may be in the process of losing their fear-reaction to snakes, since, in the absence of snakes, this behavior would have no survival value and would thus no longer be under the stimulus of natural selection.

A comparison was made between the responses of finches to birds of prey on Wenman (no birds of prey), Tower (owl only), and Indefatigable (owl and hawk). The finches used for these tests on Wenman and Tower were different subspecies of the Sharp-beaked Ground Finch (*Geospiza difficilis*), whereas those used on Indefatigable were of a different species of ground finch (*Geospiza fuliginosa*). Models of owls and hawks elicited a reaction nearly twice as strong on Indefatigable, where both birds of prey occur, as they did on Wenman, where these two predators do not occur. The hawk is now almost extinct on Indefatigable; the finches' strong reaction to the hawk on that island is thus unlikely to be the result of reinforcement by experience. Surprisingly, the finches tested on Tower showed a weaker reaction to the owl than did those on Wenman, although the owl is fairly common on Tower but is absent from Wenman. However, on Tower the owl apparently preys chiefly on other birds (storm petrels) that are common on the island, and very little on finches.

The results of these tests with birds of prey are rather inconclusive. The result of the Tower-Wenman comparsion remains unexplained, and the three-island comparison (Tower-Wenman-Indefatigable) suffers from the defect that a different finch species was used on Indefatigable. This latter test might have been more instructive if Abingdon could have been used instead of Indefatigable. On Abingdon the Sharp-beaked Ground Finch occurs, as it does on Wenman and Tower, and both hawk and owl are present, so that the same comparison with respect to the predators' occurrence could have been made, but using the same species of finch.

BEHAVIORAL VARIATIONS

There was a great deal of variation in the finch populations' reactions to a control object (an electric torch) to which they could not have become adapted, and of which they had no previous experience. For example, the variation in response to the torch was greater than that to the stuffed owl. Moreover, the Indefatigable finches' response to the torch was eight or nine times as great as the response of the finches of the other islands. Thus it is possible that the Indefatigable birds show a greater fear-reaction to any strange object presented to them than do the finches of the other islands. Indefatigable differs from Tower and Wenman in that it is inhabited by man; Abingdon, which like Indefatigable, has both owl and hawk, is uninhabited, and for this additional reason would perhaps have been a better choice for this experiment. In addition, the ecological premise that hawks and owls prey on finches to a large extent has no foundation at present, as we have seen. The predator situation in the past is completely unknown, of course.

Lack saw finches "mobbing" a Short-eared Owl on the Galápagos; on several occasions we observed the same thing and also finches mobbing hawks. However, this may be simply the retention of an ancestral response to predators that has little significance today but has been retained since it is not actually disadvantageous. The "feigned-injury" response of the Galápagos Dove to man's presence (see CHAPTER 7) may be a parallel case. The finches show no fear of man, or of cats, which thus easily prey upon them.

There is no doubt that behavioral differences do exist between island populations of the same species. Bowman (1965) has discovered that the songs of certain finch species differ from island to island, each island population having its own "dialect," as it were. The function of such interisland differences in song is obscure, just as is the function of the differences in display behavior of the lava lizards on different islands, and the explanation may be the same in both cases. However, Bowman has found that male finches only produce the typical adult song if they can listen to their father's song in their youth; the adult song is thus at least in part the result of learning.

A unique feeding habit has evolved in the Hood Island sub-species of *Geospiza conirostris* (DeBenedectis, 1966). The birds have a peculiar method of scraping gravel aside to get at food underneath. This habit has not been observed in the subspecies on Tower, and Lack (1969) suggests that this may be related to the absence from Hood of a competitor, *G. magnirostris*, which is present on Tower.

Recently a most peculiar kind of behavior has been dis-covered in the Wenman population of the Sharp-beaked Ground Finch. Bowman and Billeb (1965) reported that the finches frequently hop on to the Masked Boobies and peck at the soft skin at the bases of the wing feathers in the elbow region, until they have drawn blood. The finches then feed on the blood as it oozes down the base of the feathers. The boobies, for their part, appear to be only mildly disturbed by this unusual activity, occasionally swinging round with their beaks as though somewhat halfheartedly trying to brush off an an-noying fly. This is the only known instance of a bird habit-ually feeding on the blood of another bird. Bowman and Billeb suggest that the blood-eating habit may have arisen from an association of mutual benefit, the finches originally feeding on parasitic hippoboscid flies, which infest the boobies. The ectoparasites are particularly conspicuous on the white plumage of the Masked Boobies and the white phase of the Red-footed Boobies (this phase seems to be unusually common, for the Galápagos, on Wenman). It is suggested that the finches may have acquired the taste for blood by accidentally punc-turing the boobies' skin during overenthusiastic searches for the flies or after feeding on flies which were already engorged with booby blood. These authors believe that after the blood-eating habit arose the attack became concentrated on the el-bow region. This area is not a good source of parasites, being easily preened, but the skin here is lightly feathered and rel-atively easily accessible to the finch, which has maximum time to escape the swinging beak of the booby. Blood, of course, is an excellent source of protein for the finches, and such a habit no doubt has survival value for them. However, this does not seem to be a primary method of feeding; it only occurs sporadically, and when I was watching these finches, they usually attacked a booby that had just alighted from a flight or boobies that were in the process of courting.

The American botanist Fosberg, on the same day that Bowman and Billeb made their observations, saw finches drawing and drinking blood from the bases of the tail feathers of a Red-footed Booby on Wenman (Fosberg, 1965); the behavior is not therefore specifically directed at the Masked Boobies, although during the few hours that I was on the Wenman plateau I did not see Red-footed Boobies attacked in this way.

The habit, which so far as is known is restricted to the Wenman population of the species, is parallel to that of tits in Great Britain, which began piercing milk-bottle tops to feed on the contained milk. This habit of the tits rapidly spread throughout the British population of tits and into Europe. In the Galápagos, such spreading of the blood-eating habit cannot take place because of the isolation of the Wenman population in which the habit arose. It is not known to what extent the blood-eating habit is learned or innate.

The same behavior could equally occur in the population of the Sharp-beaked Ground Finch on Culpepper, which is the same subspecies as the Wenman population, or in the population of the closely related subspecies on Tower. On both of these islands there are breeding colonies of Masked and Red-footed Boobies, yet the habit has never been observed on these two islands. Snakes and lizards are absent from all three islands, Wenman, Culpepper, and Tower, and Wenman differs from the others in having a gecko that is unusually large and very distinct, and thus possibly has been on the island a long time. The Galápagos Hawk and the Barn Owl do not occur on any of these islands, and Wenman also lacks the Short-eared Owl, which is present on Tower and Culpepper.

The behavior of the Wenman population of Sharp-beaked Ground Finches is, in general, extremely exploratory and bold.

This is the only population of the species that feeds on cactus flowers and pads, for example. Curio has seen the Sharp-beaked Ground Finches on Wenman flocking to a booby nest on hearing the begging call of the young, and eating the half-digested fish that the returning adult regurgitated for its off-spring (Curio, 1965). He has seen them eating shore crabs and picking ectoparasites from the breasts of nesting boobies, and also states that they will eat both raw and cooked fish. Bowman and Belleb noticed one examining the cloaca and feces of a nestling Masked Booby just after it had defecated, and another overturning with its feet a stone one inch in diameter. Gifford reported that Wenman finches immediately surround and peck at any of their number that has been shot, drinking its blood, and C. M. Harris (in Rothschild and Hartet, 1899:10) saw them feeding on a seal carcass. The finches of Wenman will quickly surround any exposed egg of the Swallow-tailed Gull or Noddy Tern and hammer away at it with their beaks (M. P. Harris, 1968), and Curio states that they actually break open gulls' eggs and eat the contents. On two occasions I have seen them attempting to roll a frigate bird's egg off the nest platform by levering at it with their beaks or standing on it and turning it with their feet in the manner of a performing bear on a circus barrel.

Certainly the Wenman population of these finches was the boldest and most inquisitive I experienced in the Galápagos. Numbers of them would surround me and, alighting on me, would peck at shoelaces and probe in pockets and hair in a most disconcerting manner, reminiscent of Hitchcock's film, *The Birds*. There is little doubt that the behavior of the Wenman population is generally different from that of other populations of the species, and it would be interesting to discover whether the acquisition of the blood-eating habit is a purely chance effect or whether it is related to some facet of the Wenman environment, such as the presence of the gecko or the complete absence of avian predators.

M. P. Harris has observed the Small Ground Finch on South

Plaza Islet feeding on blood left on rocks following the birth of sea lions and pecking at the afterbirth. This is evidence of a similar kind of exploratory behavior, though evidently less developed, in a related species. Both sea lions and fur seals occur on Wenman, and Harris suggests that the Wenman finches' "taste for blood" could have arisen in this way.

Probably the most famous behavioral adaptation of Galápagos finches is the tool-using habit of the two closely related species, the Woodpecker Finch (*Cactospiza pallidus*) and the Mangrove Finch (*Cactospiza heliobates*), which feed mainly on insects. The behavior was first observed in the Woodpecker Finch. This finch has been observed to knock the branches of trees and shrubs with its beak, and listen in the manner of a woodpecker detecting hidden insects. The bird selects a suitable cactus spine or stiff slender twig, and uses this as a tool with which it probes insects out of holes or crannies too deep to be explored by its beak. The tool is held lengthwise in the beak, inserted into the crack or hole and moved about. If the concealed insect is an active one and emerges, the tool is quickly dropped and the insect seized with the beak. If the insect is a sluggish grub, the finch may use the stick to lever the grub out of the hole and slide its beak down the stick as the larva is levered higher toward the surface. Finches have been seen to improve tools which were unsatisfactory, breaking a piece off a stick which was too long or cumbersome. One finch, having obtained a stick with a Y-shaped end, the side branch of which hampered its efficiency, was seen to grasp the stick with its feet, breaking off the offending side piece. It then resumed probing with the improved tool—this time with more success. There is also evidence that once a finch has found or "made" a good tool it will retain it and carry it about from tree to tree.

The tool-using habit may not be general throughout the populations of these species. In captivity, some individuals will use tools and others will not, and the distinction seems to be quite clear-cut. In order to photograph the tool-using activity, hungry birds were allowed to watch while insects were stuffed into holes which had been drilled into a length of branch, and the finches were then individually introduced into the cage containing the branch. One bird might fly about in a frustrated manner and then, on being provided with a tool, immediately set about using it to extract the insects. Another would vainly attempt to reach the insects with its beak and would ignore any tool provided. Much more field observation is needed in order to find out whether these two distinct types of behavior occur in separate individuals of the natural populations.

Eibl-Eibesfeldt (1966) reports Woodpecker Finches in captivity using their tools for an activity that can only be described as play. After being fully fed on meal worms, a pair of these birds hid the surplus food in cracks, then proceeded to probe the meal worms out with their sticks once more, only to hide them again immediately. This type of activity is usually only seen in higher animals.

MULTIPLICATION OF SPECIES

When considering the finch fauna of the various islands, Lack observed that there was a marked correlation between the number of forms that are endemic (restricted to an island) and the degree of isolation of the island (FIGURE 24), the outlying islands having a greater proportion of endemic forms than those less isolated. This seemed to suggest that geographical isolation was an important factor in the production of new forms. Bowman disagreed, and attempted to show that differences in the plant environments of the various islands had played the chief role in the evolution of differences between the various forms, rather than geographical isolation, which he measured as distance from a central island, Indefatigable. However, mathematical analyses by Hamilton and Rubinoff (1963, 1964) have upheld Lack's contention. The average distance of an island from all the others in the archipelago is evidently the chief factor determining the total number of finch species on it, and

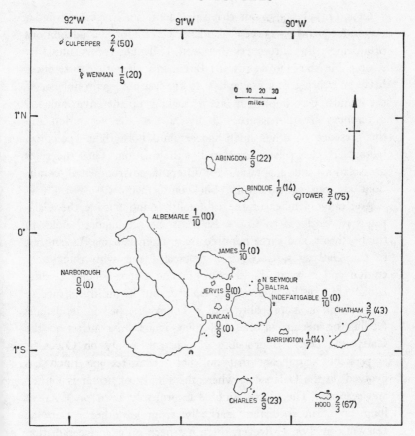

FIGURE 24. Darwin's finches. Number of subspecies endemic to a particular island, total number of species present on that island, and percentage of island endemism. Data from Bowman, 1961. e.g. 1/5 (20)=1 subspecies endemic to the island, 5 species present on the island, endemism for that island 20 per cent.

its distance from the nearest island is the most important factor determining the number of its endemic forms (Thornton, 1967; Hamilton and Rubinoff, 1967). Darwin's finches thus display extremely well the importance of the isolation of populations in the formation of new species.

Lack (1969) points out that since some finch species wander rather frequently between islands, selection for the adaptations producing the differences between endemic forms must be strong. He thus moves toward Bowman's view that differences between subspecies are adaptive to the various environments of the islands. Two important factors making up the environmental differences are the nature and diversity of the vegetation and the presence of other finch species, and both these ecological factors are themselves correlated with isolation. Thus the roles of isolation and adaptation to different environmental conditions are not contradictory, but complementary.

The only member of the subfamily found outside the Galápagos is restricted to Cocos Island, some six hundred miles to the northeast, and three hundred miles from Panama. In contrast to the Galápagos, Cocos is a tropical island with thick vegetation and a warm, moist climate. The Cocos Finch's feeding habits are not known with certainty, but from the structure of its beak it is probably like a honey creeper in its habits, feeding on nectar, insects, and some fruits. In contrast to the Galápagos, nectar is probably in constant supply on Cocos. It is probably significant that no such nectar-feeding finch has evolved on the Galápagos, where the supply of nectar is limited and seasonal. The Cocos Finch has probably been on Cocos a long time, for it differs markedly from all other species of Darwin's finches. However, there has been no adaptive radiation similar to that on the Galápagos archipelago. In spite of the favorable environment and the variety of foods and habitats, there is still only a single species on Cocos. Why should this be so? It seems most likely that it is because Cocos is a single island, not an archipelago, and there has been no opportunity for the origin of distinct forms from populations geographically isolated from one another.

The original ancestor of the Galápagos finches is unknown, nor is it known from where it came. It seems likely, however, that it originated in continental America and became established on the Galápagos Islands before any other land birds. Through the isolation of populations on different islands, comparatively free from predators and competitors, distinct forms were evolved. These became adapted to different environments and diets and in some of them unfinchlike habits arose. When these forms were later able to reinvade islands and thus meet, they may have interbred, and the differences which had so far evolved would then be eliminated. Perhaps this was the usual outcome of such reinvasions. Occasionally, however, and particularly in the case of populations that had managed to reach the more isolated islands, so much time would have been spent in isolation that when the populations came together again, they would have diverged so much that they would be unable to interbreed. In other words, separate species would have been evolved.

The barrier to interbreeding was most probably behavioral. Eibl-Eibesfeldt reports (1966) that species of different genera can be made to interbreed successfully in conditions of captivity, and Lack has shown that the existing species recognize each other by beak differences in the wild.

When two or more species came to be living in the same region, selection would operate so as to accentuate any differences between them that would reduce competition, and the species would diverge further, becoming isolated from each other ecologically, either by habitat or by food specialization. Such processes were probably repeated a number of times. As reinvasions gradually succeeded one another, species would extend their range to several islands, not just one, and the resulting island populations would also tend to diverge, both because of the operation of chance factors and because of the differing environments. MacArthur and Levins (1967) have shown, however, that the trend toward a multiplication of more specialized forms may sometimes be reversed. Where there is little diversity of food, little overall productivity, and the available resources are variable or unequal in abundance, these authors have postulated that a single more generalized form will replace two more specialized ones. Lack(1969) suggests that this may have occurred on small and outlying Galápagos islands where there is less diversity of foods, and where there is some evidence to suggest that the finch species are more generalized in their food requirements than are those on large central islands.

The evolution of the finches has already reached this stage of divergence in island populations of the various species, but there is no reason to believe that it will stop there. If the Galápagos finches are allowed to survive, it seems likely that, as these processes continue, the radiation may proceed even further. The existence of a remarkable behavioral plasticity in the stock, as seen, for example, in the tool users and in the Wenman finches, suggests that in the future there will possibly occur a radiation at least as extensive as that of the Hawaiian honey creepers, whose ancestor is also thought to have been finchlike.

CHAPTER NINE

Native Mammals

LIKE most truly oceanic islands, the archipelago is very poor in native land mammals. Only eight species are present, and these are either bats or rats, both groups well known for their powers of crossing stretches of sea water.

The two bats of the Galápagos are members of the widespread New World genus *Lasiurus*, which has species on many Pacific islands, including Hawaii. Many of the *Lasiurus* species have migratory tendencies. One of the Galápagos species is also present on the mainland of South and North America and on Bermuda, while the other is evidently endemic to the archipelago.

RODENTS

The Galápagos rodents are rice rats of the genus *Oryzomis*, which is widely distributed in the Americas, from South America to the United States. These brown native rats are almost the size of the gray Norway rat, and appear to live solitary lives; they dig burrows beneath stones and make round nests of leaves and grass. They are omnivorous, and are found in the dry zone as well as on the heights.

Of the six species, four form a close-knit group, which has

been designated as a subgenus, *Nesoryzomis*, found only in the Galápagos. They are recorded from the large central islands, Narborough (*narboroughi*), James (*swarthi*), Indefatigable (*indefessus* and *darwini*), and Baltra (*indefessus*), which is very close to Indefatigable. The other two species probably resulted from a later invasion and, although found only in the Galápagos, they do not differ sufficiently from the continental forms to be placed in a different subgenus. These have been recorded from Barrington (*bauri*) and Chatham (*galapagoensis*) (FIGURE 25).

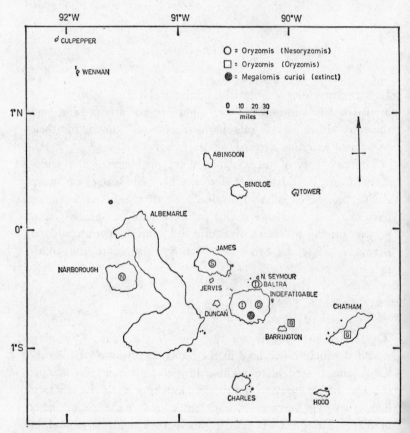

FIGURE 25. Distribution of native Galápagos rats. Letters indicate different species.

It is quite possible that these rodents reached the Galápagos on natural rafts, for, as a group, they are forest dwellers on the mainland and may have had fairly easy access to logs, branches, etc., floating down rivers. Orr (1966) believes that there were probably two separate invasions, the earlier one giving rise to the *Nesoryzomis* species. Species of *Oryzomis* have successfully invaded óther islands, for example Jamaica and The Tres Marias Islands off Mexico. Recently, evidence of a third invasion has come to light. Fragmentary remains of uncertain age that were discovered in a cave on Indefatigable were of a related group of rats that is only known otherwise from a few West Indian islands. They were considerably larger than the other species. The species that left these subfossil remains has been described under the name *Megalomis curioi*, and is almost certainly now extinct (Niethammer, 1964).

By the time of Darwin's visit in 1835 the well-known black rat, *Rattus rattus*, was already present on James, and by 1898 is was also on Albemarle, Duncan, Chatham, and Charles. Thirty years ago the black rat was introduced to Indefatigable; the native rat, which was abundant at the time, rapidly disappeared, and is probably now on the verge of extinction on that island. The black rat is now also present on Baltra. On James and Chatham the native rats are very seriously threatened by competition from the introduced black rat. The James Island rat, *O. swarthi*, was thought to be extinct in 1959, but Peterson reported its presence in 1966. However, the Chatham rat, *O. galapagoensis*, has not been seen since the time of Darwin. Native rats were exterminated on Baltra during the Second World War. Leleup (1965) suggested that some species of native rat may have become extinct as a result of virus diseases transmitted by the introduced black rat. However, the black rat cannot be blamed for the absence of native rats on the peripheral and uninhabited islands of Culpepper, Wenman, Abingdon, Bindloe, Tower, and Hood, where the black rat does not occur. Probably these islands never received native rats.

Native rats still occur in numbers on Barrington, where they are active during the day and where Peterson (1966) estimated that the population was one or two thousand, and on Narborough, where they are found from the shore to the summit crater lake. Both are islands that up to now have been free from the black rat.

On the archipelago are two interesting and highly entertaining marine mammals that spend a good deal of time ashore: the sea lion and the fur seal. Indeed, they can fairly be regarded as Galápagos animals, for the populations of both these species of pinnipeds are recognized as endemic Galápagos subspecies.

THE GALÁPAGOS SEA LION

The sea lion, *Zalophus californicus*, is primarily a species of the northern hemisphere; there are three distinct and isolated populations, each of which is regarded as a separate subspecies. The typical form is found on the west coast of North America—it breeds from northwest Mexico to southern California and out of the breeding season migrates as far north as British Columbia. The second subspecies, *japonicus*, exists as a small population in the Sea of Japan, and the third, *wollebaeki*, is restricted to the Galápagos. The latter may be distinguished from the Californian subspecies chiefly by its smaller size, and it is clearly derived from that form, which must have reached the archipelago at some time in the past when the North Pacific was colder than it is today. Were it not for the Humboldt Current, perhaps this sea lion would not have survived on these equatorial islands. The current's upwellings result in an abundance of the sea lions' food—fish, and the water temperature is lowered. As it is, the Galápagos subspecies is now effectively isolated from its ancestral stock by the warmer waters to the north.

Sea lions are abundant on the archipelago and on all the islands inhabit suitable stretches of coast except those very near settlements. These animals are quite tame: one may walk right up to them, dozing fitfully on the beach in the sun, and, covered with a thin layer of sand, looking like a row of huge bread-crumbed sausages. They are polygamous; one dominant bull, the beach master, presides over a harem of anything up to thirty cows, on a stretch of beach that he regards as his territory and jealously defends. Since as many males as females are born, and survival in early life is the same for both sexes, there are many males without harems, and these constantly challenge the beach master, who may remain in "office" for only a few weeks at a time. Thus, a beach master's life is one of constant vigilance against encounters with rivals. Such encounters may occur on the beach or in the water, and in the latter case often involve thrilling, powerful chases before one bull, usually the intruder, makes off for the open sea.

But if the beach master is something of a despot, he takes his responsibilities to his large family very seriously. A new beach master gets to know his cows and pups by scent, and this is how he recognizes them, both in the water and on the beach; he will chase off any intruding females and pups not of his group, thus keeping the group down to a manageable size. During the whole of the day, he tirelessly patrols the inshore waters of his stretch of beach, bellowing incessantly and shepherding the young frolicking pups in toward the beach and away from their arch enemies, the sharks. When he submerges, his bellows cannot be heard by the observer on shore, but they are continued under water, and presumably the pups receive signals delimiting a boundary they are not permitted to cross. When one of them does transgress, he is given short shrift, and is nudged, scolded, chastised, and chased back into the "playground."

The cows take this opportunity to rest on the beach or on flat lava rocks, but some of them are always in the water, and they are greeted individually by the bull with polite and affectionate nuzzling. The bull apparently detects by scent that a cow is in oestrus and may mate with her either in the sea or ashore, by pinning her down with his great bulk and weight and wrapping his hind quarters firmly round her to complete

the act. The female sometimes snaps and bites during this process, but evidently the bull remains amiable throughout.

The female gives birth to her single pup some distance from
the main group, and shortly after birth moves the pup away
from the placenta by carrying it in her mouth by the scruff
of the neck. Cows and pups recognize each other first by call,
then by scent. A returning cow will call incessantly and the pup
will recognize his mother and begin bleating in response. In
this way the two will home in on one another and greet each
other with ecstatic nuzzling. The pups are, of course, among
the most playful of all animals, chasing each other from one
end of their territory to the other, playing follow-the-leader
while repeatedly leaping clear of the water like dolphins, chasing
swimming marine iguanas, and even body-surfing to shore on
incoming waves like shiny living torpedoes. They are fed by
their mother until they are about two years old, by which
time they look far too big to be receiving this type of nour-
ishment.

The bull sea lion is about eight times the bulk of the cow,
and in contrast to her placid, rather surprised reaction to the
presence of man, the bull is suspicious. If he suddenly decides
the intruder might be a rival, he will make straight for the
shore at tremendous speed. His momentum carries him ashore,
and he lumbers his great bulk clumsily over the rocks or sand
in a lurching, bellowing attack. It is said that if one waits
until he is about a yard away, and then flings up one's arms
and shouts at him or throws a handful of sand, he will stop
dead in his tracks. Such is the experience of a number of stout-
hearted Galápagos naturalists, but it must be recorded in all
honesty that the present writer did not wait to try the experiment. The dominant bull, the master, his massive neck
rippling with muscle and often scarred as the result of battles
with sharks and other bulls, bellowing his challenge with what
one can only admit to be righteous fury, is a formidable opponent even ashore. At sea he would be practically invincible;

it is said that he can successfully drive away full-grown sharks, and he reacts in a flash to the presence of a rival.

Apart from his size, the bull differs from the female in having a characteristic dome on the top of his head (PLATE 34), and is often of a lighter color on the upper surface. On hot afternoons, when the sea lions sometimes retire to doze beneath the low shrubbery at the back of the beach, one may encounter groups of young bulls isolated from the cows, pups, and dominant males. On one occasion on Abingdon, I saw a couple of such "young bloods" engaged in a "trial of strength," trying to force each other over by pushing against each other's neck, much as young male humans try their strength against each other by forearm pressure. Possibly such "games" account for the tremendous development of the neck region of the older males. On Hood one hot afternoon, I saw forty sea lions lying on the rocks to leeward of the spouting of an underwater "blowhole"; the resulting spray periodically gave them an automatic cool shower.

Although, until recently, sea lions were occasionally killed by fishermen because they foul their nets, the population seems to be in no danger whatever at the present time. In some parts, even on the small islet of Jensen, a few miles from the Academy Bay settlement, they are extremely numerous, and the "lobos," as they are called by the inhabitants, are a characteristic feature of the islands. Brosset (1963) estimated their numbers as twenty thousand to fifty thousand.

THE FUR SEAL

In contrast to the sea lion, the Galápagos fur seal belongs to a species with a southern distribution, but once again the Humboldt Current is responsible for its existence on the archipelago. The southern fur seal, *Arctocephalus australis*, is found on islands near Antarctica and along both the east and west coasts of South America as far north as Brazil and southern Peru. Like the sea lion, the Galápagos population of the fur seal is accorded the rank of an endemic subspecies, *galapagoensis*. It bears much the same relationship to the southern fur seal as the Galápagos sea lion does to the Californian species: it is rather smaller. Almost certainly the species reached the archipelago by the aid of the Humboldt Current, which, however, would be a hindrance on the return journey.

The fur seals differ from the sea lions in their coat, which has an outer layer of long hairs and an inner layer of short thick fur. The head is broader and shorter (PLATE 35), resembling the head of a bear, which accounts for the name *Arctocephalus*, "bear head." The eyes are large and have a sad, gentle expression, and the "bark" is altogether different from that of the sea lion, being much more similar to the rather hoarse lowing of a cow.

Fur seals are not found on sandy beaches. Their habitat preferences are evidently narrower than those of sea lions, for they are only to be found on shores where large rocks or lava blocks form deep, shaded caves in which they spend much of their time ashore. Bartholomew (1966) has pointed out that this is a behavioral response analagous to that of a burrowing diurnal rodent, and minimizes the problems of temperature regulation. Although the sea in the Galápagos region is cool compared to that in most other equatorial areas, the islands are exposed to intense radiation from the equatorial sun. The fur seals are of a genus that is chiefly cool temperate and subantarctic in distribution, and their selection of this particular habitat allows them to live in a microclimate more suitable to the capacity of the genus. Since such shaded retreats are not available on all Galápagos shores, fur seals are not so widely distributed over the islands as are sea lions. Their requirement for a more restricted habitat may also cause them to be considered much rarer than in fact they are. Certainly they are very much less conspicuous than the sea lions and seem to live in smaller family groups. The young are weaned and swimming at three months.

Although hunted during the last century for their valuable

pelts, they are not so rare as surveys conducted in the last decade or so have suggested (Ziswiler, 1967, for example, gives the numbers as only about five hundred animals). Large numbers of them occur on Culpepper and Wenman, and they are also quite common on North Seymour, Abingdon, Bindloe, Tower, and Punta Albemarle. There are also thriving populations along the west shore of Duncan and near Buccaneer Bay on James. Fur seals have also been reported from Redonda Rock, Narborough, the north and northeast coasts of Albemarle, the coast of James south of James Bay, Jervis, the northeast coast of Indefatigable, and Baltra. They seem to be absent from the southeastern islands of the archipelago but Lévêque's estimate of four thousand individuals (Lévêque, 1963) would seem to be more accurate than that of Ziswiler. They are more retiring in their habits than sea lions, and do not seem to enjoy exposed situations as much. When disturbed at close range they will either make for the sea or retreat into rocky caves. Occasionally old bulls can be seen dozing in a characteristic attitude with the nose pointing straight up at the sky. Presumably this is the most restful way to carry the heavy weight of the relatively massive head. Occasionally sea lions may be found in company with fur seals, as on Culpepper. On this island the sea lions' preferred habitats—beaches or flat slabs of rock—are absent, so there is no marked segregation of the populations of the two mammals.

The advent of artificial furs, plus the protection afforded by the Ecuadorian government and enforced by the Research Station, appear to have allowed a reprieve for the Galápagos fur seal, and the population seems to be in a fairly healthy state at the present time.

CHAPTER TEN

Arrival

A CONTINENTAL island—that is, one which at one time was connected to a continent by land—will usually already possess a flora and fauna at the time of its origin as an island. A segment of the continent's biota will be cut off from the main land mass by the covering of the intervening land by sea, resulting in an island biota little different from that of the mainland. If the island was formed a very long time ago and at some distance from the continent, divergence of the two biotas may be expected to take place. Animals and plants will make the crossing only very infrequently from one land mass to the other, and thus genes will not flow freely between the populations on the two land areas. Under these conditions of genetic isolation, any differences in the two environments will cause further evolution to take different courses in the two areas. Those groups of genes selected in the island environment will not be the same as those selected in the continental environment. Moreover, the mutations that occur in the two isolated populations will not necessarily be identical, so that selection, already different in the two environments, will also be working on slightly different raw material, and this difference will increase with time. Mixing of the gene pools of the populations in the two environments will be reduced very drastically or completely suppressed because of the infrequency or complete lack of individuals moving from one population to the other. The two populations will thus evolve separately in genetic isolation, and the island's biota will gradually become different from that of the continent. However, because the island's original biota was in fact a sample of that of the continent, the same groups of organisms will tend to be present on both the island and the continent, and differences in the two biotas will simply be differences between the same groups of organisms.

When a continental island is extremely old, or has been subjected to very drastic environmental changes that have not occurred on the parent continent, then certain organisms present on the continent may be absent from the island. These may be animals or plants that have evolved on the continent since the birth of the island and so have not been able to colonize it. Alternatively, they may be organisms that became extinct on the island but persisted on the continent, and were unable to reinvade the island. Organisms in both these categories are usually recognizable as such, and although the biological distinction between continental and oceanic islands is by no means clear-cut, in general it may be said that a continental island has a rich and balanced biota, with a fairly good representation of the groups of organisms occurring on the continent.

In contrast to continental islands, oceanic islands, when formed by the growth of submarine volcanoes that eventually break the sea's surface as steaming, hot, sterile masses of lava, are completely devoid of living things at the time of their birth. Organisms that reach them must of necessity cross a stretch of the most inhospitable of environments for any terrestrial organism—sea water. Moreover, oceanic islands usually arise at vast distances from continents, so that the chances of land organisms reaching them, even those with good dispersal mechanisms, are extremely low.

Fisher (1954), by a striking example, has shown that even highly improbable contingencies are given an increasing probability if considered over long periods of time. He takes as his starting point the chance of a man producing at least one mature, productive son. This is by no means 100 per cent. Some men have no children, some have all daughters, some sons die before maturity and some that reach maturity are unproductive. Let us say that the odds are about five to eight— that is, slightly over 50 per cent. Taking this figure, it is possible to calculate the prior probability that a hundred generations of any particular man's descendants in the direct male line will leave at least one mature son. The odds of this happening, as they would have appeared to the reader's ancestor a hundred generations ago for example, are something like one in 1,000,000,-000,000,000,000,000,000,000,000,000 billion. And yet this highly improbable sequence of events must have occurred in the case of the hundredth ancestor of every man alive today, or the man would not be here. Thus, over very long periods of time, events that were *a priori* extremely unlikely can and do occur. This example helps us to see how organisms could have reached even the most isolated of oceanic islands, given sufficient time. The existing native plants and animals of Hawaii are living testimony that this has occurred many times in the case of this extremely isolated volcanic archipelago.

Naturally, those groups of animals and plants with good dispersal abilities will have a greater chance of reaching oceanic islands than those poorly endowed with such mechanisms. It might be expected, therefore, that oceanic islands would have a preponderance of the former and a dearth of the latter type of organism in their biota. The result would be a flora and fauna that were unbalanced as compared to a continental area, and the word "disharmonic" has been used to describe this condition.

The Galápagos Islands provide good examples of such biotic disharmony. The dominant vertebrates are the reptiles and birds; there is a paucity of native mammals, and amphibia and freshwater fish are entirely absent. Wheeler (1919) remarks that there is not a single species of the Doryline ants, which are an important element of the South American ant-fauna. Many groups of cryptozoic insects, which require dark, humid environments, are lacking on the archipelago, although they are widespread on the continent. Of the insects, no native aphids, scale insects, caddis flies, stone flies, may flies, fleas, sucking lice, Phasmida, or Megaloptera have been recorded from the islands, and butterflies, scarab beetles, tiger beetles, leaf beetles, and blister beetles are poorly represented. In contrast, the ground beetles, darkling beetles and long-horned beetles are well represented. Many groups of land birds that are well represented on the mainland are entirely absent from the Galápagos. Among the plants, lichens, ferns, grasses, sedges, and the family of composites are unusually well represented, while certain other groups like the gymnosperms, palms, aroids, figs, and several monocotyledonous families are entirely lacking. There are very few true forest trees native to the islands, and several important families of American flowering plants, such as the Lythraceae, Melastomaceae, Myrtaceae, Onagraceae, and Sapindaceae, have only a very few species. The same is true of families like the orchids, Bignoniaceae (probably entirely lacking), Scrophulariaceae, Labiatae, and Acanthaceae, which are highly specialized for insect pollination.

It is evident that groups of animals or plants well represented in the islands are often those best fitted for crossing a barrier of hundreds of miles of sea water. There are three main ways by which such a crossing could have been made: by floating on the sea—either free-floating or on natural rafts, by dispersal in the air, or by being carried on or in the body of some organism that made the crossing by air or sea.

RAFTING

Objects could reach the Galápagos by floating on the sea either from Peru and Ecuador with the Humboldt Current, or from the Panama area. The Humboldt Current, flowing northward from the Antarctic, parallel to the coast of South America, turns westward between 20 and 10 degrees south, and is then known as the South Equatorial Current, which flows through the Galápagos (FIGURE 1). It is strongest and fastest from July to November, but is supported at all seasons by the prevailing sea-level winds. From January to April, strong currents originating in the Gulf of Panama move south and west, merge with the South Equatorial Current, and thus also pass through the Galápagos.

Both in the Panama region and near the coast of Ecuador and Peru, natural rafts of vegetation have been seen floating out to sea. Living rafts of matted vegetation are a common sight at Guayaquil, at the mouth of the Rio Guayas in Ecuador, and may be seen in hundreds in the early part of the year. Some of these are ten feet or more in diameter, and would be capable of supporting plants, insects, and small animals. Agassiz (1892) reported large drift-rafts off Panama floating toward Cocos Island and the Galápagos at the rate of seventy-five miles in a day. The speed of the South Equatorial Current is one to two knots, and for most of the year the movement of a floating raft would be assisted by the southeast trade winds. It is therefore at least theoretically possible that a floating object could drift from the mainland to the Galápagos, six hundred miles away, in well under two weeks.

Usually these natural rafts become waterlogged and founder before they have drifted many miles, and there are no reports that such rafts were ever seen far out at sea between the Galápagos and South America. Indeed, Agassiz states that the *Albatross* expedition found the ocean floor to be covered with decaying vegetable matter far out to sea, and this may have been the rotting remnants of sunken natural rafts. But, as I pointed out above, we are dealing with millions of years, and only very few successful landfalls would have been necessary to account for the part of the Galápagos biota that could have reached the islands only by raft.

There are reports that such rafts have been seen in other areas, and sometimes their occupants are known. Wood Jones (1910) records that a tree with a wheelbarrow load of soil in its base was washed ashore at Cocos-Keeling, and Wheeler (1916) found a colony of ants in a log from Brazil washed up on San Sebastian Island. Zimmerman (1948) reports that Pemberton saw lush, green, floating islands with erect palms twenty to thirty feet high when out of sight of land between Celebes and Borneo. Matthew (1915) states that natural rafts have been seen over one hundred miles from the mouths of large tropical rivers and that occasionally living mammals have been seen on these rafts. Powers (1911) reports a floating island of vegetation 9000 square feet in area, which included trees thirty feet high, traveling for a thousand miles in the North Atlantic. A large boa constrictor twisted round a cedar tree came ashore on the island of St. Vincent in the West Indies, and Wallace (1880) says it "was so little injured by its voyage that it captured some sheep before it was killed." The nearest possible sources of this snake, Trinidad or South America, are almost two hundred miles away from St. Vincent.

Reptiles, which possess a relatively impermeable skin and drink very little fresh water, probably arrived on the archipelago by means of these drifting natural rafts. Their eggs are much more resistant to desiccation and sea water than those of amphibia, which are absent from the Galápagos Archipelago, and less easily broken than those of birds, which, however, have another excellent means of dispersal. The tortoises, as we have seen in an earlier chapter, are capable of floating in the sea for several days at least and can survive very long periods without food or water. They may have drifted to the islands by floating freely with the South Equatorial Current, or their eggs or young may have been carried on rafts of vegetation. Moreover, gigantism is a feature of island life, and the original tortoise colonists may not have been the size of those of today, though there is evidence that very large tortoises did exist on the South American continent in the past. Only five successful journeys in, say, a million years—that is, one every 250,000 years —would suffice to account for the existence of the present Galápagos reptiles.

The only terrestrial mammals native to the Galápagos are rats. Although these animals are notorious for their capabilities of crossing stretches of sea water on anything that will provide transport, the Galápagos rats hold the mammalian world record.

Fresh-water fish, which are absent from the Galápagos, would of course be subjected to drastic osmotic disturbances in sea water and would be incapable of crossing to the archipelago by sea.

The large Galápagos land snails, such as species of *Bulimulus* (over fifty species in the Galápagos) probably reached the islands by rafting. They are hibernating animals and can remain alive for long periods under adverse conditions. Before aestivation these snails seek out hidden and sheltered situations. They then attach themselves to the substratum by a thick, membranous layer of mucus and retire a little into their shell to secrete a second, thinner layer. These two layers effectively prevent desiccation. Species of *Helicina* have a thin, shelly operculum, which seals the shell opening tightly during aestivation, and Smith (1966) believes that these snails too could survive a long sea voyage hidden in the dry crannies of tree trunks or branches. Prevention of water loss also entails prevention of water entry, and such aestivating habits clearly fit these forms very well for survival on sea-borne rafts of vegetation.

Darwin (1872) found that hibernating individuals of several species of land snail could withstand seven days immersion in sea water. One individual of *Helix pomatia* that he tested withstood a second immersion of twenty days. Darwin then removed the calcareous operculum and, after a new membranous one had been formed, he immersed the snail in sea water for a third time. After two weeks of further immersion, it recovered completely and crawled away. Other operculate land snails were found to survive fourteen days' immersion easily, a length of time sufficient to drift from the mainland to the Galápagos.

Bark-inhabiting and heavy-bodied wood-boring insects such as weevils and other beetles, and some hemipterans, could also have reached the islands by such occasional transport, and so could the eggs of many of the insects inhabiting the vegetation composing the rafts. As long ago as 1877, Wollaston noted that the beetles that had successfully colonized the island of Saint Helena were chiefly weevils belonging to groups that are wood borers or are adapted to clinging to vegetation and bark. Beetles of the family Oedemiidae breed in driftwood and are found on most tropical islands; the family is represented in the Galápagos by five endemic species. The carpenter bee, which nests in wood, could have reached the Galápagos in a floating log. Longicorn beetles of the family Cerambycidae, which bore into dead twigs, branches, and trunks, are well represented in the Galápagos and might well have reached the islands in the same way. The closely related Chrysomelidae, leaf beetles, which on continents usually have more species than the longicorns, are poorly represented on the archipelago. Many of the leaf beetles live, as larvae, in more exposed situations than the longicorns, such as on roots or leaves, and would be less well protected on a sea-borne crossing. Moreover, they are shorter-lived and less sclerotized and require more food as adults than do the longicorns, all features that render successful dispersal over the sea less likely (Gressitt, 1961).

DISPERSAL OF PLANTS BY SEA

On the question of the dispersal of plants by sea, as with so many other biological problems, Darwin made his own pertinent observations. He noted that the natives of many Pacific coral islands use, for their tools, stones obtained solely from the roots of drifted trees. He also saw that between and behind such stones small lumps of earth were often enclosed "so perfectly that not a particle could be washed away during the longest transport: out of one small portion of earth thus completely enclosed by the roots of an oak about 50 years old, three dicotyledonous plants germinated." He continues: "Again, I can show that the carcasses of birds, when floating on the sea, sometimes escape being immediately devoured: and many kinds of seeds in the crops of floating birds long retain their vitality: peas and vetches, for instance, are killed by even a few days' immersion in sea-water; but some taken out of the crop of a pigeon, which had floated on artificial sea-water for 30 days, to my surprise nearly all germinated."

Darwin also experimented with the dried stems and branches of ninety-four plants with ripe fruits, to find out how long they would float on sea water. He found that eighteen distinct species floated for more than twenty-eight days, some for much longer. Of eighty-seven species tested for seed germination after immersion in sea water, sixty-four germinated successfully after twenty-eight days' immersion. From these and other tests Darwin concluded that one in ten "plants of a flora, after having been dried, could be floated across a space of sea 900 miles in width, and would then germinate."

Wace and Dickson (1965) list four flowering plants native to Gough Island (Tristan group) that are known to have diaspores capable of remaining afloat in periodically stirred sea water for one hundred days or more. During this length of time such specimens could have drifted 2000 miles, from South America to Gough Island.

The fruits and seeds of a few plants could have floated freely to the Galápagos Islands. For example, legumes, although intolerant of immersion, possess an air space between the embryo and the seed coat. The seeds of tropical legumes are so commonly washed up on the beaches of Tristan da Cunha that they are called "sea beans" by the islanders. *Sophora microphylla* occurs on Gough Island (Tristan da Cunha) in the south Atlantic, and also in southern Chile and in New Zealand. Sykes and Godley (1968) have shown that both buoyant and non-buoyant seeds are produced throughout the plant's range. Of three seeds that had been floated on sea water for three years, two germinated after chipping, and one of the resulting plants survived to maturity. The plant does not grow on the Kermadec Islands, some 500 miles northeast of New Zealand, but Sykes and Godley found thirty-two seeds in beach drift on these islands in 1966. Of these, thirteen were chipped, and twelve germinated within a week. Although ocean currents could disperse seeds from New Zealand to the Kermadecs in about fifty days, establishment there would be very difficult because of the nature of the coastline, and in fact has not occurred. In contrast to the wide-ranging *S. microphylla, Sophora prostrata* is confined to the South Island of New Zealand, and *Sophora chrysophylla* is confined to the highlands of the Hawaiian Islands. These two latter species, with restricted distributions, have seeds that do not float. Although some plants, such as *S. microphylla* and *Sophora tomentosa*, which is a pantropical littoral species with buoyant seeds, are very well adapted for dispersal by sea and thus are present on most remote islands, the very ease with which they are continually reinforced by immigrants of the same species usually prevents them from evolving into endemic island forms. Examples of this type of plant in the Galápagos are *Rhizophora* and *Avicennia*, for the seedlings of these mangroves can float across vast distances on the sea. Occasionally, however, such long-range dispersal is so infrequent that endemic forms may evolve. The Galápagos cottons are probably examples of this.

The cotton species *Gossypium klotzschianum* occurs in the Galápagos and also around the Gulf of California, where it exists as a separate variety. Its seeds have hard, impermeable coats, without the long free fibers ("lint") found in cultivated cottons. When still enclosed in the mature but unopened seed capsules, the seeds will float on the surface of sea water for about two weeks. When removed from the capsule, the seeds sink, but they are able to retain their viability after prolonged immersion. Since the Mexican variety grows some 1500 miles from the Galápagos, long-range dispersal to the Galápagos could have taken place only if the capsule-bearing branches traveled as components of a floating raft of vegetation. However, the present sea currents from the Gulf of California do not flow in the appropriate direction; possibly the Mexican form had a wider range in the past and extended farther south; rafting would be more plausible from Panama.

The other Galápagos cotton, G. *darwinii*, is very similar to a cultivated South American cotton, and both have a long "lint." Some authorities believe *darwinii* to be only a variety of G. *barbadense*, the South American cotton, while others grant it full specific status. G. *barbadense* grows wild near the coast of Peru. The seeds of *darwinii*, like those of *klotzschianum*, will withstand prolonged immersion in sea water, and their long attached lint gives them buoyancy. They are thus capable of floating on sea water for at least ten weeks, and probably for much longer (Stephens, 1958; Stephens and Rick, 1966). The Humboldt and South Equatorial currents could carry such floating cotton seeds to the Galápagos from Peru well within this period of time.

DISPERSAL BY AIR

Birds, bats, some insects, the spores of fungi and ferns and very small seeds or seeds with some device giving them buoyancy could have reached the Galápagos by air. Although birds, bats, and some of the larger and strongly flying insects could have made the journey under their own power, probably they were assisted by being blown off course and out to sea by winds. Land birds do not normally make sea excursions unless they are migrants, which few tropical land birds are, and the same applies to insects. However, there is evidence that occasionally these animals are carried out to sea.

Wallace reported a barn owl flying on to a whaling ship some five hundred miles south of the Azores, and Zimmerman mentioned another owl flying on to a ship a thousand miles out in the Atlantic. Stray visitors are reported from many remote islands, such as New Zealand, Tristan da Cunha, and Hawaii. Thirty-four species of stragglers have been recorded from Hawaii, the majority being land birds. Ducks banded in Utah found their way in 1943 to Palmyra Island, a thousand miles south of Hawaii, and every year American "waifs," having been carried across the Atlantic by the prevailing westerlies, make landfalls on the shores of Europe.

The number of such stragglers observed to reach Tristan in the last century amounts to 10 per cent of the total native fauna. A fisherman on Tristan da Cunha reported the arrival of a stray dragonfly (dragonflies are absent from this archipelago) in 1962, and three species of stray Lepidoptera were also probably blown there from South America (Holdgate, 1965). Holdgate also cites the famous case of a swarm of locusts alighting on a vessel 1500 miles out in mid-Atlantic.

In birds, distribution records over several hundred years are often available, and Mayr (1965) has given several striking examples of the natural colonization of islands by birds. Over a quarter of the nineteen species of native land birds of Lord Howe Island, about 350 miles east of Australia, immigrated there naturally during the last century, and eight out of ninety-one species of land birds established themselves in New Zealand in historical times (Wodzicki, 1965). The arrival of the Tasmanian White-eye in New Zealand before the 1850s required a journey of more than 1000 miles. It is now the commonest songbird in New Zealand and has spread to the Chatham Islands, various sub-antarctic islands including Campbell and Macquarie, Kermadec Island, Norfolk Island, and Lord Howe Island.

The Cattle Egret of Africa crossed the Atlantic about thirty to forty years ago, probably by natural means, and established itself in Brazil. It has since spread all over the West Indies, northern South America, and along the east coast of North America, breeding as far north as Rhode Island. It has also spread southward, has been recorded in the Falkland Islands, and migrates from South America to the Galápagos Islands. A different species of egret, banded in Spain, was shot in Surinam, northern South America, showing that such transatlantic flights are possible.

The same species, though a different subspecies, was brought into the Northern Territory of Australia, probably from Indonesia, in the 1920s. It spread southward, reaching New South Wales by the 1950s, and in 1963 the first Cattle Egret arrived in New Zealand, some 1200 miles away.

At least twenty species of non-resident birds have been recorded from the Galápagos, some regularly, some occasionally, and others only very rarely. These include shore birds such as Franklin's gull, turnstones, sandpipers, and sanderlings, but also two species of teal, plovers, phalaropes, the Wandering Tattler, Hudsonian Curlew, bobolink, barn swallow, Pomarine Jaeger, willet, and osprey. All but one of the teals are North American birds that winter in South America. According to Dorst (1962), the Galápagos Islands are not on the main migration routes for such migrants, and at least some of them appear to have been blown off their usual course by winds.

The Galápagos bats are related to bats with well-marked tendencies for long flights, and the butterflies, hawk moths, and dragonflies probably reached the islands at least partly by voluntary flight. Van Dyke (1953) believes that the dytiscid water beetle, *Eretes sticticus*, could have flown to the Galápagos from the mainland; the grasshopper genus *Schistocerca*, which is well represented on the archipelago, includes one of the most well-known of insect long-distance fliers, the desert locust. The commonest hawk moth of the islands, the pink-spotted hawk, has been caught at sea 500 miles from land (Williams, 1911). French (1964) has shown that the long-range movement of many species of Lepidoptera depends on assistance from wind. In July 1967, a dark cloud of insects, mainly dragonflies, was seen in the eye of a typhoon 310 miles south of Japan, and a week earlier several thousand leaf hoppers, carried by the wind, descended like snowfall on the weather ship located at this point. In reporting these facts, Asahina (1968) mentioned that in the daytime migrating dragonflies and butterflies occasionally visited the ship, and at night many moths, Hemiptera and Diptera were attracted by the ship's light. On the Galápagos, the prevailing winds are from the direction of the South American continent and would assist insects flying toward the archipelago.

Passive dispersal by air currents will be most effective when the disseminule is light and small and has a large surface area compared to volume. Zimmerman states that ships 400 miles out at sea have been littered with sand from the Sahara desert during storms. Wace and Dickson mention small numbers of pollen grains of *Ephedra* and *Nothofagus* found in peat deposits of the Tristan da Cunha group. These two genera are most unlikely to have been present on the islands when these particular deposits were formed, and Wace and Dickson conclude that the *Nothofagus* pollen was probably carried in the air from South America over at least 2500 miles of ocean. The pollen-trapping work of Maher (1964) has shown that *Ephedra* pollen can be carried at least 600 miles.

The spores of fungi and ferns are very small and light, and studies using sticky glass slides high in the air have shown that there is a continuous floating population of fungal spores in the air. They have been found in large numbers and variety at heights above 10,000 feet, and many had not lost their powers of germination. Gregory (1961) cites an instance of spores of mosses falling in rain water in Finland which may have traveled 1250 miles from Siberia, yet successfully yielded moss plants when germinated. Gregory states that most spores are resistant to desiccation and will survive longer at the temperatures found in the upper air than they will at ground level. Spores have even been found germinating in clouds. Ultraviolet radiation is a danger, however. This may be reduced in clouds, and there is evidence that exposure to visible light reverses the damaging effects of radiation received at high altitudes by bacteria, spores, and protozoa. However, the survivors might be expected to have an increased mutation rate on their return to earth.

Air-borne spores are removed from the atmosphere chiefly by rain; droplets of water collect spores by impaction and fall with them to the ground. Over the sea, rain is not uniformly distributed, but is much more likely to form over islands; spores carried over the sea are thus more liable to be deposited in the vicinity of high islands than in the open sea. These considerations make it easy to understand why the spore-producing ferns constitute the group of vascular plants with the greatest number of species on the Galápagos and at the same time the fewest endemic forms.

Parachute-like devices are of common occurrence on the light fruits of the Compositae, a family of flowering plants particularly well represented on oceanic islands and one having the greatest number of species of any flowering-plant family on the Galápagos. The grasses, which are also very high on the list of well-represented families, are also to some extent dispersed by wind, for which they possess similar, though less obvious, adaptations. Nevertheless, many plant geographers, including Cain (1944) and Good (1953), have pointed out that flowering plants with such seeds are no more widely distributed than are plants with heavier seeds less obviously adapted for aerial dispersal, and it seems that long-distance dispersal in the air is not of very great importance in the dispersal of flowering plants to oceanic islands (Carlquist, 1967).

Glick (1939, 1957) collected insects by trapping from an aircraft at 14,000 feet over Louisiana and caught spiders at 15,000 feet. Gressitt and his co-workers (Gressitt and Yoshimoto, 1963; Yoshimoto and Gressitt, 1959, 1960; Yoshimoto, Gressitt, and Mitchell, 1962; Yoshimoto, Gressitt, and Wolff, 1962) have operated traps on ships and aircraft over the Pacific for a number of years and have trapped well over a thousand insects by this means at heights up to 19,000 feet, many of them hundreds of miles from the nearest land. Most of the insects trapped were dead, but some were definitely alive when trapped. Taylor (1960) has shown that aerial journeys at heights of 1000 to 5000 feet are not particularly detrimental to insects. He trapped insects at these heights in nets on a balloon cable in southern England and found that less than 2 per cent died in transit. Many of these insects, including some of the most fragile, subsequently reproduced successfully.

Wingless adults, larvae, and nymphs, as well as winged insects, have been caught in the upper air. The insects captured in

Gressitt's project were mostly small and were weak fliers, with low specific gravity and fairly high surface area to volume ratio. These are just the kinds of insects that commonly occur on oceanic islands, and the families well represented in the captures are largely those that are also well represented in the Hawaiian Islands and Tristan da Cunha, for example. Holdgate points out that the relationships of the arthropod fauna of Tristan da Cunha are not with Africa, but with South America, which is in the direction of the prevailing winds.

The preponderance on the Galápagos of Cerambycid longicorn beetles over the related Chrysomelid leaf beetles may be in part the result of the relative ease with which these forms are dispersed by air. Many of the longicorns are nocturnal, and it is likely that they would be on the wing in the overcast weather accompanying storms. Moreover, their larvae bore in dead branches and twigs, which might be taken up by storm winds and in which the larvae could continue their feeding. The leaf beetles, on the other hand, are diurnal and unlikely to be flying in bad weather, and their larvae feed in more exposed situations (Gressitt, 1961).

The poor representation of butterflies on the Galápagos is probably partly because the adults have fragile wings and the larvae are extremely sensitive. Many of the small moths (microlepidoptera) that are well represented on the islands have larvae that develop as miners in leaves, borers in seeds or twigs or in bark and debris, which all could be dispersed by wind. Weevils too, which are among the toughest of insects, feed in seeds, twigs, etc., and these could be carried in the air.

Zimmerman (1948) states that the Hawaiian spider fauna is made up entirely of groups that in the juvenile stage spin silken parachute balloons that assist aerial dispersal. Spider groups that are not adapted in this way are absent from Hawaii.

The studies of Gressitt and his colleagues have shown that aerial dispersal is probably the chief method by which insects reach oceanic islands. These workers have concluded that cyclonic storms and high-speed upper-air currents (jet streams), flowing in the opposite direction to the trade winds, are responsible for the spread of insects across wide stretches of ocean in the west and central Pacific. The jet streams occur at heights of 16,000 feet and may reach speeds of 300 miles per hour. The temperatures in these streams, however, are in the range of 14 to minus 94 degrees Fahrenheit, and many insects would not survive such extreme cold. Today, the Galápagos is in an area of calms, and storms are very rare. Moreover, in contrast to the situation in Hawaii, the trade winds in the Galápagos are from the direction of the presumed source area (South America). Possibly the colonization of these two archipelagos by air has taken place in different ways.

Land snails, too, may be carried in the air. Snails were carried by hurricanes from Cuba to Florida, where they successfully established themselves. Gulick (1932) has discussed the dispersal of the minute land snails, which are such a feature of the fauna of remote Pacific islands. Many of these, when alive, weigh less than a thousandth of a gram and have shells that measure less than a millimeter in length. Gulick believed that these snails could be distributed, like small seeds, by aerial storms. Such a land snail, a species of *Tornatellides*, is found in the Galápagos. This genus is distributed over the Pacific basin from Hong Kong, Taiwan, and New Zealand in the west, to Hawaii and the Marquesas in the east. The genus is found elsewhere only in the Revillagigedo Islands, off the west coast of Mexico. Thus this small Galápagos species did not originate from the American continent, and a journey of at least 2000 miles seems to have been successfully accomplished. It is highly likely that this journey was by air.

DISPERSAL BY OTHER ORGANISMS

Darwin, who whenever possible built up his theories on the basis of personal observation, did not neglect to examine the possibility of small organisms being dispersed by birds. The leg of a woodcock sent to him by a friend had attached to it a small cake of dry earth weighing only nine grains. This earth contained the seed of a rush, which Darwin successfully germinated, and the resulting plant eventually flowered. Another colleague sent him the leg of a partridge with a larger, six-ounce ball of earth attached to it, which had been stored for three years. Darwin broke up this earth, placed it under a bell jar, and by careful watering succeeded in raising no less than eighty-two seedlings of at least five different species of plants. As he says, "With such facts before us, can we doubt that the many birds which are annually blown by gales across great spaces of ocean, and which annually migrate . . . must occasionally transport a few seeds embedded in dirt adhering to their feet or beaks?"

Taylor (1954) writes that unidentified seeds, apparently not belonging to any of the local species, were found adhering to the feet of albatrosses on Macquarie Island, between New Zealand and Antarctica. These seeds were so encased in a hardened coating formed from the regurgitate of the albatrosses that they "could be carried almost indefinitely in flight and could withstand immersion in sea water if the bird alighted to rest, yet on landing the seeds would be easily rubbed off." Taylor also cites the water milfoil, *Myriophyllum elatinoides,* which occurs in New Zealand and South America and also on the island of Macquarie. On Macquarie the water milfoil has lost its ability for fruit and seed production, reproducing only by vegetative means. Taylor suggests that migrating petrels may have been the original means of transport to Macquarie. Neither the water milfoil nor the Macquarie petrels occur on the Galápagos Islands. Carlquist (1965) reports that seeds of twenty-one species of plants, mostly associated with ponds, were obtained from mud on birds caught on Christmas Island near Java and suggests that the wide distribution of sedges and marsh plants may be the result of transportation by water birds. The sedges, together with the grasses, make up practically all the monocotyledonous flora of the Galápagos—there are twenty-five forms and most of them are widespread in the tropics of the Americas.

When we were visiting El Junco, the small fresh-water crater lake of Chatham, Doctor Eliasson discovered the bladderwort, *Utricularia foliosa*, not previously known to grow in the Galápagos (Eliasson, 1968). In a subsequent letter to me he said, "No doubt this species has reached Galápagos from the mainland attached in some form (probably as a vegetative shoot) to a waterfowl." A score or so of Galápagos pintails were seen on this lake during our visit, and frigate birds were also dipping on to the surface for a second or so, keeping their wings well out of the water. Doctor Eliasson continues, "The small water fern *Azolla caroliniana* is known from scattered fresh-water pools in the archipelago. Like *Utricularia* it lives free-floating and is certainly dispersed by waterfowl (Galápagos pintails)."

Many plants have fruits that are "sticky," possessing barbs, hooks, and other structures that cause them to adhere to anything they touch. These plants are of course ideally adapted for dispersal by birds. On Macquarie, Taylor says that all the vascular plants have propagules suited to bird transport. These are seeds less than 1 mm. in length, seeds with hooks, bristles or barbs, and sticky berries or large hard fruits that might be carried internally. *Pisonia aculeata* is distributed widely across the Pacific and is found on many small islands. Its fruits are remarkably adhesive and have been found on the feathers of a bird in the Cocos (Keeling) Islands. The most common forest tree of the Galápagos is another species of *Pisonia*, the endemic *Pisonia floribunda*, which is found in the moist and intermediate zones of the high islands. Species of *Bidens* have fruits with barbed appendages, well suited for bird transport; three species are found in the Galápagos, all occurring elsewhere in North and South America.

Carlquist (1965) cites other examples of seeds being found on birds, such as the hooked seeds of *Acaena* found in the down of petrels on Juan Fernandez and on other petrels in New

Zealand. These petrels make a 7000-mile migration from Western Australia to South America and live in close contact with vegetation. They may well be responsible for the peculiar distribution of *Acaena*, which, like the milfoil, grows in New Zealand and on distant Juan Fernandez. Wace and Dickson point out that the ranges of some sea birds and some flowering plants include both the Tristan da Cunha archipelago in the south Atlantic and the Amsterdam-St. Paul group in the Indian Ocean. Coincidences like these are strongly suggestive of bird transport. These authors conclude, after a thorough survey of the plants of the Tristan da Cunha group, that bird transport has been of much greater importance in the dispersal of flowering plants to the islands than has dispersal by sea or air.

Several plants could have reached the Galápagos archipelago in this way, apart from the *Bidens* species, sedges, and the ancestor of *Pisonia floribunda*. Species of *Desmodium*, *Cenchrus* (having hooked seeds), and *Mentzelia aspera* (having small, carrot-shaped, hooked fruits) could well have been carried by birds, as could species of *Tribulus* and *Bastardia viscosa*. The *Desmodium* species and *M. aspera* are also found in the Americas; one of the *Cenchrus* species is also found in Cuba, while another is endemic. *Tribulus cistoides* is widely distributed, and there is an endemic Galápagos variety and a closely related endemic species. *Bastardia viscosa* occurs in Mexico, the West Indies, and mainland South America. *Plumbago scandens*, which is widely distributed in the tropics, and species of *Boerhavia*, which occur also in the southern United States, Mexico, West Indies, and South America, have glandular fruits that are extremely adhesive and probably reached the islands on birds. Carlquist illustrates a Sooty Tern captured with viscid *Boerhavia* fruits on its feathers. The Sooty Tern also occurs in the Galápagos. Other Galápagos plants that may have reached the islands by adhering to birds are species of *Digitaria*, *Oplismenus*, *Paspalum*, *Sonchus*, *Sporobolus*, *Peperomia*, and *Lepidium*.

Darwin believed that not only seeds but also land snails were occasionally transported by the feet of birds, for he had shown that many snails can withstand prolonged immersion in sea water (see above). Perkins found a small land snail of the family Achatinellidae alive on a Hawaiian bird (Zimmerman, 1948), and Gislen (1948) states that a mallard duck, shot down over the Sahara desert, had snail eggs stuck to its feet. Gressitt and Yoshimoto (1963) believe that most of the transport of the Pacific land snails to remote islands occurs through their attachment by excrement, mud, or secretions to the feet and feathers of birds. Snails of the genus *Succinea*, which live on many Pacific islands, have been found on the plumage of birds.

Arthropods too are occasionally carried by birds, although there are few recorded observations. Zimmerman removed a living bark beetle from an owl knocked down in flight in the mountains of Fiji, and owls have been recorded to wander for great distances. Dunnet (1964) records that a flea recovered from an albatross on Nightingale Island, Tristan da Cunha, was of a subspecies characteristic of St. Paul, in the Indian Ocean, but not of Tristan da Cunha. Hartmann (1964) has reported the occurrence in Finland of a parthenogenetic population of South African copepods, presumably carried by migrating Arctic terns.

Birds can also transport seeds internally, in their alimentary tracts. Sea birds do not normally eat berries, but occasionally they do (Carlquist, 1967), and we have seen that land birds, including many wide-ranging shore birds, are recorded as occasional strays on oceanic islands. Carlquist points out that such shore birds as the Bristle-thighed Curlew, Ruddy Turnstone, Sanderling, and Stilt are recorded to eat seeds, and of course ducks could carry a wide variety of seeds and fruits. Regular migrants to the Galápagos, listed as common by Lévêque *et al.* (1966), include the Franklin's Gull, Northern Phalarope, Blue-winged Teal, Bobolink, and eight shore birds. Another thirty-eight birds are listed as rare or accidental visitors. Many island plants have brightly colored fleshy fruits, which are attractive to birds. In the Galápagos for example, *Momordica charantia*, an introduced cucurbit, has very conspicuous, reddish-orange fruits, and the berrylike fruits of species of *Tournefortia* and the berries of *Castela galapageia* may be attractive to birds, although no actual investigations to test this have been made. However, birds also eat fruits that are inconspicuous and less palatable, at least to humans; for example, they have been seen eating the bitter fruits of *Scaevola*, the acrid ones of *Freycinetia*, and the white berries of poison ivy.

It might be thought that the seeds would be destroyed on being eaten. In many cases this is not so, and in some cases chances of germination are even improved. The improved germination powers of seeds of the Galápagos tomatoes after they have passed through the gut of the Galápagos mockingbirds is a pertinent example. Darwin germinated several of twelve kinds of seeds picked out of the excrement of small birds in his garden. He even forced seeds into the stomachs of dead fish, which were then fed to fish eagles, storks, and pelicans; several of these seeds were found to have retained their powers of germination.

It is also said that seeds pass through the gut of birds too quickly to be retained for the full length of a long journey (see, for example, Ridley, 1930, and Cruden, 1966). However, Darwin asserted positively that after a bird has taken a large meal, the grains do not all pass into the gizzard for twelve or even eighteen hours. Here again, he made pertinent tests. "Some seeds of the oat, wheat, millet, canary hemp, clover, and beet germinated after having been from twelve to twenty-one hours in the stomachs of different birds of prey; and two seeds of beet grew after having been thus retained for two days and fourteen hours." Many migratory birds reach speeds of from thirty to fifty miles an hour, some much more, and with the assistance of winds—such as those occurring in storms—could easily make the passage from the continent to the Galápagos Islands in twelve to eighteen hours.

Carlquist (1965) mentions that Scarlet Grosbeaks on the island of Heligoland in the North Sea feed on the dry fluffy fruits of the sow thistle, *Sonchus oleraceus*, which is widely distributed and occurs in the Galápagos. Although such seeds would seem to be well fitted for external transport, internal transport is thus also a possibility. Carlquist also states that a few ptarmigans killed on Spitzbergen were found to contain propagules of one-quarter of the plant species native to that island, including even small bulbs capable of growth. Wace and Dickson state that a "small hard seed" found in the gizzard of a Cape Pigeon, *Daption capensis*, 550 miles east of Tristan da Cunha, was presumably carried 1250 miles, from the Scotia Arc Islands, the Crozet group, or Kerguelen, the nearest breeding grounds of this bird.

Finally, there is the possibility that insects reaching the Galápagos by air could carry seeds and spores. Polunin (1960) states that "ants frequently transport seeds with edible appendages, while flies and many other insects often carry spores of cryptogams adhering to their bodies—especially when the latter are hairy." Darwin himself has shown that large grasshoppers such as locusts may transport plant seeds internally. From the excretory pellets of locusts sent to him from South Africa, he extracted several seeds "and raised from them seven grass plants, belonging to two species, of two genera. Hence a swarm . . . might readily be the means of introducing several kinds of plants into an island lying far from the mainland." Large short-horned grasshoppers, one a species closely related to the desert locust, have succeeded in colonizing the Galápagos Islands.

In general, it can be said that aerial dispersal is of great importance in the distribution of cryptogamic plants, birds, and terrestrial arthropods, and transport by birds is probably the most important method of long-range dispersal of terrestrial flowering plants.

The effectiveness of various methods of long-distance dispersal has been demonstrated by a natural experiment, which, although not ideal, came close to copying the appearance of a sterile volcanic island in the sea, and its subsequent colonization by living things. In 1883, Krakatau, a volcanic island between

Java and Sumatra, erupted with such violence that two-thirds of the island was blown off, a hole 1000 feet deep was formed in the sea bed, and the remnants, four small islets, were covered with a layer of lava and hot ash 100 to 200 feet deep. The fine dust from the explosion rose seventeen miles into the air and circled the earth for months, causing spectacular sunsets in far-distant countries. Two months after the explosion, the volcanic debris was still hot enough to turn rain into steam. The resulting islets were effectively devastated, and, if any life survived, it did not affect the following succession of events. Krakatau, though only fifteen and twenty-five miles from Sumatra and Java respectively, was recolonized by living things in a manner much like an accelerated version of the original colonization of oceanic islands.

Three years after the eruption, eleven species of ferns were present, and the only flowering plants were two species of Compositae and two grasses. Eleven years later (1894), the interior was largely grassland, with a few shrubs. Nine years after that, in 1903, a woodland was beginning to develop and this subsequently became a fairly luxuriant mixed forest. Twenty-five years after the eruption (1908), there were already 13 species of birds, including pigeons, kingfishers, orioles and a bulbul, a species of monitor lizard and a gecko, and 192 species of insects, chiefly ants and flies, but including 31 beetle species, six butterflies and two dragonflies. Spiders, scorpions, wood lice and two species of snails were also present. In 1919, 621 animal species were found in three days of searching and mixed forest was beginning to appear. The number of species of animals had tripled in eleven years, and the first mammals, two species of bats and a rat, had arrived. The birds were now represented by 29 species, and another gecko, a skink and a python, as well as two species of earthworm, had become established. By 1930, 144 species of flowering plants had been recorded, and Ridley concluded that 24 per cent of these were distributed by wind, 42 per cent sea-borne on floating rafts, and the remainder had mostly been carried by birds. There were also 48 species of ferns and 19 mosses and liverworts, all probably wind-borne. By 1933, the mixed forest was dominant and two more species of bat had arrived, one of them insectivorous. Another rat, skink and gecko and more birds—including a flycatcher—had arrived, and a crocodile was present. Most of the colonists had come from Sumatra, but some were from Java. The insects and spiders were mainly wind-borne, for they were found in the upper air currents. The reptiles probably arrived by rafting, or perhaps, in the cases of the crocodile and monitor, swam the fifteen miles. There were now 720 species of insects, 30 kinds of resident birds, land snails, reptiles, a few mammals, but—significantly—no frogs or toads. Altogether 1100 species of living organisms had established themselves on the Krakatau remnants in fifty years. Compared to nearby islands of similar size, there were almost the expected number of birds, nine-tenths of the spiders and molluscs, two-thirds of the insects, but only a quarter of the terrestrial vertebrates. Insects, other invertebrates, and birds were clearly more rapid colonizers than mammals. By 1940 it was reported that there were 283 species of flowering plants, 61 pteridophytes, and 13 lichens. The lichens were all epiphytes, probably carried by driftwood; none of them was rock-inhabiting.

It is clear, then, that colonization by animals and plants by what Darwin called "occasional means" is still going on. This colonization could be observed on Krakatau, because it was quite rapid. Also, since the island was sterile at the start of the "experiment," arrivals were easily noticed. With more remote existing islands the process must be much slower and the chances of witnessing it very slight.

There is one remarkable case of the birth of a volcanic island being witnessed and its subsequent colonization by organisms being studied. The island of Surtsey arose by volcanic action from the ocean floor in 1963. Its subsequent colonization has been rapid. Many plants and about 50 species of invertebrates—insects, spiders, and mites—had established themselves in five years (Lindroth, 1968). Surtsey is close to Iceland, so that one might expect colonization to be much more rapid than it would be on an isolated island.

Darlington (1957) has pointed out that ability to cover distances by passive means (such as in a steady wind over the sea) is not just inversely proportional to distance or even to the square of the distance. If only one individual in a thousand succeeds in crossing, say, a hundred miles of sea, then only one in a thousand of the successful ones will be able to cross a further hundred miles, and so on. Thus, if the chance of a given organism reaching an island isolated by one hundred miles of sea is 1 in 1000, its chance of reaching an island two hundred miles away will be 1 in 1,000,000 and of reaching one three hundred miles away 1 in 1,000,000,000, etc. Thus the chance of arrival of a passive propagule, such as an air-borne seed, will decrease exponentially with distance.

Propagules that fly or swim actively until their energy reserves are used up and then sink or die would have a dispersal distribution approaching the normal, rather than the exponential (MacArthur and Wilson, 1967). This would also apply to organisms floating on natural rafts, which persist for a time and then sink.

MacArthur and Wilson have shown that, providing the distance to be crossed is greater than the mean dispersal distance of the propagule, the chance of arrival of a propagule whose dispersal has a normal distribution would decrease with increasing distance even more rapidly than would the chance of arrival of a propagule whose dispersal is exponential.

The dispersal distributions of most organisms are probably more complex than either of these two theoretical models, but it seems clear that they would only very rarely result in successful landfalls in the case of remote islands. Indeed, if they were often successful, the biotas of oceanic islands would have a monotonous uniformity, and endemic species would not be evolved at all.

Zimmerman has calculated that only about 250 successful colonizations would have been necessary to account for the

3000 or more species of endemic Hawaiian insects, and Fosberg (1948) estimated that only 272 original immigrants could have given rise to the 1700 species of native seed plants. In the Galápagos such estimates cannot yet be made for the insects, many of which are still undiscovered, but clearly only about thirty successful colonizations are required to account for all the native land vertebrates including land birds, and probably less than a hundred for approximately 250 endemic vascular plants.

CHAPTER ELEVEN

Establishment

THERE are two reasons why certain plant or animal groups may be absent from oceanic islands. The first, which was discussed in the previous chapter, is the failure of an organism to arrive at all. The second is that, having arrived, the organism fails to establish itself on the island. Establishment is just as vital as arrival for the successful colonization of an island; arrival in itself is not enough.

The terrestrial organism arriving by sea must make a landfall in what is usually a highly unsuitable habitat, the intertidal zone, which is alternately covered by sea water and exposed to the air twice a day and where there is very little or no soil. Although Carlquist (1967) cites instances of nesting sea birds bringing plant disseminules from the shore to their nests further inland, the disseminule of a plant either has to "make do" with the conditions obtaining in the place where it happens to land, or perish. Animals, which can move and thus to a certain extent select their own habitat, have an obvious advantage over plants in this respect. When the animal has survived the landfall with sufficient energy (and sea-borne waifs are likely to have used up much of their energy reserve) and suitable food and habitats are within range, it can immediately seek them out. Reptiles, and in particular tortoises, have less immediate needs than most other land vertebrates in these respects. They probably survive the journey and its immediate aftermath relatively well, and this may be another reason, in addition to their fairly good dispersal abilities, why they have successfully colonized a number of isolated islands. However, seeds, the vegetative parts of plants, and the eggs of insects, molluscs, or reptiles, in contrast to adult animals, must remain for a time in the place where they land, and germination, rooting, or hatching must be accomplished at the site of their landfall. Thus most sea-borne organisms perish very soon after arrival.

An organism arriving by air will usually have traveled faster than a sea-borne one and will not have used up as much of its energy reserve. Also, the air-borne organism, in contrast to the sea-borne one, is not restricted in its landfall to one particular island environment but may fall to the ground in any habitat. For these reasons air-borne organisms might be expected to establish themselves more easily than those carried on the sea. Organisms with rather broad habitat tolerances and high reproductive potential are the best equipped for building up populations immediately after arrival, and plants with a pioneering, weedy nature clearly have an advantage in taking hold in the aftermath of lava flows. Many of the indigenous Galápagos plants are of such a type. Carlquist found that the actual colonization of lava flows was primarily related to method and ability of short distance dispersal and secondarily to ability to grow in the relatively dry sites. He found that in Hawaii the early occupants of new lava flows were wind-dispersed, whether they were trees, herbs, or lichens, and these were soon followed by plants with fleshy, attractive fruits eaten by birds.

Organisms carried to islands by birds will usually be deposited in a habitat closely similar to their original one, for the bird itself will usually seek out its own optimum environment. Thus a bird that has fed on a certain type of fruit on the mainland will search for an area where such fruits are likely to be found, and this is the area in which the seeds will be deposited. Similarly, a bird of marshes and swamps, carrying disseminules from such a habitat, will be likely to deposit them in a habitat as closely similar to their original one as the bird can find.

Carlquist studied the fruit and seed morphology and made field observations of the native angiosperm plants of Pacific islands to assess the possible modes of dispersal of the original immigrants. He found that the ecology of the recipient island was of greater importance than its distance from the source area in determining the colonizing success of plants arriving by various means of dispersal. For example, internal transport by birds is regarded as the most important mode of arrival of the floras of the major high islands of Polynesia, and the link between this means of transport and the wet forest habitat was found to be rather strong. In contrast, dispersal by repetitive drift was thought to account for the majority of plants on atolls, with internal transport by birds being of negligible significance. On dry volcanic islands, Carlquist found a large proportion of species that he regarded as having arrived by external transport on birds, by means of dry fruits caught in feathers by barbs or hairs. The Galápagos Islands fell into this category, along with the Revillagigedo Islands and possibly Easter Island. Carlquist thought the proportion of seeds and fruits brought internally in birds to be notably low in the Galápagos flora, and the drift element rather large.

REPRODUCTION

Once an organism has successfully overcome the immediate difficulties following its landfall, it must reproduce its kind if the species is to survive on the island. In most plants, even if only a single individual arrives as a founder, it will be able to reproduce, provided it grows to maturity, for most individual mature plants carry the organs of both sexes, either within the same flower or at least on the same plant. However, dioecious plants and most animals consist of individuals of either one sex or the other. Such organisms can become established only if an individual of the other sex has also successfully reached the island, and has happened to land within range of the first one. Animals can actively seek out the opposite sex, while plants cannot. It is thought that organisms do sometimes arrive in small groups, rather than as single individuals; within recent times a *pair* of kingfishers was recorded arriving in Hawaii. However, an animal species that arrives as a single female bearing eggs or young can, of course, become established from this single founding female.

After its arrival, a single seed of a self-compatible plant, in which natural fertilization of the ovum by pollen of the same plant is possible, can, if it becomes established and mature, produce a colony of plants. Moreover, if several seeds of such a plant arrive on an island at different times or at different places, populations can be formed from each of these seeds. These populations will grow and spread, thus increasing their chances of meeting other populations derived from similar propagules. When the meeting does take place, crossing between individuals of the populations will enhance the variability of the species, and thus its evolutionary potential on the island.

In contrast, two seeds of self-incompatible plants would have to arrive at about the same time, and close together, in order for a population of plants to be formed. This follows because in self-incompatible plants there is a chemical barrier preventing pollen from the flowers of one plant from germinating on the stigma of flowers from the same plant. Natural self-fertilization is thus precluded, and cross-fertilization is obligatory. This would apply to plants the individual flowers of which were hermaphrodite (monoclinous) and carried the organs of both sexes. It would also apply theoretically to plants in which the flowers were either of one sex or the other (diclinous) but both types of flowers were carried on an individual plant (monoecism); however, self-incompatibility is almost unknown in such plants. With dioecious plants, in which the individual plant carries flowers of either one sex or the other, *at least* two propagules would have to arrive together, for the chances are only even that the two propagules would carry flowers of the same or of different sex.

From such considerations as these, Baker (1955) has argued that in the establishment of organisms following long-distance dispersal, self-compatible individuals rather than self-incompatible ones would be favored. This has been called Baker's Law (Stebbins, 1957). Baker points out, however, that in plants, apomixis and vegetative reproduction could possibly assist in the initial establishment of self-incompatible or dioecious individuals.

Carlquist (1965, 1966a and b), however, maintains that dioecism is extremely important in island immigrants. It imposes on the population obligatory outbreeding, and this increases the limited variability contained in the small number of immigrants. The variability within a population is the raw material upon which natural selection acts. He suggests that dioecism is so valuable in this way that the need for the simultaneous establishment of at least two propagules is not a severe disadvantage for self-incompatible or dioecious plants. Carlquist estimates that 27.5 per cent of the species of the Hawaiian flora and 14.5 per cent of the species of the New Zealand flora are dioecious. These proportions are unusually high; the proportion for the Californian fauna being 2.6 per cent (Baker, 1967). Dioecism in island species may have been present in the original colonists, or it may have arisen after establishment. If it was present in the original colonists, Carlquist asserts, Baker's Law must be abandoned, at least in part.

Carlquist has cited ten Hawaiian plant genera in which dioecism is likely to have been present in the original founding stock. However, Baker (1967) points out that this is only 3.7 per cent of the minimum number of immigrants (272) estimated by Fosberg (1948) as being necessary to have given rise to the 1500 to 2000 species of native Hawaiian flowering plants. This is not an unusually high proportion of the presumed founders. One of the genera cited by Carlquist, *Pandanus*, might have been carried to the Hawaiian Islands by man, and in any case the propagule is a many-seeded fruit, which would increase the chances of the simultaneous establishment of adjacent staminate and pistillate plants.

Baker convincingly argues that the evolution of dioecism *after* arrival actually supports Baker's Law. According to the Law, there would have been selection among the immigrants in favor of self-compatibility. If, later on, selection favored outcrossing, the outcrossing could not be reinforced by self-incompatibility unless there was an evolutionary change from self-compatibility to self-incompatibility. In its most efficient (physiological) form, self-incompatibility involves a multiple allele system, and the genetic changes necessary for the evolution of self-incompatibility would have to be complex. Dioecism would also ensure outcrossing, although less efficiently than self-incompatibility because dioecism is often imperfect and incomplete. However, it could be evolved by a simpler process of genetic change than could self-incompatibility. Baker also points out that aids to outcrossing such as protandry and protogyny, in which the male and female sex organs of an individual plant become mature and functional at different times, are common in the Hawaiian flora. None of these systems are as efficient in ensuring outcrossing as self-incompatibility, and Baker believes their prevalence in Hawaiian plants implies that the original founders could not have been self-incompatible, but were in fact self-compatible.

As was mentioned earlier (CHAPTER 4), Rick (1966) and Linsley and his colleagues (1966) found that the earlier plant immigrants to the Galápagos were probably self-fertilizing, and although later the presence of the carpenter bee and the few other pollinating insects allowed the existence of outcrossing species, there is still no evidence of self-incompatibility in the flora.

It appears then that, in the initial establishment of plants, self-pollinating and self-compatible species will be favored by natural selection. Later, after establishment, outcrossing will be favored, and this would be reinforced, as a rule, by the evolution of dioecism and other mechanical aids to outcrossing, rather than by the evolution of self-incompatibility.

Wind-pollination would promote outcrossing over a wide area, without the need for an animal pollinating agent. A wind-pollinated species would thus be fairly easily established, and yet outcrossing would be promoted. It is thus not surprising that 32.4 per cent of the Hawaiian flora, 34 per cent of the Juan Fernandez flora and 29 per cent of the New Zealand flora are characterized by wind-pollination. There is no figure available for the Galápagos flora for comparison, but it might be expected to be of about the same order.

Plants which are highly specialized for insect pollination can only reproduce successfully if the appropriate pollinators are already present. A classic example of this is the orchid family. Orchid seeds are powder seeds, very small and light, and easily dispersed by wind, yet orchids are very poorly represented in the Galápagos. Their poor representation is thus not due to failure to disperse but more probably to difficulties of establishment in an environment with very few of the right kind of pollinating insects.

Figs, which are completely absent in the Galápagos, have an intimate and obligatory relationship with certain small chalcid wasps, which are essential for the setting of the seed within the individual figs. The very existence of figs is thus entirely dependent upon the presence of these insects, as is the existence of the insects on the presence of figs. Moreover, each species of fig has, with very few exceptions, its own particular species of fig insect. If a whole fig rather than individual seeds or fruits were dispersed to an island, then the insect, which passes much of its life cycle inside the fig, would be likely to be brought, too. However, this would not enable the insect to become established, since, on emergence from the fig, the insects would very quickly require more figs in which the next generation could develop. Such figs would not be available for several years, until the fig plant had reached maturity, by which time the insect would have become extinct. Thus, for successful colonization of both the fig and the insect, the fig plant must first become established, and then, several years later, the appropriate insect must arrive. This double requirement probably accounts for the absence of native figs from such isolated archipelagos as the Galápagos and Hawaii.

Because they can actively seek out their optimal habitats, and also a mate, and because fertilization does not involve a vector such as a pollinating insect, animals probably establish themselves more successfully than plants. However, plants are probably more successful at reaching islands, and more individuals will therefore be available to take part in the wasteful, and usually unsuccessful, trials at establishment.

ENVIRONMENTAL REQUIREMENTS

Certain physical requirements are necessary before some groups of organisms can successfully establish themselves. Most land plants require soil, and will not become established on a very new island on which soil formation has not yet begun. Exceptions are the lichens, which, as we have seen, are well represented on the laval shores of the Galápagos. Bailey (1967) believes that the lack of established sod discourages certain kinds of thrips, insects which inhabit soil and roots and which have a "pseudopupal" stage normally found in soil.

Fresh water is necessary for certain organisms, such as those insects which have aquatic larvae. Were these forms dispersed to waterless islands, they would have no chance of reproducing themselves. The Galápagos Islands, many of which are waterless, are poor in such aquatic insects, and completely lack fresh-water snails and fishes.

Organisms must thus be preadapted to the island conditions if they are to become successfully established. Obvious examples of such preadaptation to the extreme conditions of volcanic islands, are the tree *Metrosideros*, in Hawaii, and the small cereoid cactus *Brachycereus*, in the Galápagos. Both these plants are capable of taking hold and surviving on very recent

31. A juvenile Galápagos Hawk, Narborough. Adults often have a uniform dark brown breast.

32. The Hood Island species appears to be the most fearless and inquisitive of all the Galápagos mockingbirds. Photo U. Eliasson.

33. A ground finch, Chatham. These rather insignificant-looking birds have an important place in the history of evolutionary biology and are still the subject of intensive study. Photo U. Eliasson.

34. The shape of the head is characteristic of adult bull sea lions.

35. Galápagos Fur Seal, Culpepper. In contrast to the sea lions, the fur seals are restricted to rocky shores with cool, shaded retreats.

36. Male goats being ferried to the carrier at Academy Bay for transport to the continent. On this voyage 335 live goats were shipped in the hold; only two were females, and both died within two days.

lava flows which can support no other vegetation (PLATE 22). Bowman (1961), after making a detailed study of the jaw musculature of Darwin's finches, has concluded that the ancestral finches were preadapted for their various specialized feeding methods. "Weedy" plants, with broad habitat tolerances, are of course preadapted in a very general way to a variety of situations, and are common on the Galápagos.

The timing of the arrival in relation to that of other organisms which serve as food also affects the chances of successful establishment. Animals depend either directly or indirectly on plants for their food, and sometimes also for shelter, so plants must first become established on an island before any land animals can do so. Sea lions and fur seals, and those sea birds which roost on land but do not require plants as nesting material, could of course become established on barren, plantless islands.

Plant-eating insects will only become established if they find the right kind of food plants, and many of them, for example the larvae of butterflies, are quite specific in these requirements. A *Nysius* plant bug became established on the island of Guam in the Marianas only after the garden plant *Emilia* had been introduced there, and the widely ranging Monarch butterfly succeeded in establishing itself on Arno Atoll in the Marshall Islands shortly after its food plant, the milkweed, was established. The Academy Expedition of 1905–6 found the milkweed plentiful on some of the Galápagos Islands, but in spite of systematic collecting for Lepidoptera, the Monarch butterfly was not found. However, Beebe noted it on Chatham in 1923, and it has since been found on Charles (Linsley, 1966). Probably it has only recently become established. It is likely that many insects are prevented from establishing themselves because the right food plant is not present.

Vegetarian vertebrates, such as tortoises and land iguanas, could only become established on the Galápagos after a good plant cover had developed, and even nest-building sea birds could not have established themselves on barren rocky islands which possessed no nest material. Forest dwellers are unlikely to survive on an island until after a forest has developed on it. The carpenter bee could not have colonized the Galápagos until after woody plants were available to provide wood for its nest building, as well as pollen and nectar for food.

Social bees and wasps are absent from the Galápagos, although on the coast of Ecuador they are among the most conspicuous and abundant of insects. These insects require a large amount of plant and insect food for their survival, and Williams (1926) believed the lack of variety and quantity of such food in the archipelago to be the reason for their absence.

Nectar-feeding birds, such as hummingbirds, which are so abundant in South America, have not colonized the islands at all. Nectar is in short supply in the Galápagos, flowers being of only seasonal occurrence.

Similarly, predators can only survive on an island where the requisite prey species have already become established. Oceanic islands, including the Galápagos, are well known for their general lack of large vertebrate predators. Predaceous birds (two species of owl and a hawk) are present on the Galápagos, but the owls have not developed into endemic Galápagos species, and although the hawk has done so, it has not diversified at all within the archipelago. Thus, compared to other land birds, such as the finches, doves, and mockingbirds, all of which are of genera peculiar to the archipelago, these birds of prey have diverged but little on the Galápagos. Possibly they are more recent arrivals; their food requirements would only be available at a late stage in the development of the Galápagos biota. The Short-eared Owl does not occur on Wenman, although it is present on Culpepper, a neighboring island of about the same size, both islands being well isolated from the main group. Culpepper has a large population of Sooty Terns, which provide an abundance of food for the owls. Although there are breeding colonies of boobies on Wenman, there is no tern colony, and it has been suggested that the population of birds of a small enough size is insufficient to support a pair of owls.

Insectivorous birds, such as flycatchers, require a large population of flying insects, probably of a number of species, on which to feed their young. There are about 110 genera of the large flycatcher family in the Americas, and yet only two have successfully colonized the Galápagos.

Parasites, too, must have an appropriate host available to them. Native fleas and sucking lice are absent from the Hawaiian archipelago and also, so far as is known, from the Galápagos, where their hosts, land mammals, were absent or very poorly represented until the arrival of man.

The timing of the arrival is also important in relation to the arrival of other, competing species. The ecological niche of an arriving organism may already be filled by another, previously established in the community. MacArthur and Wilson (1967) have demonstrated, from theoretical models devised by Brosset, that when one of two interacting species is much scarcer than the other, and character displacement occurs (see next chapter), the rare species will contribute a very large share to the joint displacement and be in danger of going extinct very quickly. MacArthur and Wilson cite evidence that natural extinction has occurred in this way in the flora of the Dry Tortugas, an archipelago of the Florida Keys. They also mention the experiments of Doctor Ruth Patrick, who found that the extinction process in diatom species on artificial "islands"—glass slides suspended in Roxborough Spring, Pennsylvania—paralleled that of the plants of the Dry Tortugas. Thus all the advantage will initially be with the competing species which is already "in possession." Entry to such "closed" communities is often extremely difficult; many attempted introductions into islands like Hawaii have failed, presumably for this reason. The large herbivorous reptiles have been successful in the Galápagos, where there is a complete absence of large herbivorous mammals which might compete with them for food. The tortoises and iguanas have thus taken the place of such mammals in the ecology of the island community. Similarly, on Gough Island, of the Tristan da Cunha group, marine forms—an isopod crustacean and a planarian—have been able to colonize fresh water in the absence of competition from fresh-water species (Holdgate, 1965).

Various authors have ascribed the successful radiation of Darwin's finches to an absence of predators and the presence of but few competing land birds. Lack (1947) notes that finches on the continents do not normally evolve into warbler-like forms, since efficient warblers are present and the warbler niche is thus filled. He believes that it was possible for the Galápagos finches to evolve a warbler type because no mainland warbler occurred on the islands at the time of their arrival. Lack argues that had the mainland warbler been present already, it would have provided competition much too stiff for any developing warbler finch, which would not have been able to enter this niche successfully.

It cannot be assumed that the yellow warbler of the Galápagos is a recent arrival simply because it has not evolved into a distinct Galápagos species. Nevertheless, when one compares the markedly different degrees of divergence in finches and in yellow warblers, it is certainly reasonable to suppose that the finches did not arrive after the warblers.

The finches have not evolved flycatcher types, cuckoo types, mockingbird types, or swallow types. This is usually explained by assuming that competition from flycatchers, cuckoos, mockingbirds, and swallows already present on the archipelago has prevented the radiation of the finches into the niches of these species. But here we are getting into deep water. The swallows and cuckoos have diverged no more from their mainland relatives than has the yellow warbler. Evolutionists do not all agree that the degree of divergence is a good measure of relative arrival times; there is, of course, no direct evidence of the relative times of arrival of any of these birds on the archipelago.

Entry of a foreign organism into an island which is already fully "saturated" is only possible when species on the island become extinct, much as promotion in many government departments must depend upon the retirement or death of senior employees. The island can be said to be in equilibrium; immigration is balanced by extinction. Large islands, near to a source area, have a high immigration rate and a low extinction rate, and thus become saturated relatively quickly. Remote islands, with a low rate of immigration, will become saturated more slowly, particularly if they are small islands, on which extinction is likely to be more rapid. MacArthur and Wilson (1963), who are responsible for this equilibrium theory, suggest that the Krakatau fauna had approached equilibrium thirty-six years after the explosive eruption, and cite examples of new bird colonists (flycatchers), in the 1930s, and the probable extinction at about that time of other birds (kingfisher, bulbul, shrike) which had previously become established.

In spite of the "double sieve" created by difficulties of both arrival and establishment, a number of plants and animals, albeit an unbalanced and impoverished assemblage, have succeeded in colonizing the Galápagos Islands. In their subsequent evolution the same factors which are involved in the evolution of continental organisms have played their part, but with different emphases and in different patterns, with some remarkable and unpredictable results.

CHAPTER TWELVE

Archipelago Evolution

THE factors involved in evolution are mutation, recombination, selection, isolation, and the effects of chance. These factors operate on islands and continental areas alike, but on islands the emphasis on the various factors may be different.

Islands differ from continental areas most obviously and importantly in their isolation, and the increased isolation, as we shall see, affects both the roles of selection and chance in the evolutionary process, and increases the likelihood of the multiplication of species.

ISOLATION AND THE MULTIPLICATION OF SPECIES

The full title of Darwin's great work was *The origin of species by means of natural selection or the preservation of favoured races in the struggle for life,* but very little of the book was devoted to the origin of species by the splitting of one species into several daughter species. Darwin's great theme was natural selection, as the means whereby organisms gradually become better adapted to their environments. He devoted almost the whole of his effort to demonstrating evolutionary change within single lineages—what Simpson called "phyletic evolution."

In a sense, this results in the gradual origin of a "new" species from a previously existing one, but as Mayr (1963) has pointed out, true speciation, the multiplication of species, occurs when a single species breaks up into two or more reproductively isolated populations.

This second aspect of evolution, the multiplication of species, is of vital importance in providing the raw material, the starting points from which further evolutionary changes of great magnitude may proceed. Although the majority of species will eventually become extinct without opening up new evolutionary pathways, very occasionally one will become an "evolutionary pioneer," the basis for changes which will lead eventually to the invasion of an entirely new adaptive zone and thus the evolution of a whole new group of organisms. It is precisely because such successful "pioneers" are very rare that it is so important that the multiplication of species should continue, in order to provide a large number of entries in the sweepstakes of major evolutionary advance. Mayr puts forward this idea with particular force when he says: "The species are the real units of evolution, as the temporary incarnation of harmonious, well-integrated gene complexes. And speciation, the production of new gene complexes capable of ecological shifts, is the method by which evolution advances. Without speciation there would be no diversification in the organic world, no adaptive radiation, and very little evolutionary progress. The species, then, is the keystone of evolution."

Darwin realized that species multiplication occurred, and that new species originated from what he called "varieties" of preexisting species, but he did not believe that the isolation of populations had any great importance in this particular aspect of evolution. Wagner (1868), however, nine years after the publication of the *Origin of Species*, pointed out the vital importance of isolation in this process. "The formation of a real variety which Mr. Darwin considers as incipient species, can succeed in nature only where some individuals can cross the previous borders of their range and segregate themselves for a long period from the other members of their species" (quoted from Mayr). Karl Jordan was the first to assert that both isolation and mutation were necessities in species multiplication. The importance of this mode of speciation is now generally accepted, and Mayr has underlined the overwhelming importance of geographic isolation in the multiplication of species.

Of course, isolation is an important factor in speciation on continents, wherever discreet habitats are separated from others by stretches of country which are less habitable for the species concerned. Mountain tops, forest clearings, patches of swamp, caves, and desert oases, for example, are all "islands" ecologically for the species which are specifically adapted to live in such places. In a broad sense, all species originate as "island" forms, for the population which may later achieve specific status must first undergo a period of isolation from other sister populations.

For terrestrial organisms, however, true geographical islands are the most completely isolated areas, being surrounded by sea water, that most inhospitable of environments. For aquatic organisms, inland lakes or any landlocked body of water are equally effective geographical islands. Geographical islands differ from ecological islands in one important respect. Both competitors and immigrants may live in habitats adjacent to ecological islands and may persistently overflow into them. The area around and between geographical islands, however, is devoid of competitors and has no permanent reservoir of potential immigrants. Thus on geographical islands, there is a higher degree of isolation and a lower immigration rate. Peninsulas are, of course, intermediate in these respects. On archipelagos, which may be of lakes or islands, isolation plays an unusually important part, for it is multiple, and it is not surprising therefore that an unusual degree of speciation is such a feature of archipelago evolution.

Natural Selection on Islands

In an earlier chapter, we saw that some species of organisms are better equipped for island colonization than others, because their specific characteristics fit them better for successful dispersal to and establishment on remote islands. Some organisms have become specialized in colonizing, for they have evolved attributes which enable them to colonize "empty," disturbed habitats with great ease. Workers have studied these attributes in various groups of organisms (Baker and Stebbins, 1965), and the most important appear to be good dispersal, the ability to reproduce on arrival, and wide ecological tolerance or great ecological plasticity. Baker has said that such organisms have a "general purpose genotype," fitted for a wide variety of environmental conditions. They are Jack-of-all-trades species. However, the habitats which such species can most easily colonize are usually temporary and, in order to survive, their populations must constantly move out of such habitats as they are filled up and stabilized and into new ones which are ripe for colonization. Their "general purpose genotype" does not allow them to persist successfully in the competitive situations of stable habitats, and such fugitive species can be said to be Jack-of-all-trades but master of none. Many weeds are in this category (Baker, 1965).

Not all good colonizers, however, are confined to such temporary, disturbed habitats. Carson (1965) has studied the genetic systems of eight successful cosmopolitan species of *Drosophila* and has found, surprisingly, that they are characterized by a *reduction* of chromosomal polymorphism. Possibly genic polymorphism has replaced chromosomal polymorphism in these species, but the interesting feature of Carson's study is that the reorganization of the genetic system in these species has not reduced the ecological tolerance, at least of some of the species: one or two of them are able to compete with native species in some of the natural habitats which they have invaded.

Clearly, a good number of such extreme colonizing specialists will be able to reach and colonize remote islands, and may in fact do so very early in the island's history and play an important part in the early development of island communities. But because they are such specialists in colonization, rarely are they sufficiently isolated from their parent population to allow speciation to proceed unhampered by a constant influx of immigrant genes.

Endemic island forms probably more frequently evolve from not-so-good colonists, those species which have been able to reach and establish themselves on the islands but which have not been able to do so often enough to destroy the genetic isolation of the colonizing population. Put another way, islands which are near the limits of dispersal of parent species are more likely to be the sites of endemic species formation than are islands which are well within the range of dispersal of the parent species.

Islands which are well isolated as far as a particular organism is concerned will not only have few colonizing episodes, but also will probably receive only a few propagules when colonization does take place. The small size of the original founding population has effects on both the course of natural selection and the role of chance in the subsequent evolution of the island population.

If a founding population of small size enters a new environment, population pressure within the species will, at first, be small, and the population will grow exponentially, unimpeded by crowding. Under these conditions, those genotypes which are able to rear the largest families will increase in frequency; selection will favor a raising of the intrinsic rate of population increase (r). Lewontin (1965) has shown that, on theoretical grounds, the same increase in r can be achieved by relatively small changes in development rate (about 10 per cent) or by larger increases in fertility (about 100 per cent), and that we might expect that during this phase of density-independent growth, selection will act more efficiently by shortening the developmental period than by increasing fecundity.

Very soon the population size will have reached a ceiling, determined by the carrying capacity of the environment (K). Once this ceiling is reached, crowding will begin to take place and individuals of the population will begin to compete with one another in various ways. Lewontin has pointed out that it cannot be assumed that those genotypes selected during the early phase of logarithmic growth will necessarily be those selected during the later phase of crowding and intraspecific competition. The direction of selection will have shifted slightly. MacArthur and Wilson (1967) have developed the argument that in a crowded situation those genotypes which manage to replace themselves even when food is scarce will have a selective advantage; thus selection will now favor efficiency of the process of turning food into offspring, rather than mere productivity.

Thus the successful colonizing population must be able to maintain first a positive rate of increase and later a rate of increase of zero. Not all founding populations will be capable of responding to these demands in the new environment, and there will be frequent failures of colonization. Those founding populations which are successful, as Lewontin pointed out, will be "a selected sample of the essentially random genetic collections that have attempted colonization." There will thus be selection for colonizing ability *between* such founding populations, and this selection will be for characteristics of the population as a whole, such as the type of genetic system.

Once the colonizing population has reached a size where competition within it has begun to occur and what MacArthur and Wilson call K-selection has begun, the future evolution of the population will be dominated by selection for the particular ecological requirements of the new environment. One way in which the island environment usually differs from a mainland environment is that there are fewer competing species. MacArthur and Wilson have shown that in this situation both r-selection and K-selection will result in an expansion of the species' habitat, rather than an expansion of the range of foods taken within the habitat. There is very little empirical evidence in support of such a conclusion, however. In the Galápagos, as we have seen, there are as many examples of shifts and expansions in food as there are of habitat expansion.

The small initial size and the isolation of the founding population have other important effects on the course of selection, effects which have been brilliantly expounded by Mayr (1954, 1963) and Dobzhansky (1960, 1963). They have reasoned that certain genetic effects are a consequence of a sudden and drastic reduction in population size.

The gene pool of a large population that is constantly receiving immigrants from other adjacent populations is an adaptive system, which, as a result of selection on the gene pool itself, has acquired certain characteristics. Most of the genes of such a population will occur in the heterozygous condition, and these will have been selected so that they operate efficiently in this condition and also yield efficient combinations with most of the many other genes present or which may enter the system. Mayr has called such genes "good mixers," and a gene pool which has been evolved with a large proportion of such genes is a coadapted, well-compensated system with "built-in" stability.

When the population is suddenly reduced to a very small size by the arrival of founders on an island, although a good deal of heterozygosity might well be retained, inbreeding must inevitably replace the previous outbreeding system, at least during the first few generations, while the population is still small. Moreover, the continuous inflow of genes which occurred in the parent population will have suddenly ceased completely. Under these conditions, the "good mixers" will have no particular advantage. Instead, selection will favor those genes which are highly effective in the homozygous condition—the "soloists," as Mayr calls them. Also, with complete isolation from immigrant genes, the need for a closely integrated, self-balancing system is gone, and the new population can now indulge in the biological "luxury" of utilizing novel gene combinations, of "experimenting," as it were. The cohesion of the well-integrated parental gene pool has been suddenly disrupted, and natural selection operating on the isolated population can now cause drastic shifts and departures in new directions which would have been resisted by the well-compensated parental population (Fraser, 1965). Fraser has suggested that the reconstitution of the well-balanced integrated system by natural selection will be a relatively slow process, thus allowing selection to act more effectively on the "liberated" gene complex, for several generations, fitting the organism to its new environment. Under this theory a small number of founders may actually enhance the chances of successful colonization.

Because the gene complex is a unified coadapted system, any change in the selective advantage of one gene will affect all the others in the system. A drastic change in the whole gene complex will thus result, and Mayr has aptly termed this a "genetic revolution." Carson has studied the detailed nature of such genetic changes in *Drosophila* species. Few populations will survive such a radical genetic reorganization, but, when one does, it may be expected to diverge strongly from its parental population, even irrespective of any environmental differences.

The Role of Chance in Island Evolution

Chance affects the course of island evolution in a number of ways, and it may be effective from the very beginning of the colonization process.

We have seen that some organisms are better adapted than others for successful arrival and establishment on islands. Nevertheless there is also an element of chance in these early processes particularly with respect to the timing of the arrival, which can be of crucial importance for successful establishment. Also, an organism must be preadapted to the island's environmental conditions, at least to some degree, in order to become established, and it is largely a matter of chance whether or not the organisms which reach the island are those which are preadapted to the conditions there.

Having become established, an organism's future evolution on the island is immediately subject in considerable measure to the vagaries of chance. This is because the founding population, even if it consists of more than a single immigrant, will almost certainly be small, and the small size of the initial colony means that chance effects are immediately operative in two respects.

The first of these is that if the founder population is very small in comparison with its parent population, it can only carry with it a small fraction of that population's gene pool. Moreover, the particular sample of the gene pool which is carried to the island by the few founders will be determined largely by chance. This randomly determined assortment of gene combinations will be the raw material on which subsequent selection in the new island environment must act. Thus, in addition to entering a new environment, and therefore encountering new selection pressures, the founding population is endowed at the outset with only a biased sample of its parent population's rich gene pool, and in this sample there will be a radical change in gene frequencies. With almost complete isolation from the parent population, the genetic peculiarities of this sample will be preserved, and may even become exaggerated in succeeding generations.

Parsons and his colleagues have demonstrated experimentally how this may occur (Parsons, 1970). By breeding from single inseminated females taken from one wild population of *Drosophila melanogaster* in Victoria, Australia, they produced strains which differed from one another consistently and very considerably in seven different quantitative traits. Three of the traits were morphological, two behavioral, and two represented the ability of flies to withstand environmental stress (high temperature, and desiccation). These differences in quantitative traits in the various strains are due to the fact that the original wild population was polymorphic for polygenes controlling the traits, and thus the various founder females differed in their complement of these polygenes. Hosgood and Parsons (1967) further showed that for one of the morphological characters the difference between strains could be exploited by directional selection—some strains responded to such selection and others did not. Thus, in the colonization of islands, strains from some founders may quickly respond to the new selection pressures which they encounter, and thus adapt to the new environment, while strains from other founders may not, and the response, or lack of it, will depend on the particular genetic make-up that the initial founders chanced to possess.

Another effect of chance resulting from the small size of the initial population is the random loss and fixation of genes. When populations are small, many of the possible gene combinations that are produced by recombination in sexual reproduction at each generation cannot be realized. There are too few individuals present for all the possible combinations to be represented in the population. Some alleles may become lost completely and others become "fixed." It is a matter of chance which ones are lost and which ones are fixed.

Moreover, new mutations arising in the island population are unlikely to be the same as those in the parent population, and are unlikely to arise at the same time. Chance, therefore, also determines to a large extent the production of *new* genetic material in the two populations.

Dobzhansky has underlined the fact that adaptation to the environment is unpredictable. The environment does not impose a specific response on the population like a mold determining the shape of a cast. Instead, the environment presents the population with a challenge, and populations may meet this challenge in a number of different ways. Dobzhansky cites as an example the many diverse ways in which desert plants have responded to the environmental challenge of desert conditions. Thus, where there is isolation between populations, even if the environmental conditions are the same, the course of evolution in the populations concerned may be different for this additional reason.

All the above chance effects and genetic factors will tend

to cause divergence of the populations, even if the environments of the populations are identical, provided there is isolation. But of course the environments are never identical, and the difference between a continental environment and that of an oceanic island may be very great. The oceanic island, as we have seen, usually has an origin, geological history, and climate very different from a continental area, and the organisms present on the island and continent are likely to differ both in kind and relative representation. Thus the physical, climatic, and biotic factors of the environments are usually markedly different in the two areas, and differential selection will operate together with all the factors discussed above, resulting in very different courses of evolution.

Wace and Dickson (1965) have remarked that the production of endemic forms on Tristan da Cunha and other islands is less in plants than in animals. They believe this may be because of the generally better dispersal ability of plants. The colonizing group would be larger, so that the founder effect would be less marked and there would be more subsequent immigration from the source area. Both of these factors would tend to retard the formation of endemic forms.

UNUSUAL ADAPTATIONS

Considering the array of circumstances which may act to promote divergence on islands, there is no wonder that it is on islands that the most unusual adaptations are often found. Ecological shifts and changes in behavior, as well as unusual structural alterations, are particularly prevalent on oceanic islands.

In Hawaii there are non-parasitic bees which have developed species which are parasitic on other bees and have lost the pollen-gathering apparatus, and there are dragonfly larvae which instead of living in water occur in trees and undergrowth and among ground litter. Delicately winged lacewing flies have evolved tough armourlike forewings and cannot fly, but creep and leap about on the ground. Among the plants are shrubby violets, woody treelike Lobelias, and highly peculiar composites. The owl hawks in broad daylight, the Hawaiian goose has completely forsaken water even for the rearing of its young, breeds on high lava flows and feeds on berries and grass, and honey creepers have developed the habits of parrots or woodpeckers (Zimmerman, 1963).

On the Galápagos archipelago there is a lizard which feeds on seaweed some five fathoms below the surface of the sea, and relatives of sunflowers have developed into trees. Finchlike birds have developed warblerlike habits and feed on insects, while others feed on the blood of other birds or use tools to extract insects from twigs or bark. Mockingbirds on the Galápagos Islands have the habits of jays and appear to be in the process of changing from songbirds to a new kind of predatory bird. There are tortoises which have reached gigantic proportions, a cormorant which has completely lost the power of flight, and a gull which is nocturnal. The Green Heron of the Galápagos, which is not particularly distinct from its mainland relatives, sometimes dives, kingfisherlike, from a perch two feet above the water. Curio (1968) describes an unusual shore fish which has a bipartite cornea and which is not only amphibious but sometimes feeds by lunging at flying insects from land and falling back into the sea.

SPECIATION ON ARCHIPELAGOS

Neither Hawaii nor the Galápagos are single islands; they are archipelagos, and this has had a great influence on the course of evolution in the two areas. On archipelagos, isolation is multiple and the population is subjected to all the above factors of chance and differential selection as it passes through various numerical bottlenecks in the course of its dispersal to, and its establishment on, the various islands of the archipelago.

A classical experiment, performed by Dobzhansky and Pavlovsky (1957), is pertinent here. Twenty populations of *Drosophila*, each derived from the same parental population, were exposed to the same selection pressure. Ten of these were started with four thousand individuals each, and ten were founded by only twenty individuals each. After seventeen months, there was divergence between the various lineages in both groups, but the divergence was very much greater among the ten populations descended from a small number of founders than it was between the ten populations which had not passed through a "bottleneck" of small population size. Here is a striking parallel with small groups of founders, possibly from the same parental population, establishing themselves on the various islands of a remote archipelago. The chief difference between the laboratory experiment and the natural situation on an archipelago is that the various founding populations on an archipelago would *not* be subjected to the same selection pressures, for the various island environments would not be identical. Thus in the natural situation an even greater divergence might be expected. When the distance between islands is a sufficiently effective barrier to allow evolution to proceed independently on the different islands, the initial result of the compounding of all these factors will be the formation of endemic island forms on the various islands of the archipelago, as is seen at an early stage in the vermilion flycatchers of the Galápagos, and even in the shore crabs (Kramer, 1966).

The island forms may eventually acquire reproductive isolation, that is, become full species, incapable of interbreeding with other such populations. On archipelagos, the acquisition of this vital step, from which there is no turning back, is often difficult to recognize. This is because the populations are physically separated from each other, and under natural conditions are not put to the test of reproductive isolation. Groups of distinct forms occurring in isolation on different islands of the archipelago may be recognized in many Galápagos animals and plants, such as the lava lizards, tortoises, land iguanas, geckos, mockingbirds, vermilion flycatchers, flightless grasshoppers, and the plants *Jasminocereus* and *Bursera*.

At a later stage, a distinct island population may reinvade

an island already occupied by a population of its parent species. If the two populations have not yet acquired reproductive isolation, they will interbreed. However, if full specific status has been achieved during their isolation, they will maintain their identity. It is only when full reproductive isolation has been demonstrated in this way that one can be certain that the two populations have become distinct species. In practice, taxonomists often assign the rank of species to island populations which have diverged to the same extent as those in which reproductive isolation is known to have been achieved, although this may not have been demonstrated for the populations concerned.

The ecological requirements of the invading species, for example for food or territory, might be very similar to those of the species already in occupation, and if these requirements overlap to any extent then competition may occur between the two species. Under such circumstances, natural selection will operate so as to minimize competition, by favoring in one or both species characters that allow the two species to diverge ecologically as much as possible. Brown and Wilson (1956) showed that there is usually greater difference in phenotypic characters between pairs of related species, particularly of insects and vertebrates, where they occur together, than there is in places where they occur separately. This process of further divergence, which in its initial stages involves interspecific competition but eventually leads to its reduction, has been called "character divergence" or "character displacement."

Character displacement can also occur for another reason. If the two populations hybridize (i.e. reproductive isolation is imperfect), and the hybrids are at a disadvantage relative to the two parents, it will be advantageous to both populations if the hybridization is prevented. Any behavioral or other character which makes hybridization less likely, and thus reduces the chance of wastage of gametes, will be selected for. The perfection of reproductive isolation by the enhancement of behavioral or ecological isolating mechanisms between the two species will thus lead to divergence.

Character displacement does not occur invariably wherever two species interact. Van Valen (1965) showed that the exact opposite, namely "character release," can occur when a colonizing species enters a small or remote island which has fewer competing species than has the source region. He found that in five selected bird species, island populations showed much greater variability in bill size than did mainland populations of the same species. Such "character release" could occur when the selection pressure of mainland competitors, leading, for example, to a stabilized bill size, is removed; characters which permit a wider exploitation of the environment, e.g. a more variable bill size, may then be selected for. This phenomenon may explain two fairly frequent characteristics of island populations, namely, great variability and a tendency toward increased size.

MacArthur and Wilson have pointed out that when competing species come together they may, under certain circumstances, converge rather than diverge from one another in evolution, at least in theory. Species which spend much time and energy searching for food items, rather than pursuing them once they are found, can reduce the searching time simply by enlarging their diets. They will thus converge by "generalizing." In contrast, species in which pursuit of food is much more important, in terms of time and energy, than is searching for it may increase the efficiency of pursuit by specializing. If the food of the two pursuer species is rather different, they will diverge.

These authors have also shown that where character displacement and divergence does occur, it will often accelerate the divergence of the older, resident population, rather than that of the newcomer. This is because many organisms invade islands through ecologically marginal habitats, and later on gradually adapt and shift to the more central habitats where many species occur. Any character displacement will thus result in an even greater shift of the resident population toward the central habitats, thus reducing its capacity for dispersal, and increasing its divergence from the original parent population. Wilson (1959, 1961), working on ant species in Melanesia, showed that some of the species that in New Guinea became adapted to the inner rain forests may have readapted to the marginal habitats and expanded secondarily, so that the whole cycle may begin again.

In an earlier chapter, when discussing Galápagos plants, mention was made of loss of dispersal ability. This is of fairly frequent occurrence in island organisms, and is found not only in plants, but also in insects (loss or reduction of wings, or functionless wings) and birds (loss of flying ability). Darwin accounted for this by suggesting that natural selection would act against individuals which had a greater likelihood of being inadvertently carried from islands out to sea, where they would perish. However, Darlington (1943) found that species of carabid beetles on low small islands tend to be fully winged, while those in more sheltered, mountain and island habitats tend to be wingless. He thus concluded that negative selection was responsible for loss of dispersal ability. On the low small islands the population is subjected to high winds and is in great danger of extinction; ability to disperse to other islands is thus extremely important. On larger, more mountainous islands, however, long-distance dispersal is less important, and the selection pressure for it is relaxed. Loss of dispersal ability, of course, is conducive to the fragmentation of island populations into smaller, isolated units and thus accelerates the speciation process.

There are two other fairly common characteristics of island populations which also tend to cause fragmentation and thus accelerate speciation. The first, which was discussed above, is the tendency of a colonizing population, once established, to move out of the marginal habitats, which are the best "staging areas" for departing organisms, into the more central ones, reducing the population's capacity for dispersal. The second is that island organisms tend to exist as small, restricted, very local populations. Both in Hawaii and in the Galápagos, many endemic forms are only found as very small populations, adapted to very specialized local habitats. Both the ecological specialization and the reduction in population size reduce the colonizing capacity of the populations concerned, and tend to keep them separate from one another.

Once a species is present on more than one island, a second round of divergence may follow in its island subpopulations. In the Galápagos, apparently this is beginning in the winged grasshoppers of the genus *Schistocerca*, and has proceeded further in the snakes, ants of the genus *Camponotus*, and species of the plant genus *Mollugo*. In all these organisms, multiple invasions have resulted in more than one form being present on an island, and fine differences in the various island subpopulations of the same species have been recognized.

There is no theoretical reason why divergence should stop at this point if the island environments are sufficiently diverse to support a large number of related forms which have differing ecological requirements. A further round of full speciation may be completed, and then another and another, and so on. Probably several such cycles have taken place in the evolution of the Galápagos finches, Hawaiian honey creepers, and many groups of beetles and other insects both in the Galápagos and Hawaii.

Quite obviously, endemic forms are likely to be formed on well-isolated oceanic islands. If the island is single, like Cocos Island, then there can be no archipelago speciation, and there will be little opportunity for the various populations to achieve geographic isolation. Thus the Cocos Finch, although endemic to Cocos and very different from the other species of Darwin's finches, has not speciated further on Cocos.

On larger islands there may be more opportunity for the isolation of populations, and some speciation may occur. For example, Madagascar has seven genera of Vanga Shrikes, a family of shrikelike birds peculiar to the island and all possibly derived from a single founder population.

On archipelagos, divergence is facilitated by the isolation produced by the islands themselves, and even on small archipelagos consisting of only a few islands speciation may proceed to a considerable degree. Thus on the extremely isolated Tristan da Cunha group, consisting of only four islands, the beetle genus *Tristanodes* has evolved into eleven endemic species, only one of which occurs on more than one of the three islands of the northern group, which are no more than twenty-five miles apart (Holdgate, 1965). This species multiplication is almost certainly the result of reinvasions.

THE GALÁPAGOS SITUATION

There are sixteen or so islands in the Galápagos archipelago, and many examples of endemic species complexes (a group of related species derived from a common ancestral species). The ease with which the complexes are formed depends on the degree of isolation of the various island populations. This in turn depends upon the distance between the islands and the dispersal ability of the species concerned. The effects of isolation on the Galápagos archipelago can be seen by an examination of the distribution there of several groups of animals and plants, the systematics of which have been well studied.

The tortoises, which, of course, have fairly limited ranges, have evolved fifteen distinct subspecific forms on the eleven islands on which they have occurred (FIGURE 19). No two forms occur together, and reinvasions do not seem to have taken place. A distinct endemic form was evolved on each of the five major volcanoes of Albemarle, and it has been suggested that these volcanoes were separate islands in the past. Whether or not this is the case, there is no doubt that they are now, and have been for some time, "ecological islands," effectively separating the populations of tortoises from one another.

In contrast to the tortoises, the land iguanas (FIGURE 18) are limited to the central islands of the archipelago, with the exception of Duncan, and a distinct species has evolved on the most southeasterly of these, Barrington.

In the flightless grasshopper genus *Halmenus* (FIGURE 12), the most divergent population of the four which are recognizable is that on the distant island of Wenman.

There are three species of Galápagos snakes (FIGURE 16), two of which occur on the central group of islands, and the third is restricted to the three southeasterly islands, Charles, Hood, and Chatham. Reinvasions have occurred only on the central islands.

The geckos show a pattern similar to that of the snakes (FIGURE 17), but there have been no reinvasions. A single species occurs on the central group of islands, distinct species on the more peripheral southeasterly islands, Barrington, Charles, Hood, and Chatham, and one very divergent species is restricted to Wenman. Geckos have not reached the other northern islands.

The lava lizards (FIGURE 14) also have distinct forms on Charles, Hood, and Chatham, as well as on the northern islands of Abingdon and Bindloe. A single species occupies all the central islands with the exception of Duncan, which has its own endemic species. Once again, reinvasions have not resulted in more than one species per island.

The mockingbirds, which are, of course, more easily dispersed than the reptiles, occur on all the islands except Charles, where they may have become extinct, and Duncan, where they are of only occasional occurrence (FIGURE 23). As in the case of all the reptiles except the snakes, reinvasions have not resulted in the existence of more than one form on each island. Three of the species are each restricted to one of the three southeastern islands on the windward periphery of the archipelago, the Charles Island species being represented only on adjacent islets. The fourth species is present on all the remaining islands except Duncan and has distinct subspecies restricted to the more peripheral of these.

Two endemic complexes of plants, which have been well studied systematically, have distribution patterns similar to those of the reptiles and mockingbirds. The seven *Mollugo* species (FIGURE 7) include endemic species on Wenman, Barrington, and James, one occurring only on Charles and Chatham, one on Charles and Duncan, and two others which are rather widespread on the central group. Of the ten endemic species of *Alternanthera* (FIGURE 6), seven occur on peripheral islands. In both these plant genera, reinvasions have resulted in more than one species occurring on some islands.

The fully winged grasshopper genus, *Schistocerca*, has two species (FIGURE 13). One of these is widespread on the archipelago and the second is confined to the southeastern islands of Tower, Chatham, Charles, and Hood. On Chatham, Charles, and Tower, two species are present.

The distributions of these various animals and plants have several points of interest in common. The peripheral islands usually either have distinct endemic forms or have not been reached at all. The sea currents flow through the Galápagos roughly from east to west, and the prevailing winds are from the southeast. Thus organisms arriving on the archipelago by sea or air which "miss" the southeastern islands of Charles, Hood, and Chatham, but make a landfall farther northwest, are less likely to spread later to the southeastern islands against the prevailing winds and current. The isolation of these three southeastern islands, therefore, is probably greater, as far as the organisms are concerned, than mere distance on the map might suggest.

THE PROBLEM OF DUNCAN

Another feature of the distributions outlined above is the anomalous position of Duncan. This is a small but fairly high island, quite central in position, and yet time and again the distributional data are such that if one did not know it to be central in position one would believe it to be a peripheral island. The "problem of Duncan," as we may call it, was what led Van Denburgh and Slevin (1913) to suggest that the central group of islands was once a continuous land mass with a large baylike crater lake, and Duncan was a central cone in the crater. This theory fits the bathymetrical data (FIGURE 3) and would account for the unusually isolated nature of Duncan biologically. There is at present no geological evidence to support such a theory, but geological studies on the archipelago have been extremely limited.

In spite of the lack of geological support for this theory, the fact remains that there is something decidedly odd about Duncan. It is biologically much more isolated than one would expect from its geographical position. The distribution of three more groups of organisms further illustrate its unusual biological

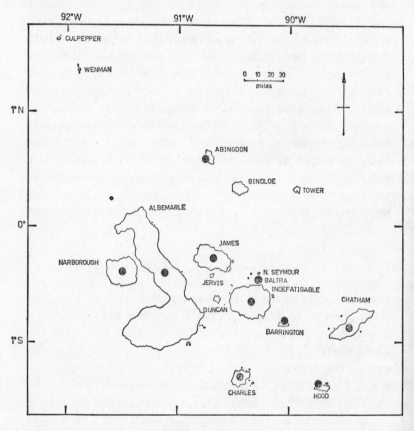

FIGURE 26. Distribution of the endemic grasshopper *Sphingonotus fuscoirroratus*. Data from Hebard, 1920.

isolation. The grasshopper genus *Sphingonotus* has an endemic Galápagos species which, however, has not speciated within the archipelago (FIGURE 26). It is widespread, but has not reached the peripheral islands of Culpepper, Wenman, Bindloe, and Tower (Dirsh, 1969). Nor does it occur on Duncan. The candelabralike, night-flowering *Jasminocereus*, an endemic genus, has three species, and these are represented on all the islands except those of the northern line, Barrington, the isolated southeastern island of Hood, and Duncan (FIGURE 8). Finally, the "palo santo" tree, *Bursera*, which is almost a Galápagos trademark, so commonly is it found in the lowlands of the archipelago, occurs on every single island except Duncan (FIGURE 10).

While there are several measures of geographical isolation, two of which are given in TABLE 3, biological isolation is much more difficult to express quantitatively. The number of forms peculiar to the island, and the total number of forms present, are often used as assessments of biological isolation. However, we have seen that geographically isolated islands often lack certain groups altogether, and the number of endemic forms will take no account of these absent groups, which, nevertheless, are an indication of biological isolation. In TABLE 3, Column A includes not only the number of single-island endemics, but also the number of cases where groups are totally absent from the island in question. Percentage endemism (Column B, TABLE 3) also takes this additional factor into account. In Column B, the single-island endemic forms are expressed as a percentage of the total number of forms which have succeeded in reaching the island. Clearly, a biologically isolated island may be expected to have fewer non-endemics, that is, forms present also on other islands, than an island less isolated biologically (Column C, TABLE 3). However, it is conceivable that an island may have many non-endemic forms, these being present only on the island in question and on one other island, possibly its nearest neighbor. This is likely to be the case when two islands are fairly close to each other but remote from the other islands of the archipelago. An island which has, for example,

TABLE 3

Indices of biological isolation of six central and six peripheral Galápagos islands, based on the distributions of 141 species and sub-

	Average distance from all other islands (arbitrary units).	Distance from nearest island (miles).
Central islands:		
Albemarle	45	3
James	48	3
Jervis	56	3
Duncan	56	7
Indefatigable	48	1
Baltra	56	1
Peripheral islands:		
Culpepper	153	21
Wenman	134	21
Tower	80	29
Chatham	87	28
Hood	99	28
Charles	78	30

1. Vertebrates: native rats, tortoises, land iguanas, snakes, geckos, lava lizards, mockingbirds, vermilion flycatchers, Darwin's finches (five genera).

Insects: *Sphingonotus, Schistocerca, Halmenus, Camponotus.*

Plants: *Jasminocereus, Bursera, Opuntia, Mollugo, Alternanthera, Scalesia, Coldenia.*

ten non-endemic forms, each of which occurs on but one other
island, is biologically more isolated when the whole archipelago
is considered, than an island which has ten non-endemics, each
of which occurs on, say, twelve other islands. This consideration
is included in the index given in Column D of TABLE 3.

species, of 24 groups of native organisms,[1] the systematics of which have been well studied.

BIOLOGICAL ISOLATION

Number of single-island endemics and groups not represented on the island.	Number of endemics as a percentage of all forms present on the island.	Number of forms present which are not endemic to the island.	Sum of the number of other islands on which all non-endemic forms (Column C) occur.[2]
A	B	C	D
12	26	31	177
10	27	27	177
10	5	19	147
18	43	12	107
13	30	31	181
7	13	21	127
20	38	5	19
18	42	7	40
22	56	4	28
21	59	13	99
18	47	8	55
20	50	17	122

2. This index is derived by considering an island's non-endemic forms (Column C) and adding together the number of other islands on which each of these occurs. For example, there are 4 forms on Tower which are not restricted to Tower; one occurs on 13 other islands, one on 3, one on 11, and the fourth occurs on only 1 other island. The sum of these figures is 28 (Column D).

Whichever index of biological isolation is used, Duncan stands out as a central island which is as biologically isolated as peripheral islands. Duncan is also a peculiar island ecologically (see CHAPTER 2), and it may well be that ecological factors are partly responsible for its unusual biological isolation. This "problem of Duncan" has been presented in some detail, because it shows that, although the Galápagos have been a focus of attention for biologists since Darwin's visit, we are still a long way from explaining the course of evolution on the archipelago in many groups, and tantalizing, unsolved problems still await explanation.

GALÁPAGOS AND HAWAII

Darwin's finches, although not at such an advanced stage of evolutionary divergence as the Hawaiian honey creepers, are an extremely good example of adaptive radiation. This is the name given to the evolutionary process whereby a lineage splits, and the resulting forms become so adapted that they are able to utilize separate segments of the environment. Re-invasions and subsequent competition with related species clearly have been largely responsible for the radiation of Darwin's finches. Five genera of the finches are present on the Galápagos, each of which is wide-ranging (FIGURE 27) and each of which has distinct ecological characteristics. Within these genera, the species also show ecological differences, and, in contrast to the reptiles and mockingbirds, for example, the various species of finches are not restricted to single islands. Although the species and genera were formed very probably in isolation, they have subsequently spread, and most of them now occur widely throughout the archipelago, and therefore coexist on many islands. All islands carry three or more species, and twelve islands have seven or more. They are able to coexist because their ecological requirements are different and competition between them is minimized.

The Galápagos finches also show the beginnings of a third round of speciation. Species subpopulations which are on different islands show slight differences in their characteristics, which, Bowman believes, are correlated with fine differences in the various island environments (Bowman, 1961; Lack, 1969).

The Hawaiian archipelago offers even more striking examples

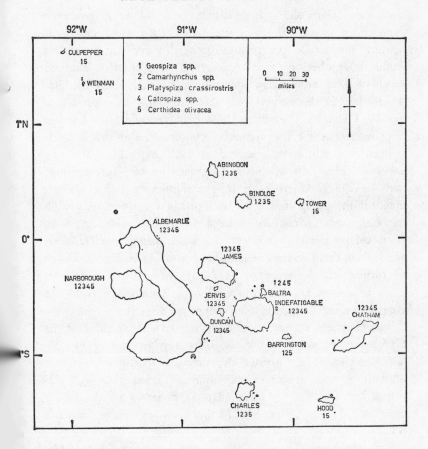

FIGURE 27. Distribution of genera of Darwin's finches in the Galápagos Islands.

of species multiplication than do the Galápagos Islands. For example, there are today more Hawaiian species of the Drosophilidae, the family of flies to which *Drosophila* belongs, than there are in the whole of continental North America (Hardy, 1960). Most of the Hawaiian fauna, apart from the birds, originated on the western borders of the Pacific and is thought to have spread gradually across the Pacific by the successive colonization of intervening high islands. Some of these have now degenerated into coral atolls or are now flat-topped seamounts beneath the sea. A progressive eastward movement from one island to another, or from one group of islands to another, would involve archipelago speciation not once, when the Hawaiian Islands themselves were reached, but many times previously. Groups and chains of high islands would have acted as stepping stones for the organisms concerned, and species multiplication would have occurred at each step. Thus the vast endemic complexes of many Hawaiian insects, for example, may be the products of a long evolutionary history which involved the compounding of archipelago speciation. Although the Galápagos Islands are isolated from the South American continent by a narrower stretch of water than is the Hawaiian archipelago from its continental source areas, there is no evidence of former islands between the Galápagos and the continent. Thus organisms reaching the Galápagos Archipelago from the continent must presumably have done so directly.

The Hawaiian Islands, though less numerous than those of the Galápagos, are much higher and offer a wider variety of ecological niches. Their greater elevation may partly explain, not only the greater degree of speciation in Hawaii than in Galápagos, but also the extensive adaptive radiation of the honey creepers, which has proceeded further than has that of Darwin's finches.

Both the Hawaiian and Galápagos archipelagos are volcanic, and on the Hawaiian islands of Hawaii and Maui, as well as on the Galápagos islands of Narborough, Albemarle, James, and Bindloe, there can be seen today "islands" of vegetation which have not been covered with lava (PLATE 2). These "kipukas," as they are called in Hawaii, may have a fairly long life, for topographical effects which lead to one area becoming a kipuka might well also result in the same kipuka being spared destruction in a subsequent flow. These ecological islands of vegetation, surrounded by barren lava or regenerating growth which is periodically subjected to destruction by succeeding flows, could be important in isolation. Populations of organisms with limited dispersal ability might become restricted to the kipuka for long periods of time, and the speciation of such organisms would thus be accelerated.

THE FUTURE

The vigorous plasticity in behavior as seen, for example, in the finches and the ecological shifts and behavioral changes that have taken place in many Galápagos forms show how an important evolutionary advance might occur. The invasion of entirely new adaptive zones might lead to the evolution of new, higher categories of organisms. Nevertheless, the odds are that all the Galápagos organisms are doomed to eventual extinction, and it is highly unlikely that their evolutionary potential will be fully realized.

There are several reasons for this pessimistic prognosis. All islands gradually deteriorate under the incessant and unrelenting forces of erosion by wind, rain, and sea. Geologically, a small island has a short, if interesting life. Many Pacific atolls now represent the coralline headstones of what were once high islands. These degenerate low islands are particularly vulnerable when a rise in sea level or submergence of the land occurs. Because these processes take place extremely slowly, the island organisms do not react by dispersing, but remain on their gradually diminishing island until it, and they, disappear.

Islands carry small populations. Wild populations of any kind usually fluctuate, and very small isolated populations are unusually sensitive to population reductions; they may be reduced in numbers to such an extent that they are unable to recover.

In the next chapter we shall see that island organisms are also particularly vulnerable to competition from later immigrants, whether these are introduced with man's assistance or by natural means.

There is very little chance of island organisms escaping back to the mainland. Loss of dispersal ability, as we have seen in earlier chapters, is one of the tendencies of island evolution. Examples from Galápagos plants, insects, and birds have already been cited. Moreover, oceanic islands such as the Galápagos rarely possess rivers, so that rafting is relatively less likely to occur from islands than it is from the mainland. As far as the Galápagos Islands are concerned, both the sea currents (FIGURE 1) and prevailing winds are in the wrong direction to assist in dispersal from the islands to the continent. Finally, continental areas, unlike oceanic islands, have rich, diversified biotas which have reached equilibrium. Establishment within these closed communities would be extremely difficult for island organisms, which, having evolved in the ecologically "sheltered" conditions of an island, have often lost their competitive ability. Thus, island organisms which did succeed in making the return journey to the mainland would in all probability find "no vacancies." For example, the West Indian White-crowned Pigeon has spread north and established itself on coastal islands of North America such as the Florida Keys, but it has been unable to invade the mainland of North America.

Island forms, therefore, will rarely, if ever, make important evolutionary contributions on a world-wide, long-term scale. Most of them are dead ends, doomed to extinction, either on the islands which they inhabit or on other newer islands which they might colonize and thus delay their inevitable end. However, for the Galápagos organisms, extinction will not occur until some time in the distant future, provided that they can be protected from the dangers associated with man's presence. These organisms offer today, as they did in Darwin's time, unusual opportunities for the study of evolutionary processes, and it is important that they should be studied under natural conditions, free from man's direct or indirect interference.

CHAPTER THIRTEEN

The Dangers

O F A L L areas of the world, the Galápagos Islands must surely have one of the best cases for the protection and conservation of native plants and animals. On the one hand, the plants and animals are of very great scientific interest and many of them are found only on the archipelago. On the other hand, the dangers to their survival are numerous and acute. Perhaps the closest parallel to the Galápagos biota is that of the Hawaiian Islands, and much can be learned by comparing the history of the plants and animals of these two archipelagos since man has reached them.

The Galápagos Islands are the home of unique organisms of quite extraordinary biological interest. The marine and land iguanas, tortoises, mockingbirds, gulls, Darwin's finches, Galápagos Dove, Flightless Cormorant, Waved Albatross, Galápagos Penguin, and many unusual plants, occur nowhere else in the world. The behavior of most of the animals is affected little, if at all, by the presence of an observer, and thus they can easily be studied in the field, and many have become adapted in structure, physiology, and behavior in ways unparalleled elsewhere.

The Galápagos biota exemplifies in a remarkable way the interdependent processes and events involved in the evolution of living organisms. The archipelago has been called a "Showcase for Evolution," and there is no doubt that in this simplified, almost stylized environment, evolutionary processes can be recognized with a clarity matched in few other parts of the world. The number of islands, their age, and their distance from the source areas, a distance neither too great nor too small, are all factors which have combined to allow these processes to proceed to just the right extent for productive scientific study. Such studies, as the previous chapters have suggested, have proceeded further in some groups of organisms than in others. The pioneer work of discovering, describing, and naming of species is still incomplete in some groups, such as the insects. In groups that are named, work can now be directed toward ecological and behavioral aspects of evolutionary problems. All such future fieldwork depends for its success on the biotic communities remaining in their natural states. To the biologist, these islands are a "laboratory" for the study of evolution.

Unfortunately, islands are notorious for the ease with which the balance of natural communities can be upset by the accidental or purposeful introduction of organisms from other areas. When such organisms are introduced to islands, the natural checks to their increase which are found in their home environments are often absent, so that they may quickly and successfully establish themselves. Having done so, their populations can increase without the usual checks, at the expense of the native flora and fauna. An island community, because it is usually simpler, incorporates fewer checks and self-balancing systems than a continental community, and there are many cases of introduced animals and plants that have developed into serious pests. Also, many island organisms, during their long period of isolation, have become so specialized in their adaptations to the simplified island environment that they are ill-fitted to withstand the competition or predation of introduced organisms.

The majority of species that have become extinct in recent times were island organisms. Ninety per cent of the extinct birds listed by Ziswiler (1967) were island forms. Flightless birds (which, we have seen, are particularly likely to be evolved on islands) feature high on the list of extinct species and probably owe their extinction to the increased vulnerability which loss of flight entails. Such are the Moas (New Zealand), Dodo (Mauritius), Solitaire (Rodriguez and probably also Reunion, both in the Indian Ocean), Great Auk (offshore North Atlantic islands), Elephant Birds (Madagascar), Flightless Owl (Cuba), and the flightless rails of the Hawaiian Islands, Wake Island, Samoa, Fiji, Chatham and Aukland Islands (both off New Zealand), Mauritius, and Rodriguez.

Another characteristic of island animals that increases their vulnerability in the presence of man and his introduced predators is fearlessness. Most of the animals mentioned in the previous chapters show this characteristic to a remarkable degree, and it is also evident in other island animals. As MacArthur and Wilson (1967) have pointed out, a given piece of land can support far fewer numbers of predators than it can prey, so that predators will be precariously rare, even on large islands. On small islands the carrying capacity may be too low to allow the existence of a permanent predator population. Also, large terrestrial predators are unlikely to be dispersed to remote islands. Thus, on islands, selection for effectiveness of escape from predators will be relaxed. Other beneficial characters, which on a continental area may be opposed by selection because of their interference with effective escape, may on islands be selected for. Thus, on many islands, in the absence of large predators, there has been no selection for behavior which leads to their avoidance, i.e. fear. When man enters the environment, with his associated rats, cats, and dogs, the island animals are at their mercy. This was probably one reason for the extinction of the Stephen Island Wren. This bird inhabited a small island east of New Zealand, and became extinct as soon as it was discovered by the lighthouse keeper's cat. The ease with which the native fauna of Baltra in the Galápagos was completely exterminated by bored U.S. servicemen during the Second World

War was no doubt largely because of the absence of any fear-reaction to man's presence.

The Hawaiian Islands are a good example of what can happen to an island fauna and flora as a result of man's activities, which have been more extensive in Hawaii than in the Galápagos.

Many island species which have become extinct in recent times have become so only indirectly as a result of man's interference. Sometimes the effects have been unforeseeable at the time, and their causes purely accidental. There are many other cases where organisms have been introduced by man for a specific purpose, and have affected the native biota in drastic and unpredicted ways.

Mosquitoes, accidentally introduced to Hawaii, carried a virus to the native honey creepers which were thereby weakened and eventually killed. The mosquitoes may also have carried bird malaria, introduced with exotic birds, to the native birds.

The mongoose was purposefully introduced into Hawaii to control the rats in the sugar-cane fields. However, it has had little effect on the rats, and eats the eggs of ground-nesting birds. The endemic Hawaiian Goose, the "nene," is of great interest since it has completely forsaken water and instead breeds on high lava flows, feeding on herbs and berries. This goose suffered particularly from predation by the mongoose and was brought to the verge of extinction; the goose population on the island of Maui was completely wiped out. Fortunately, rearing programs at the Severn Wildfowl Trust in England and also in Hawaii have saved this species. The population on the island of Hawaii has been reinforced, and the birds were reintroduced to the great Maui volcano, Haleakala. Although the mongoose occurs in Haleakala's crater, the newly established nene population was surviving when I visited the crater in 1963. Strict conservation measures are being enforced, and the mongoose is being controlled by a program of trapping.

The Japanese White-eye, a bird introduced for aesthetic reasons in 1929, has undergone a population explosion in Hawaii and competes with the native birds for insects. The Indian

Mynah was introduced into Hawaii in 1865 to control the army worm (itself an accidental introduction). This bird attacks and destroys the eggs and young of other birds, and its numbers now exceed those of all the native birds together.

Zimmerman (1948 and 1963) describes how the native Hawaiian insects have also suffered as a result of man's introductions. Generalized insect predators of caterpillars, particularly ichneumon flies introduced to control lepidopterous pests of agriculture, have ravaged the native Lepidoptera, and introduced fresh-water fish such as top minnows have reduced the once-plentiful lowland damsel flies to rarities. The greatest destroyer of native insects in Hawaii has been the voracious introduced ant *Pheidole megacephala*. As a result of its depredations, few endemic insects are now to be found in the Hawaiian Islands below about 2000 feet.

The Giant African Snail reached Hawaii from the Far East and rapidly became a pest of vegetable and garden crops. As controlling agents, predaceous snails were introduced, but their attentions were not confined to the pest, and some of them reached the hills, where the endemic Hawaiian land snail fauna, one of the most distinctive in the world, is suffering from their attacks.

The Hawaiian native forests have retreated before man's direct attack and those of his accidental or purposeful introductions. Burning and cultivation, arboreal rats which arrived with the Hawaiians and which feed on fruit and destroy seeds, browsing and grazing animals introduced after Cooke's discovery of the islands and which have since run wild, and introduced grasses which smother the seedlings have reduced the native forest to a quarter of its original extent. In the twelfth century, when the Hawaiians arrived, the forest extended down to the sea; today it is confined to the highlands, and so of course is the endemic forest fauna. Forty per cent of the known species of drepaniids (honey creepers) are now extinct, and 80 per cent of the species of land birds as a whole have recently become extinct. Thus the whole of the native lowland forest community no longer exists. It has been lost forever and can never be properly studied.

Plants too have played their part in this sad story, although more subtly. Continental plants, evolved in a diverse and complex environment, are more opportunistic than those on islands, which in the relative absence of competitors have gradually lost their competitive abilities. Plants introduced to Hawaii in the last century are even now menacing the native flora. Escapes of lantanas in the lowlands and blackberries, nasturtiums, gorse, guavas, and plums at higher elevations are gradually choking out native plants. On the island of Kauai, the blackberry is completely out of control, and its destruction now would involve very extensive disturbance of the community, thus offering any survivors even greater opportunities of expansion.

In the Galápagos, in contrast to the Hawaiian Islands, man has so far made only limited direct inroads into the native flora, on the inhabited islands of Chatham, Indefatigable, Charles, and southern Albemarle. On Indefatigable, Harris (1970) points out that the best argicultural land includes the preferred breeding areas of the Dark-rumped Petrel, which has been pushed to the upper limit of its natural habitat by agricultural encroachments. This species has declined rapidly since the arrival of man and the black rat.

Man's direct effect on the native animals of the Galápagos has been considerable, even in the space of a few centuries. The lamentable tale of his pillaging of the tortoises has been told in an earlier chapter. Today, of the original fifteen island-forms of tortoise, only four or five have any real chance of survival. The Galápagos fur seal was hunted in thousands and Townsend (1934) reports that over seventeen thousand were taken between 1816 and 1897. The fur seal was thought to be on the brink of extinction, but fortunately the population appears to be recovering. Sea lions, which were hunted for their skins and killed because they were said to foul fishing nets, are nevertheless abundant. On Baltra, the whole of the native vertebrate fauna has been destroyed by man. The Galápagos Hawk, persecuted by settlers because it was thought to prey on their livestock, is now rare in inhabited areas, and may have disappeared completely from Chatham and Charles. Doves were killed in their thousands during the last century, and even in recent years there have been reports of mass killings. Like the hawk, the dove is now rarer, and much less tame, on inhabited islands. The Flightless Cormorant, the population of which is naturally low, has been reported as being accidentally caught in the lobster traps of visiting fishermen in the Bolívar Strait. Local fishermen catch lobsters by diving for them, and do not use lobster pots. Although Ziswiler (1967) states that the Galápagos Penguin was hunted for meat, and the eggs and young collected, I have not been able to find any evidence that this occurred on a large scale. Ziswiler also makes the remarkable statement that Darwin's Ground Finch, *Geospiza magnirostris magnirostris*, became extinct in the nineteenth century because it was persecuted and captured for the live-animal trade.

As so often in the history of man's journeyings, the black rat was close on his heels when he came to the Galápagos. It is now present on Albemarle, James, Duncan, Indefatigable, Baltra, Chatham, and Charles (FIGURE 28). Duncan is the only one of these islands which has not been inhabited by man, and the spread of the rat to this island is doubly regrettable, for it was avoidable, and it has had a drastic effect on the island's tortoise population. The black rats eat tortoise eggs and young, and are the chief danger to the Duncan tortoises. The black rat is probably responsible for the severe decline of the native rat on James and the near extinction of the native rats of Indefatigable and Chatham. Black rats also eat the eggs of Galápagos birds, and Harris, studying a colony of the Dark-rumped Petrel on Indefatigable, found rat droppings "in every hole and cranny." He ascribes the very low nesting success of this petrel to the predatory activities of black rats.

Domestic animals have gone wild on several islands of the group, and many of them menace the native species. Feral pigs were seen on Charles by Darwin in 1835, and were on Indefatiga-

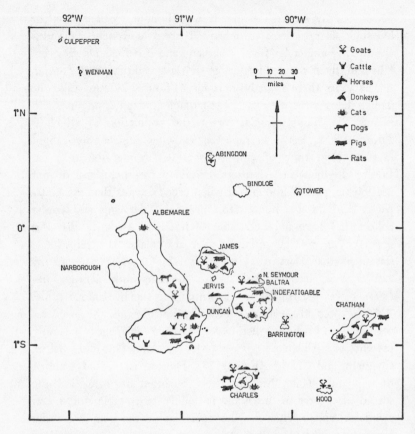

FIGURE 28. Distribution of mammals, introduced by man into the Galápagos, which have become feral or free-ranging.

ble and James in 1906. They are now feral on all the islands which have been inhabited. The pigs uproot tortoise nests and eat their young and eggs and are known to destroy the burrows and eat the adults and young of the Dark-rumped Petrel on Indefatigable. Harris states that in 1935, about eight years after pigs were introduced to Indefatigable, during the petrel's breeding season, pig fat was so tainted by the smell and taste of the petrel as to be almost unusable. The other Galápagos breeding grounds of this petrel are unfortunately on other islands where pigs have also run wild, and the bird is thus threatened on these islands too.

Wild dogs and cats are of course predacious and feed on the young of reptiles and birds. Wild dogs are present on southern Albemarle, where they hunt the calves of free-ranging cattle, and occur also on Charles and Indefatigable. Brosset (1963a) suggests that the wild dogs of Charles, which Wintour (1900) described as hunting in packs, destroyed all the goats on that island. In Harris's study of the Dark-rumped Petrel, he found that a considerable proportion of the adults were killed by feral dogs. Cats occur on all these islands, also on Chatham and possibly on James. Ziswiler (1967) states that feral dogs and cats have "denaturalized" the population of the Waved Albatross. However, this bird breeds only on Hood, an uninhabited island free from dogs and cats. The same author blames dogs, in part, for the reduction in numbers of the Galápagos Hawk, a bird which often nests in trees.

On the four islands with sizeable settlements, Albemarle, Indefatigable, Chatham, and Charles, there are feral cattle and donkeys. Wild donkeys also occur on James, and horses run free on southern Albemarle and on Chatham. Beck reported "thousands of cattle" on southern Albemarle in 1901 and this is still the main area for cattle export to the mainland. These animals roll and step on tortoise nests and iguana burrows, and, by their feeding, change the general character of the vegetation. Donkeys do not appear to have any great effect on the tortoises of Volcan Alcedo, for although the donkeys are common, the tortoise population is one of the most flourishing in the archipelago. Donkeys have some slight value in that—from a human's point of view—they form the best animal trails on the islands.

Probably the most dangerous of the feral animals are those specialists at desert formation, goats. On the island of Guadalupe, off Baja California, they have completely changed the face of the landscape, as they have in Cyprus, Egypt, and much of the

Middle East. On the Hawaiian island of Molokai very drastic vegetational changes have taken place in recent years probably as a result of the activity of goats.

Goats apparently occurred in the Galápagos as early as 1700, when the Peruvian viceroy is said to have ordered dogs to be released on the islands to put down goats left ashore by the English. Captain Porter of the *Essex* released goats on James in 1814, and Beck repeated this in 1906. They were common on Charles at the time of Darwin's visit in 1835, and the 1906 Academy Expedition found them also on Baltra, Barrington, and Hood. A few goats were released on Abingdon by fishermen some time after 1957, when there were no goats on the island. Today there are hundreds all over the southern slopes and they are penetrating into the moist zone. They are now on all the inhabited islands, as well as James, Barrington, Abingdon, and Hood.

The Galápagos goats are handsome creatures, colored uniformly brown or black, and the males have magnificent spirally spreading horns. This, however, is all that can be said on their behalf, apart from their value as an occasional source of meat. They are polygamous and have a very high rate of population increase. Voracious browsers, they leave not a vestige of a leaf when they have finished with a bush; their intensive feeding thus removes the ground cover, promotes erosion, and also delays the normal regenerative processes of plants. They eat practically anything that grows, and this includes the food of the tortoises, land iguanas, and some birds.

Because of their activities, the shrub layer of Barrington has almost completely disappeared and the vegetation of this island has been reduced to a kind of open parkland. The wild cotton and Galápagos tomato have been exterminated on Barrington by goats. Eliasson (1968) believes that *Scalesia helleri* is restricted on Barrington to cliffside sites because of the browsing pressure of goats. This island is one of the few areas in the archipelago where there is a fairly good population of land iguanas. It is unlikely that these vegetarian reptiles will be able to withstand for long the sort of competition which goats produce.

On Hood, like Barrington an uninhabited island, the tortoise population is on the very brink of extinction, and competition from goats is intense.

Eliasson (1968) has recently reported on the influence of goats on the vegetation of James. On this island he observed *Opuntia* stems nearly two feet in diameter which had been completely gnawed through. Near the shore, goats had also browsed the branches of *Cryptocarpus* as high up the bushes as they could stretch, and were seen climbing six feet above the ground and browsing on the upper branches of *Clerodendron*. Eliasson believes that the range of the endemic composite genus *Scalesia* is steadily decreasing, and that this is mainly due to browsing pressure from goats. Three species of *Scalesia* form a natural group endemic to James. The survival of two of these species is very seriously threatened. Eliasson sought in vain for *S. darwinii* in the James Bay area where it had previously been collected, and found only three small trees of *S. atractyloides*, possibly the only survivors of the species, growing on a steep cliffside out of reach of goats. The third species, *S. stewartii*, was found on the islet of Bartholomew, on which there are no goats, and on a fresh lava field on James opposite the islet. A fourth *Scalesia* species, *S. pedunculata* var. *pedunculata* is a tree-like form, growing to a height of over thirty feet, and sixty years ago there were forests of this species on James at altitudes of around 2000 feet. Eliasson found only a few scattered specimens in 1967, all fully grown, and believes that this form is also threatened with extinction.

On Indefatigable, the population of *Scalesia helleri*, as on Barrington, is largely restricted to steep cliff sites, at least on the southern side of the island.

A very rare succulent, *Calandrinia galapagosa*, was collected in 1906, and again by Eliasson in 1967. It is restricted to Chatham, and has only been found in the area around Sappho Cove. The score or so of individuals which Eliasson saw in 1967 were all sterile and severely damaged by goats, and he believes that the species will soon be exterminated unless the goats there can be controlled.

Another endemic succulent, *Portulaca howellii,* is now found on the small islets of Bartholomew, Jervis, Daphne Major, Eden, North Seymour, Plaza Islets, Brattle, Onslow, Champion, Enderby, Caldwell, and Gardner-by-Charles, but was not found by Doctor Eliasson on the larger islands, James, Indefatigable, Albemarle, and Charles, to which these islets are adjacent. He believes that the influence of goats might possibly explain this distribution, for the animals have been present on the four large islands for many years. Two small specimens only were found near the shore of Abingdon, an island to which goats were introduced in the last decade. For most of the year this plant survives as naked succulent stems, in which a large part of the plant's nutriment is stored. The stems are probably attractive to goats, and by 1967 there were hundreds of goats on Abingdon. It seems likely that very soon, Abingdon, like the other larger islands, will lack *Portulaca howellii* altogether, so that the plant will survive only on small islets which are free from goats.

The goat is probaby the greatest single threat today to the Galápagos flora and fauna.

The most serious plant pest on the islands is the guava. On Chatham the spread of this plant, combined with the grazing of cattle, has seriously modified the plant cover at high elevations. The endemic shrub *Miconia* occurs on this island as well as on Indefatigable, but on Chatham it is not present as a discreet belt, and appears to be retreating. On Charles much of the upland plateau is covered with guava, and on Sierra Negra of Albemarle, and on Indefatigable, it is spreading seriously. On all these areas cattle roam freely over the mountains or have done so until recently, and are probably responsible for the guava's rapid spread by carrying its seeds about on their hoofs.

It is difficult to reconcile a policy of conservation and protection with the often conflicting needs of human settlement. However, on the Galápagos, settlement is limited both in numbers and geographical extent by the resources of the islands. Therefore there is a good chance that a policy of conservation may not in fact conflict with human needs, but may instead be of benefit to the human population. The whole of the archipelago has been declared a National Park of Ecuador, with certain areas only of Chatham, Indefatigable, Charles, and Albemarle set aside for settlement and cultivation. Harris (1970) points out the need for control of land clearance on Indefatigable and southern Albemarle, where the Dark-rumped Petrel population is seriously threatened by habitat reduction and predation. The Ecuadorian government realizes the potential of the Galápagos wildlife as a tourist attraction, and Galápagos tours are beginning, although slowly and on a very small scale. Thanks largely to the educational program of the Research Station, the settlers are becoming proud of their islands' natural heritage, and destruction of the native animals has practically ceased. Many settlers take a real interest in the natural history of the islands and have assisted visiting scientists in many ways. Some supplement their income by providing services for scientists visiting the islands, by acting as guides, putting their boats out for charter, and providing food. Others have invested in facilities for tourists; there is a small tourist hotel on Indefatigable and another on Charles. Certainly the whole economy of the islands benefits from the visits of both scientists and tourists.

Although settlement and tourism have not reached the scale in the Galápagos that they have in Hawaii, and probably never will, there is still a danger that the sort of thing that has happened in Hawaii may occur in the Galápagos, and this danger increases with the number and frequency of visitors to the islands. The accidental introduction of a single small organism in the baggage of some visitor to the islands could rapidly upset the natural balance of the islands' ecology and wreak untold havoc on the natural attractions of the archipelago. In

Hawaii, the authorities have learned by bitter experience that prevention is better and cheaper than cure, and the plant and animal quarantine procedures of the State of Hawaii are now among the strictest and most efficient in the world. In the Galápagos, the introduction of domestic animals is controlled now on the advice of the Research Station. With the expansion of tourism, however slow, an effective plant and animal quarantine program is also badly needed. There are no quarantine procedures at all for incoming visitors at present.

Although the introduction of preventative measures and the tightening of existing controls are clearly practicable, the correction of the mistakes which have already been made will be much more difficult. The problem of goats is urgent on Barrington, Hood, and Abingdon. A program of eradication on Barrington, started a year or two ago, was going very well until there was opposition from some of the settlers on other islands. They claimed that this goat population was part of their livelihood, and a permanent source of fresh meat was being destroyed. In fact, hunting parties to Barrington were extremely infrequent in the past, and the island's goats were not a steady source of meat for the settlers. Goats have now increased in numbers again on Barrington, and continue to menace the land iguana of that island, which is an endemic species restricted to Barrington. A reasonable compromise seems called for here, and could work. Once the goat population is reduced to manageable limits, some sort of licensed culling, preferably of females, would no doubt be possible.

There seems to be no reason at all why the goat populations of Hood and Abingdon should not be exterminated, provided the money and labor are made available. Hunting by the settlers might be a sufficient population check on the inhabited islands, if the hunters could be persuaded to concentrate on females or to take females only. At present they take only males (PLATE 36); in a polygamous animal this has little effect on population control.

Altogether about six members of the staff of the Research Station are specifically concerned with conservation. The Chief Conservation Officer, based on Indefatigable, is both familiar with the islands and their native plants and animals and untiring in his efforts to preserve and conserve them. But he is working under great difficulties. With the whole of the archipelago as his responsibility, he has no independent means of transport at his disposal, and his only assistants are two wardens on Indefatigable, two on Albemarle, and a half-time one on Charles. Ideally, twice as many are needed, and the conservation side of the station's work should really have its own transport, independent of that of the other sections.

The spirit and enthusiasm are there, and the station has already, in the short space of time since its inception, done much to save the Duncan tortoises from extinction and greatly increased our knowledge of the status and ecology of the other tortoise populations. It is giving expert advice on the areas to be set aside for settlement and conducting important field research into the ecology of the birds of prey. In addition, the station is operating seismographic and oceanographic stations and assisting visiting scientists in every possible way. But it could do so much more, particularly in the field of conservation, if funds were available. The amount of money spent in one minute by the "developed" countries on armaments would equip and staff the station sufficiently for proper supervision and control of the remarkable assemblage of animals and plants in this unique area for scientific investigation.

A channel does exist whereby interested individuals who are not professional scientists can give practical help. An organization, "Friends of the Galápagos," has been established. Members pay a small annual fee and are kept up-to-date with current developments and problems by means of periodic bulletins. Details of this organization may be obtained from the Charles Darwin Foundation for the Galápagos Islands, 1, Rue Ducale, Brussels 1, Belgium. Membership of the Foundation itself is open to learned societies, institutes, universities or their departments, and to individual scientists of all countries.

If this book has awakened sufficient interest on the part of the reader for him to post an enquiry to Brussels, then it will have been well worthwhile. Darwin's islands both deserve and need the attention of educated men everywhere, and the need is urgent.

BIBLIOGRAPHY

Bibliography

THE following works may be of interest to the reader who wishes to pursue his studies of the Galápagos Islands. Those not actually seen by the author are marked †; those containing an extensive bibliography relevant to the particular chapter are marked *. The letter G indicates that a reference is of general interest and the letter S refers to specialized scientific works. Abbreviations are in accordance with the recommendations of the World List of Scientific Periodicals.

CHAPTER 1

G   Beebe, W. L., 1924. *Galápagos—World's End.* Putnam's, New York.

G   ——, 1926. *The Arcturus Adventure.* Putnam's, New York.

G   Brower, K., 1969. *Galápagos: The Flow of Wildness. Volume 1.* Sierra Club, San Francisco.

G†   Cabello de Balboa, M., 1576–86. *Miscelania Antartica.* MS in New York Public Libr., copied from lost original.

G†   ——, 1586 (1840). *Histoire du Perou. In:* Termaux—Compans, *Voyages, Relations et Memoirs originaux pour servir a l'histoire de la découverte de l'Amérique.* Paris, 1840.

G   Conway, A. and Conway, F., 1947. *The Enchanted Islands.* Putnam's, New York.

G   Darwin, C., 1845. *Journal of researches into the geology and natural history of the various countries visited during the voyage of* H.M.S. *Beagle round the world.* 2nd edition. Ward, Lock & Co., London.

279

G ——, 1872. *The origin of species by means of natural selection or the preservation of favoured races in the struggle for life.* 6th edition. Oxford Univ. Pr., London.

G Heyerdahl, T., 1952. *American Indians in the Pacific.* George Allen & Unwin, London.

S ——, 1963. Archaeology in the Galápagos Islands. *Occ. Pap. Calif. Acad. Sci.* 44: 45–51.

S —— and Skjolsvold, A., 1956. Archaeological evidence of pre-Spanish visits to the Galápagos Islands. *Am. Antiq.* 22: 1–71.

S Huxley, J., 1966. Charles Darwin: Galápagos and after. *In:* R. I. Bowman (ed.), *Proc. Symp. Galápagos int. scient. Project:* 3–9. Univ. California Pr., Berkeley and Los Angeles.

G Koford, C. B., 1966. Economic resources of the Galápagos Islands. *In:* R. I. Bowman (ed.), *Proc. Symp. Galápagos int. scient. Project:* 286–90. Univ. California Pr., Berkeley and Los Angeles.

G Livingston, J. and Sinclair, L., 1966. *Darwin and the Galápagos.* C.B.C., Toronto.

G Markham, C. R., 1892. Discovery of the Galápagos Islands. *Proc. R. geogrl. Soc., Lond.* 14: 314–16.

S Means, P. A., 1942. Pre-Spanish Navigation off the Andean Coast. *Amer. Neptune* 2 (2).

G Melville, H., 1856. The Encantadas. *In: Four Short Novels.* Bantam Paperbacks, New York (1959).

G Miller, R. C., 1965. Islands of the tortoise. *Pacif. Discovery* 18 (5): 1–2.

G† Morrell, B., 1932. *A narrative of four voyages to the South Sea, north and south Pacific ocean . . .* Harper, New York.

G Pinchot, G., 1931. *To the South Seas.* Hutchinson, London.

G† Porter, D., 1815. *Journal of a cruise made to the Pacific Ocean by Captain David Porter in the United States Frigate Essex in the years 1812, 1813 and 1814.* 2 volumes, Bradford and Inskeep, Philadelphia.

G Ritchie, J., 1943. Evolution and the Galápagos Islands. *Univ. Edinb. J.* 12 (2): 97–105.

G Robinson, W. A., 1936. *Voyage to Galápagos.* Harcourt, Brace, New York.

G Rogers, W., 1712. *Cruising Voyage Round the World.* Cassell, London, 1928.

G Sarmiento de Gamboa, P., 1572 (1907). *History of the Incas.*

(Transl. and ed. C. Markham.). Hakluyt Soc. II Ser., Vol. 22, Cambridge, 1907.

G   Shipman, J. C., 1962. *William Dampier, Seaman–Scientist.* Univ. of Kansas Publ. Library series, 15.

G   Slevin, J. R., 1955. Charting the "Enchanted Isles." *In: Essays in the Natural Sciences in honor of Captain Allan Hancock.* Univ. Southern California Pr., Los Angeles.

G* ——, 1959. The Galápagos Islands. A history of their exploration. *Occ. Pap. Calif. Acad. Sci.* 25: 1–150.

G   Strauch, D., 1936. *Satan came to Eden.* Harper, New York.

G   Townsend, C. H., 1925. The Galápagos tortoises in their relation to the whaling industry. *Zoologica, N. Y.* 4 (3): 55–135.

G   Wittmer, M., 1961. *Floreana.* Michael Joseph, London.

G   Wycherley, G., 1929. *Buccaneers of the Pacific.* Rich and Cowan, London, 1935.

CHAPTER 2

S   Anonymous, 1968. Nouvelles des Galápagos. *Notic. Galápagos* 12: 3–7.

S   Alpert, L., 1946. Notes on the weather and climate of Seymour Island, Galápagos Archipelago. *Bull. Am. met. Soc.* 27: 200–9.

S ——, 1963. The climate of the Galápagos Islands. *Occ. Pap. Calif. Acad. Sci.* 44: 21–44.

S   Banfield, A. F., Behre, C. H. Jr. and St. Claire, D., 1956. Geology of Isabela (Albemarle) Island, Archipielago de Colon (Galápagos). *Bull. geogr. Soc. Am.* 67: 215–34.

S* Bowman, R. I., 1961. Morphological differentiation and adaptation in the Galápagos finches. *Univ. Calif. Publs. Zool.* 58: 1–302.

G   Brower, K., 1969. *Galápagos: The Flow of Wildness. Volume 2.* Sierra Club, San Francisco.

S   Chesterman, C. W., 1963. Contributions to the petrography of the Galápagos, Cocos, Malpelo, Cedros, San Benito, Tres Marias, and White Friars islands. *Proc. Calif. Acad. Sci.* ser. 4, 32 (11): 339–62.

S   Chubb, L. J., 1933. Geology of Galápagos, Cocos, and Easter islands. *Bull. Bernice P. Bishop Mus.* 110: 3–44.

G   Colinvaux, P. A., 1968a. Eruption on Narborough. *Animals* 11 (7): 296–301.

S   ——, 1968b. Paleolimnological investigations in the Galápagos Archipelago. *Notic. Galápagos* 11: 13–18.

S   Cox, A., 1966. Continental drift in the southern hemipshere. *In:* R. I. Bowman (ed.), *Proc. Symp. Galápagos int. scient. Project:* 78–86. Univ. California Pr., Berkeley and Los Angeles.

S   —— and Dalrymple, G. B., 1966. Palaeomagnetism and potassium-argon ages of some volcanic rocks from the Galápagos Islands. *Nature* 209: 776–7.

S   Dall, W. H., 1924. Notes on fossiliferous strata on the Galápagos Islands explored by W. H. Oschner of the expedition of the California Academy of Sciences in 1905–6. *Geol. Mag.* 61: 428–9.

S   —— and Oschner, W. H., 1928. Tertiary and Pleistocene Mollusca from the Galápagos Islands. *Proc. Calif. Acad. Sci.* ser. 4, 17: 89–139.

S   Dalrymple, G. B. and Cox, A., 1968. Palaeomagnetism, potassium-argon ages and petrology of some volcanic rocks from the Galápagos Islands. *Nature* 217: 1–8.

G   Darwin, C., 1845. *Journal of researches into the natural history and geology of the countries visited during the voyage of* H.M.S. *Beagle round the world.* 2nd edition. Ward, Lock & Co., London.

G   Durham, J. W., 1965. Geology of the Galápagos. *Pacif. Discovery* 18 (5): 3–6.

G   Eibl-Eibesfeldt, I., 1959. Survey on the Galápagos Islands. *Unesco Mission Reports* 8: 1–31.

G   ——, 1961. *The Galápagos—Noah's Ark of the Pacific.* Doubleday, New York.

S   Lack, D., 1947. *Darwin's Finches.* Cambridge Univ. Pr., London.

S   ——, 1966. Study of a soil sequence on Indefatigable Island. *In:* R. I. Bowman (ed.), *Proc. Symp. Galápagos int. scient. Project:* 87–92. Univ. California Pr., Berkeley and Los Angeles.

S   Laruelle, J., 1963. Exploration géo-pédologique de l'île de Santa Cruz. *Notic. Galápagos* 1: 11–13.

G   Leleup, N., 1965. Commentaires sur le sanctuaire zoologique des Galápagos. *Africa-Tervuren* 9 (3–4): 85–91.

S   McBirney, A. R. and Aoki, K., 1966. Petrology of the Galápagos Islands. *In:* R. I. Bowman (ed.), *Proc. Symp. Galápagos int. scient. Project:* 71–77. Univ. California Pr., Berkeley and Los Angeles.

S   Palmer, C. E. and Pyle, R. L., 1966. The climatological setting of the Galápagos. *In:* R. I. Bowman (ed.), *Proc. Symp. Galápagos int. scient. Project:* 93–99. Univ. California Pr., Berkeley and Los Angeles.

G   Peterson, R. T., 1967. The Galápagos, eerie cradle of new species. *Natn. geogr. Mag.* 131 (4): 540–85.

S   Richards, A. F., 1954. Volcanic eruptions of 1953 and 1948 on Isabela Island, Galápagos Islands, Ecuador. *Volc. Lett. Hawaii Volc. Res. Ass.* 525: 1–3.

S   ——, 1962. *Catalogue of the active volcanoes of the world. XIV. Archipielago de Colon, Isla San Felix and Islas Juan Fernández.* International Volcanological Association, Rome.

S   Richardson, C., 1933. Petrology of the Galápagos Islands. *Bull. Bernice P. Bishop Mus.* 110: 45–67.

G   Shipton, E., 1966. Climbing a volcano. *Animals* 9 (3): 154–58.

S   Shumway, G., 1954. Carnegie Ridge and Cocos Ridge in the east equatorial Pacific. *J. Geol.* 62 (6): 573–86.

S   —— and Chase, T. E., 1963. Bathymetry in the Galápagos region. *Occ. Pap. Calif. Acad. Sci.* 44: 11–19.

S   Stewart, A., 1911. A botanical survey of the Galápagos Islands. *Proc. Calif. Acad. Sci.* ser. 4, 1: 7–288.

G   ——, 1915. Further observations on the origin of the Galápagos Islands. *Pl. Wld.* 18: 192–200.

S   Van Dyke, E. C., 1953. The Coleoptera of the Galápagos Islands. *Occ. Pap. Calif. Acad. Sci.* 22: 1–181.

S   Vinton, K. W., 1951. Origin of life on the Galápagos Islands. *Am. J. Sci.* 249 (5): 356–76.

S   Williams, H., 1966. Geology of the Galápagos Islands. *In:* R. I. Bowman (ed.), *Proc. Symp. Galápagos int. scient. Project:* 65–70. Univ. California Pr., Berkeley and Los Angeles.

S   Wilson, J. T., 1963. Evidence from islands on the spreading of ocean floors. *Nature* 197: 536–38.

S   Wooster, W. S., and Hedgpeth, J. W., 1966. The oceanographic setting of the Galápagos. *In:* R. I. Bowman (ed.), *Proc. Symp. Galápagos int. scient. Project:* 100–7. Univ. California Pr., Berkeley and Los Angeles.

CHAPTER 3

G   Bailey, A.M., 1961. Dusky and Swallow-tailed Gulls of the Galápagos Islands. *Denver Mus. nat. Hist., Museum Pictorial No. 15.*

S ——, 1962. Nesting of the Galápagos Penguin and the Galápagos Sooty Gull. *Condor* 64: 159–61.

S Beck, R. H., 1904. Bird life among the Galápagos Islands. *Condor* 6 (1): 5–11.

G Beebe, W. L., 1924. *Galápagos—World's End*. Putnam's, New York.

G Brosset, A., 1963. La réproduction des oiseaux de mer des Iles Galápagos en 1962. *Alauda* 31: 81–109.

G Cavagnaro, D., 1965. Exploring the Galápagos on foot. *Pacif. Discovery* 18 (5): 14–22.

S Couffer, J. C., 1957. Nest of the Galápagos Penguin. *Condor* 59: 399.

S Cullen, E., 1957. Adaptations in the Kittiwake to cliff-nesting. *Ibis* 99: 275–302.

S Davis, M. and Friedmann, H., 1936. The courtship display of the Flightless Cormorant. *Scient. Mon., N.Y.* 42: 560–3.

G Eibl-Eibesfeldt, I., 1959. Survey on the Galápagos Islands. *Unesco Mission Reports* 8: 1–31.

G Fosberg, F. R., 1965. Natural bird refuges in the Galápagos. *Elepaio* 25: 60–67.

G Hailman, J. P., 1963. Why is the Galápagos Lava Gull the colour of lava? *Condor* 67 (4): 354–5.

S ——, 1964a. Breeding synchrony in the equatorial Swallow-tailed Gull. *Am. Nat.* 98: 79–83.

G ——, 1964b. The Galápagos Swallow-tailed Gull is nocturnal. *Wilson Bull.* 76 (4): 347–54.

G ——, 1965. Cliff-nesting adaptations of the Galápagos Swallow-tailed Gull. *Wilson Bull.* 77: 346–62.

G ——, 1966. Strange gull of the Galápagos. *Audubon Mag.* 68: 180–4.

S ——, 1967. The ontogeny of an instinct: the pecking response in chicks of the Laughing Gull (*Larus atricilla* L.) and related species. *Behav. Suppl.* 15, 196 pp.

S ——, 1968. Behavioural studies of the Swallow-tailed Gull. *Notic. Galápagos* 11: 9–12.

S Harris, M. P., 1967. Sea-bird research in Galápagos 1965–67. *Notic. Galápagos* 9/10: 11–14.

S ——, 1969a. Age at breeding and other observations on the Waved Albatross *Diomedea irrorata*. *Ibis* 111: 97–98.

S ——, 1969b. Food as a factor controlling the breeding of *Puffinus l'herminieri*. *Ibis* 111: 139–56.

S ——, 1969c. Breeding seasons of sea-birds in the Galápagos Islands. *J. Zool., Lond.* 159: 145–65.

St ——, 1969d. The biology of storm-petrels in the Galápagos Islands. *Proc. Calif. Acad. Sci.* Ser. 4, 37 (4): 95–166.

S ——, 1970. The Biology of an Endangered species, the Dark-rumped Petrel (*Pterodroma phaeopygia*) in the Galápagos Islands. *Condor* 72 (1): 76–84.

St ——, in press, a. Breeding ecology of the Swallow-tailed Gull *Creagrus furcatus*. *Auk*.

St ——, in press, b. Factors influencing the breeding cycle of the Redbilled Tropicbird in the Galápagos Islands. *Ardea*.

S Howell, T. R. and Bartholomew, G. A., 1962. Temperature regulation in the Red-tailed Tropic Bird and the Red-footed Booby. *Condor* 64: 6–18.

S Lack, D., 1950. Breeding seasons in the Galápagos *Ibis* 92: 268–78.

G Lévêque, R., 1963. The status of some rarer Galápagos birds. *Bull. int. Coun. Bird Preserv.* 9: 96–98.

S ——, 1964. Notes sur la réproduction des oiseaux aux îles Galápagos. *Alauda* 32 (1): 5–44.

S Moynihan, M., 1962. Hostile and sexual behavior patterns of South American and Pacific Laridae. *Behav. Suppl.* 8, 365 pp.

G Murphy, R. C., 1936. *Oceanic birds of South America*. American Museum Natural History, New York.

G* Nelson, B., 1966a. Boobies. *Animals* 9 (3): 144–49.

S ——, 1966b. Flighting behaviour of Galápagos storm petrels. *Ibis* 108: 430–32.

S ——, 1967a. The breeding behaviour of the White Booby, *Sula dactylatra*. *Ibis* 109: 194–231.

S ——, 1967b. Etho-ecological adaptations in the Great Frigate-bird. *Nature* 214: 318.

G* ——, 1968a. *Galápagos: Islands of birds*. Longmans, Green & Co., London.

S ——, 1968b. Galápagos 1964. *Notic. Galápagos* 12: 8–12.

S ——, 1968c. Breeding behaviour of the Swallow-tailed Gull in the Galápagos. *Behav.* 30: 146–74.

S ——, 1969a. The breeding ecology of the Red-footed Booby (*Sula sula* L.) in the Galápagos. *J. Anim. Ecol.* 38: 181–98.

S ——, 1969b. The breeding behaviour of the Red-footed Booby, *Sula sula. Ibis* 111: 357–85.

G Palmer, R. S., 1962. *Handbook of North American Birds.* Volume 1, Yale Univ. Pr., New Haven.

G Peterson, R. T., 1967. The Galápagos, eerie cradle of new species. *Natn. geogr. Mag.* 131 (4): 540–85.

S Risebrough, R. W., 1968. Observaciones sobre las aves fregatas, *Fregata minor* y *Fregata magnificens,* en las Islas Galápagos. *Notic. Galápagos* 11: 3–8.

S Rothschild, W., 1898. A communication. *Bull. Br. Orn. Club* 7: 51–53.

S —— and Hartert, E., 1899. A review of the ornithology of the Galápagos Islands. With notes on the Webster-Harris expedition. *Novit. zool.* 6: 85–205.

S —— and ——, 1902. Further notes on the fauna of the Galápagos Islands. Notes on the birds. *Novit. zool.* 9: 381–418.

S Snodgrass, R. E. and Heller, E., 1904. Papers from the Hopkins-Stanford Galápagos expedition, 1898–99. XVI. Birds. *Proc. Wash. Acad. Sci.* 5: 231–372.

S Snow, B. K., 1966. Observations on the behavior and ecology of the Flightless Cormorant *Nannopterum harrisi. Ibis* 108 (2): 265–80.

S —— and Snow, D. W., 1968. Behavior of the Swallow-tailed Gull of the Galápagos. *Condor* 70 (3): 252–64.

S —— and ——, 1969. Observations on the Lava Gull, *Larus fuliginosus. Ibis* 111: 30–35.

S Snow, D. W., 1965a. The breeding of Audubon's Shearwater (*Puffinus l'herminieri*) in the Galápagos. *Auk* 82: 591–97.

S ——, 1965b. The breeding cycle of the Red-billed Tropic Bird in the Galápagos Islands. *Condor* 67: 210–14.

G ——, 1967. Movements of Galápagos sea-birds. *Notic. Galápagos* 9–10: 15.

S —— and Snow, B. K., 1966. The breeding season of the Madeiran Storm Petrel *Oceanodroma castro* in the Galápagos. *Ibis* 108: 283–4.

S —— and ——, 1967. The breeding cycle of the Swallow-tailed Gull *Creagrus furcatus. Ibis* 109: 14–24.

S Streets, T. H., 1912. The Fork-tailed Gull (*Xema furcatum*). *Auk* 29: 233–4.

S   Townsend, C. H., 1929. The Flightless Cormorant in captivity. *Auk* 46: 211–13.

S   Wynne-Edwards, V. C., 1962. *Animal dispersion in relation to social behaviour*. Oliver and Boyd, Edinburgh.

G   Ziswiler, V., 1967. *Extinct and vanishing animals*. Longmans, Green & Co., London.

Chapter 4

S   Bailey, S. F., 1967. A collection of Thysanoptera from the Galápagos Islands. *Pan-Pacif. Ent.* 43: 203–10.

G   Carlquist, S., 1965. *Island Life*. Natural History Pr., New York.

S   Cockerell, T. D. A., 1935. The carpenter bees of the Galápagos Islands. *Proc. Calif. Acad. Sci.* ser. 4, 41 (28): 379–82.

S   Dawson, E. Y., 1962. Cacti of the Galápagos Islands and of coastal Ecuador. *Cactus Succ. J.* 34 (3): 67–74. 34 (4): 99–105.

S   ———, 1963. Additional note on *Jasminocereus howellii*. *Cactus Succ. J.* 35 (2): 42.

S   ———, 1964. Cacti in the Galápagos Islands. *Notic. Galápagos* 4: 12–13.

S   ———, 1965. Further studies of *Opuntia* in the Galápagos Archipelago. *Cactus Succ. J.* 37 (5): 135–48.

S   ———, 1966. Cacti in the Galápagos Islands, with special reference to their relations with tortoises. *In:* R. I. Bowman (ed.), *Proc. Symp. Galápagos int. scient. Project:* 209–14. Univ. California Pr., Berkeley and Los Angeles.

S   Dirsh, V. M., 1969. Acridoidea of the Galápagos Islands (Orthoptera). *Bull. Br. Mus. nat. Hist. (Ent.)* 23 (2): 27–51.

S   Hagerup, O., 1950. Rain pollination. *Biol. Meddr.* 18 (5): 1–19.

S   ———, 1951. Pollination in the Faroes in spite of rain and poverty in insects. *Biol. Meddr.* 18 (15): 3–48.

S†   Harling, G., 1962. On some Compositae endemic to the Galápagos Islands. *Acta Horti Bergiani* 20: 63–120.

S   Hebard, M., 1920. Dermaptera and Orthoptera. *Proc. Calif. Acad. Sci.* ser. 4, 2, Part 2 (17): 311–346.

S   Holdgate, M. W., 1965. The fauna of the Tristan da Cunha Islands. *Phil. Trans. R. Soc.* B 249 (759): 361–402.

S   Hooker, J. D., 1847a. Enumeration of the plants of the Galápagos Islands, with descriptions of those which are new. *Trans. Linn. Soc., Lond.* 20: 113–233.

S ——, 1847b. On the vegetation of the Galápagos Archipelago, as compared with that of some other tropical islands and of the continent of America. *Trans. Linn. Soc., Lond.* 20: 235–62.

S Howell, J. T., 1933a. The genus *Mollugo* in the Galápagos Islands. *Proc. Calif. Acad. Sci.* ser. 4, 21 (3): 13–23.

S ——, 1933b. The Amaranthaceae of the Galápagos Islands. *Proc. Calif. Acad. Sci.* ser. 4, 21 (9): 87–116.

S ——, 1934. Cacti in the Galápagos Islands. *Cactus Succ. J.* 5: 515–18, 531–32.

S ——, 1941. The genus *Scalesia*. *Proc. Calif. Acad. Sci.* ser. 4, 22 (11): 221–71.

S Kroeber, A. L., 1916. Floral relations among the Galápagos Islands. *Univ. Calif. Publs. Bot.* 6: 199–220.

S Kuschel, G., 1963. Composition and relationships of the terrestrial faunas of Easter, Juan Fernández, Desventuradas, and Galápagos Islands. *Occ. Pap. Calif. Acad. Sci.* 44: 79–95.

S Leleup, N., 1965a. Commentaires sur le sanctuaire zoologique des Galápagos. *Africa-Tervuren* 9 (3-4): 85–91.

S ——, 1965b. Existence d'une faune cryptique relictuelle aux Iles Galápagos. *Notic. Galǎpagos* 5–6: 4–16.

S Linder, D., 1934. Lichens of the Galápagos Islands. The Templeton Crocker Expedition of the California Academy of Sciences. *Proc. Calif. Acad. Sci.* ser. 4, 21: 211–21.

S Linsley, E. G., 1965. Notes on male territorial behavior in the Galápagos carpenter bee. *Pan-Pacif. Ent.* 41 (3): 158–61.

S ——, 1966. Pollinating insects of the Galápagos Islands. *In:* R. I. Bowman (ed.), *Proc. Symp. Galápagos int. scient. Project:* 225–32. Univ. California Pr., Berkeley and Los Angeles.

S —— and Chemsak, J. A., 1966. Cerambycidae of the Galápagos Islands. *Proc. Calif. Acad. Sci.* ser. 4, 32 (8): 197–236.

S ——, Rick, C. M., and Stephens, S. G., 1966. Observations on the floral relationships of the Galápagos carpenter bee. *Pan-Pacif. Ent.* 42: 1–18.

S* —— and Usinger, R. L., 1966. Insects of the Galápagos Islands. *Proc. Calif. Acad. Sci.* ser. 4, 33 (7): 113–36.

S Meyrick, E., 1926. On Micro-lepidoptera from the Galápagos Islands and Rapa. *Trans. ent. Soc. Lond.* 1926: 269–78.

S Ono, M., 1967. The systematic position of *Scalesia* from the viewpoint of chromosome number. *Notic. Galápagos* 9-10: 16–17.

S   Rick, C. M., 1956. Genetic and systematic studies in accessions of *Lycopersicon* from the Galápagos Islands. *Am. J. Bot.* 43: 687–96.

S   ——, 1963. Biosystematic studies on Galápagos tomatoes. *Occ. Pap. Calif. Acad. Sci.* 44: 59–77.

S   ——, 1966. Some plant-animal relations on the Galápagos Islands. *In:* R. I. Bowman (ed.), *Proc. Symp. Galápagos int. scient. Project:* 215–24. Univ. California Pr., Berkeley and Los Angeles.

S   —— and Bowman, R. I., 1961. Galápagos tomatoes and tortoises. *Evolution* 15: 407–17.

S   Robinson, B. L., 1902. Flora of the Galápagos Islands. *Proc. Am. Acad. Arts Sci.* 38: 77–269.

S   —— and Greenman, J. M., 1895. On the flora of the Galápagos Islands, as shown by the collection of Dr. G. Baur. *Am. J. Sci.* ser. 3, 50: 135–49.

S   Stebbins, G. L., 1966. Variation and adaptation in Galápagos plants. *In:* R. I. Bowman (ed.), *Proc. Symp. Galápagos int. scient. Project:* 46–54. Univ. California Pr., Berkeley and Los Angeles.

S*   Stewart, A., 1911. A botanical survey of the Galápagos Islands. *Proc. Calif. Acad. Sci.* ser. 4, 1: 7–288.

S   ——, 1912. Notes on the lichens of the Galápagos Islands. *Proc. Calif. Acad. Sci.* ser. 4, 1: 431–46.

S†   ——, 1915. Some observations concerning the botanical conditions in the Galápagos Islands. *Trans. Wis. Acad. Sci. Arts Lett.* 18: 272–340.

S   Svenson, H. K., 1935. Plants of the Astor expedition (Galápagos and Cocos Islands). *Am. J. Bot.* 22: 208–77.

S†   ——, 1945. A brief review of the Galápagos flora. *In:* F. Verdoorn, *Plants and plant science in Latin America.* Waltham, Mass: Chronica Botanica.

S   ——, 1946. Vegetation of the coast of Ecuador and Peru and its relation to the Galápagos Archipelago. *Am. J. Bot.* 33: 394–426.

S   ——, 1963. Opportunities for botanical study on the Galápagos Islands. *Occ. Pap. Calif. Acad. Sci.* 44: 53–58.

S   Van Denburgh, J. and Slevin, J. R., 1913. The Galápagoan lizards of the genus *Tropidurus;* with notes on the iguanas of the genera *Conolophus* and *Amblyrhynchus. Proc. Calif. Acad. Sci.* ser. 4, 2 (1): 133–202.

S   Van Dyke, E. C., 1953. The Coleoptera of the Galápagos Islands. *Occ. Pap. Calif. Acad. Sci.* 22: 1–181.

S   Weber, W. A., 1966. Lichenology and bryology of the Galápagos Islands. *In:* R. I. Bowman (ed.), *Proc. Symp. Galápagos int. scient. Project:* 190–200. Univ. California Pr., Berkeley and Los Angeles.

S   Wheeler, W. M., 1919. The ants of the Galápagos Islands. *Proc. Calif. Acad. Sci.* ser. 4, 2 (2): 259–97.

S   ——, 1924. Formicidae of the Harrison Williams Galápagos Expedition. *Zoologica, N.Y.* 5 (10): 101–22.

S   ——, 1933. Formicidae of the Templeton Crocker Expedition. *Proc. Calif. Acad. Sci.* ser. 4, 21 (6): 57–64.

S   Wiggins, I. L., 1966. Origins and relationships of the flora of the Galápagos Islands. *In:* R. I. Bowman (ed.), *Proc. Symp. Galápagos int. scient. Project:* 175–82. Univ. California Pr., Berkeley and Los Angeles.

S   Williams, F. X., 1911. The butterflies and hawk-moths of the Galápagos Islands. *Proc. Calif. Acad. Sci.* ser. 4, 1: 289–322.

S   ——, 1926. The bees and aculeate wasps of the Galápagos Islands. *Proc. Calif. Acad. Sci.* ser. 4, 2: 347–57.

CHAPTER 5

S   Bartholomew, G. A., 1966a. Interaction of physiology and behavior under natural conditions. *In:* R. I. Bowman (ed.), *Proc. Symp. Galápagos int. scient. Project:* 39–45. Univ. California Pr., Berkeley and Los Angeles.

S   ——, 1966b. A field study of temperature relations in the Galápagos marine iguana. *Copeia* 1966 (2): 241–50.

S   —— and Lasiewski, R. C., 1965. Heating and cooling rates, heart rate and simulated diving in the Galápagos marine iguana. *Comp. Biochem. Physiol.* 16: 573–82.

G   Beebe, W., 1924. *Galápagos, World's End.* Putnam's, New York.

G   Blomberg, R., 1951. Strange reptiles of the Galápagos. *Nat. Hist.* 60 (5): 234.

S   Carpenter, C. C., 1966a. Comparative behavior of the Galápagos lava lizards (*Tropidurus*). *In:* R. I. Bowman (ed.), *Proc. Symp. Galápagos int. scient. Project:* 269–73. Univ. California Pr., Berkeley and Los Angeles.

S   ——, 1966b. The marine iguana of the Galápagos Islands, its behavior and ecology. *Proc. Calif. Acad. Sci.* ser. 4, 34: 329–76.

G ——, 1967. Some findings on Galápagos lizards. *Notic. Galápagos* 9-10: 18–20.

G† Colnett, J., 1798. *Voyage to the South Atlantic and round Cape Horn into the Pacific Ocean, for the purpose of extending the spermaceti whale fisheries.* Printed for the author by W. Bennett, London.

G Darwin, C., 1845. *Journal of researches into the natural history and geology of the countries visited during the voyage of H.M.S. Beagle round the world.* 2nd edition. Ward, Lock & Co., London.

G Dowling, H. G., 1962. Sea dragons of the Galápagos: the marine iguanas. *Anim. Kingd.* 65 (5): 169–74.

S Eibl-Eibesfeldt, I., 1955. Der Kommentkampf der Meerechse (*Amblyrhynchus cristatus* Bell) nebst einigen Notizen zur Biologie dieser Art. *Z. Tierpsychol.* 12 (1): 49–62.

S ——, 1956. Ein neue Rasse der Meerechse *Amblyrhynchus cristatus venustissimus. Senckenberg. biol.* 37: 87–100.

G ——, 1961. *Galápagos—Noah's Ark of the Pacific.* Doubleday, New York.

S ——, 1962. Neue unterarten der Meerechse *Amblyrhynchus cristatus,* nebst weiteren Angaben zur Biologie besonderer Art. *Senckenberg. biol.* 43 (3): 177–99.

S ——, 1963. Meerechsen in Gefangenschaft. *Natur. Mus., Frankf.* 93: 410–14.

G ——, 1964. The art of keeping marine iguanas. *Anim. Kingd.* 67: 75–77.

G ——, 1965. A revisit of the Galápagos. *Notic. Galápagos* 5-6: 23–27.

G ——, 1966. Marine iguanas. *Animals* 9 (3): 150–52.

S Garman, S., 1892. The reptiles of the Galápagos Islands. *Bull. Essex Inst. (Massachusetts)* 24: 1–5, 73–87.

G Hagen, V. W. von, 1937a. Galápagos land iguanas. *Nature Mag.* 29 (6): 368–70.

G ——, 1937b. Sea iguanas of the Galápagos. *Nature Mag.* 29 (3): 147–49.

G Hendrickson, J. R., 1965. Reptiles of the Galápagos. *Pacif. Discovery* 18 (5): 28–36.

S Hobson, E. S., 1965. Observations on diving in the Galápagos marine iguana, *Amblyrhynchus cristatus* (Bell). *Copeia* 1965 (2): 249–50.

S   Mackay, S., 1964. Galápagos tortoise and marine iguana deep body temperatures measured by radio telemetry. *Nature* 182: 783–85.

S   Mertens, R., 1960. Uber die Schlangen der Galápagos. *Senckenberg. biol.* 41 (3-4): 133–41.

S   ——, 1963. Die Weiderentdeckung der Geckonengattung *Gonatodes* auf den Galápagos. *Senckenberg. biol.* 44 (1): 21–23.

G   Pawley, R., 1965. Housekeeping for marine iguanas. *Anim. Kingd.* 69: 146–50.

G   Pinchot, G. 1931. *To the South Seas.* Hutchinson, London.

S   Schmidt, K. P., 1935. Notes on the breeding behavior of lizards. *Field Mus. Nat. Hist., Publ. Zool. Ser.* 20: 71–76.

S   Schmidt-Nielsen, K. and Fange, R., 1958. Salt glands in marine reptiles. *Nature* 182: 783–85.

G   Shurcliff, S. N., 1930. *Jungle Islands, the "Illyria" in the South Sea.* Putnam's, New York.

S   Slevin, J. R., 1935. An account of the reptiles inhabiting the Galápagos Islands. *Bull. N. Y. zool. Soc.* 38: 3–24.

S   Stebbins, R. C., Lowenstein, J. M. and Cohen, N. W., 1967. A field study of the lava lizard (*Tropidurus albemarlensis*) in the Galápagos Islands. *Ecology* 48 (5): 839–51.

S   Van Denburgh, J., 1912a. The snakes of the Galápagos Islands. *Proc. Calif. Acad. Sci.* ser. 4, 1: 323–74.

S   ——, 1912b. The geckos of the Galápagos Archipelago. *Proc. Calif. Acad. Sci.* ser. 4, 1: 405–30.

S   —— and Slevin, J. R., 1913. The Galápagoan lizards of the genus *Tropidurus;* with notes on the iguanas of the genera *Conolophus* and *Amblyrhynchus. Proc. Calif. Acad. Sci.* ser. 4, 2 (1): 133–202.

CHAPTER 6

G   Agassiz, A., 1892. General sketch of the expedition of the *Albatross* from February to May, 1891. The Galápagos Islands. *Bull. Mus. comp. Zool. Harv.* 23 (1): 56–74.

S   Anderson, E. F. and Walkington, D. L., 1968. A study of some neotropical opuntias of coastal Ecuador and the Galápagos Islands. *Notic. Galápagos* 12: 8–22.

S   Baur, G., 1890. The gigantic land tortoises of the Galápagos Islands. *Am. Nat.* 23: 1039–57.

G   Beck, R. H., 1903. In the home of the giant tortoise. *Rep. N. Y. zool. Soc.* 7: 1–17.

S   Breder, C. M. Jr., 1925. A relative of the Galápagos tortoise. *Bull. N. Y. zool. Soc.* 28 (3): 64–65.

S   Brosset, A., 1963. Statut actuel de la faune aux îles Galápagos. *Notic. Galápagos* 1: 5–8.

G   Brown, B., 1931. The largest known land tortoise. *Nat. Hist.* 31 (2): 183–87.

S   Carpenter, C. C., 1963. Notes on the behavior and ecology of the Galápagos Tortoise on Santa Cruz Island. *Proc. Okla. Acad. Sci.* 46: 28–32.

S   Cary, B., 1834. Note on a large specimen of the Galápagos tortoise. *Proc. zool. Soc. Lond.* Part 2, 1834: 113.

G   Castro, M., 1970. Chatham Island tortoise. *Animals* 13 (1): 43–45.

G   Cochran, D. M., 1928. Turtles of Galápagos. *Nature Mag.* 12: 322–24.

G   Darwin, C., 1845. *Journal of researches into the natural history and geology of the countries visited during the voyage of H.M.S. Beagle round the world.* 2nd edition. Ward, Lock & Co., London.

S   Dawson, E. Y., 1962. Cacti of the Galápagos Islands and of coastal Ecuador. *Cactus Succ. J.* 34 (3): 67–74; 34 (4): 99–105.

S   ——, 1964. Cacti in the Galápagos Islands. *Notic. Galápagos* 4: 12–13.

S   ——, 1965. Further studies of *Opuntia* in the Galápagos Archipelago. *Cactus Succ. J.* 37 (5): 135–48.

S   ——, 1966. Cacti in the Galápagos Islands with special reference to their relations with tortoises. *In:* R. I. Bowman (ed.), *Proc. Symp. Galápagos int. scient. Project:* 209–14. Univ. California Pr., Berkeley and Los Angeles.

S   Gans, C. and Hughes, G. M., 1967. The mechanism of lung ventilation in the tortoise *Testudo graeca* Linné. *J. exp. Biol.* (1967) 47: 1–20.

S   Garman, S., 1917. The Galápagos tortoises. *Mem. Mus. comp. Zool. Harv.* 30: 261–96.

G   Gaymer, R., 1967. Aldabra's giant tortoises. *Animals* 10: 192–93.

S   ——, 1968. The Indian Ocean giant tortoise *Testudo gigantea* on Aldabra. *J. Zool., Lond.* (1968) 154: 341–63.

S   Gressitt, J. L., 1966. Epizoic symbiosis. *Proc. 11th Pacif. Sci. Congress, Tokyo,* 5: 32.

S   Günther, A., 1876. Description of the living and extinct races of gigantic land-tortoises. Parts I–II. Introduction, and the tortoises of the Galápagos Islands. *Phil. Trans. R. Soc.* 165: 251–84.

G   Hagen, V. W. von, 1937. Centenarians of the Galápagos. *Travel* 49 (1): 32–33, 46.

G   Hamilton, F., 1903. Hunting the giant tortoise. *Wide Wld. Mag.* 11: 25–30.

S   Heller, E., 1903. Papers from the Hopkins Stanford Galápagos Expedition, 1898–99. XIV. Reptiles. *Proc. Wash. Acad. Sci.* 5: 39–98.

G   Hendrickson, J. R., 1965. Reptiles of the Galápagos. *Pacif. Discovery* 18 (5): 28–36.

G   ——, 1966. The Galápagos tortoises, *Geochelone* Fitzinger 1835 (*Testudo* Linnaeus 1758 in part). *In:* R. I. Bowman, (ed.), *Proc. Symp. Galápagos int. scient. Project:* 252–57. Univ. California Pr., Berkeley and Los Angeles.

G   Holder, C. F., 1901. The turtles of the Galápagos. *Scient. Am.* 85 (9): 139–40.

G   Honegger, R. E., 1960. Giant tortoise survey. *Am. first Zoo* 12 (2): 19.

S   ——, 1964. Die letzten Riesen von Galápagos. *Aquar. -u. Terrar. -Z.* 17 (9): 275–78.

S   Howell, J. T., 1934. Cacti in the Galápagos Islands. *Cactus Succ. J.* 5: 515–18, 531–32.

S   Hughes, G. M. and Gans, C., 1966. Electromyographic analysis of respiratory movements in *Testudo graeca. Am. Zool.* 6: 566–67.

G   Loveridge, A., 1945. *Reptiles of the Pacific World.* Macmillan, New York.

S   —— and Williams, E. E., 1957. Revision of the African tortoises and turtles of the suborder Cryptodira. *Bull. Mus. comp. Zool. Harv.* 119 (6): 163–557.

G   Lucas, F. A., 1922. Historic tortoises and other aged animals. *Nat. Hist.* 22 (4): 301–5.

S   Mackay, S., 1964. Galápagos tortoise and marine iguana deep body temperatures measured by radio telemetry. *Nature* 182: 783–85.

G†   Porter, D., 1815. *Journal of a cruise made to the Pacific Ocean by Captain David Porter in the United States Frigate* Essex *in the years 1812, 1813 and 1814.* 2 volumes. Bradford and Inskeep, Philadelphia.

G Shaw, E. C., 1967. Breeding the Galápagos tortoise—success story. *Oryx* 9 (2): 119–26.

G Shipman, J. C., 1962. *William Dampier, Seaman–Scientist.* Univ. of Kansas Publ. Library Series, 15.

S Simpson, G. G., 1942. A miocene tortoise from Patagonia. *Am. Mus. Novit.* 1209: 1–6.

S Slevin, J. R., 1935. An account of the reptiles inhabiting the Galápagos Islands. *Bull. N. Y. zool. Soc.* 38: 3–24.

G Snow, D. W., 1966a. Giant tortoises. *Animals* 9 (3): 140–42.

G ——, 1966b. The giant tortoises of the Galápagos Islands. Their present status and future chances. *Oryx* 7 (6): 277–90.

G Street, P., 1961a. *Vanishing Animals.* Faber & Faber, London.

G ——, 1961b. Can the Giant Tortoise survive? *Discovery* 21–22: 158–60.

S Townsend, C. H., 1924. Impending extinction of the Galápagos tortoises. *Bull. N. Y. zool. Soc.* 27 (2): 55–56.

G ——, 1925. The Galápagos tortoises in their relation to the whaling industry. *Zoologica, N. Y.* 4 (3): 55–135.

G ——, 1931. Giant tortoises nearing extinction are being propagated in the United States. *Scient. Am.* 144 (1): 42–44.

S Van Denburgh, J., 1907. Preliminary descriptions of four new races of gigantic land tortoises from the Galápagos Islands. *Proc. Calif. Acad. Sci.* ser. 4, 1: 1–6.

S* ——, 1914. The gigantic land tortoises of the Galápagos Archipelago. *Proc. Calif. Acad. Sci.* ser. 4, 2 (1): 203–374.

CHAPTER 7

S Abs, M., Curio, E., Kramer, P. and Niethammer, J., 1965. Zur Ernahrungsweise der Eulen auf Galápagos. *J. Orn., Lpz.* 106: 49–57.

G Amadon, D., 1966. Insular adaptive radiation among birds. *In:* R. I. Bowman (ed.), *Proc. Symp. Galápagos int. scient. Project:* 18–29. Univ. California Pr., Berkeley and Los Angeles.

S Beck, R. H., 1904. Bird life among the Galápagos Islands. *Condor* 6 (1): 5–11.

S Brosset, A., 1963. Le comportement de la buse des Galápagos, *Buteo galapagoensis. Alauda* 31: 5–21.

G   Curio, E., 1966. How finches react to predators. *Animals* 9 (3): 142–43.

G   Fosberg, F. R., 1965. Natural bird refuges in the Galápagos. *Elepaio* 25: 60–67.

S   Gifford, E. W., 1919. Field notes on the land birds of the Galápagos Islands and of Cocos Island, Costa Rica. *Proc. Calif. Acad. Sci.* ser. 4, 2 (2) (13): 118–258.

S   Gilliard, E. T., 1958. *Living Birds of the World.* Doubleday, New York.

G   Hagen, W. von, 1937. The flamingoes of the Galápagos Islands. *Nat. Hist.* 39: 136–39.

S   Harris, M. P., 1968. Egg-eating by Galápagos mockingbirds. *Condor* 70 (3): 269–70.

S   Hatch, J. J., 1965. Only one species of Galápagos mockingbird feeds on eggs. *Condor* 67 (4): 354–55.

S   Lack, D., 1947. *Darwin's finches.* Cambridge Univ. Pr., London.

S   Lévêque, R., 1963. The status of some rarer Galápagos birds. *Bull. int. Coun. Bird Preserv.* 9: 96–98.

S   ——, 1964. Notes sur la réproduction des oiseaux aux îles Galápagos. *Alauda* 32: 5–44, 81–96.

S   ——, Bowman, R. I. and Billeb, S. L., 1966. Migrants in the Galápagos area. *Condor* 68 (1): 81–101.

G   Nelson, B., 1968. *Galápagos: islands of birds.* Longmans, Green & Co., London.

S   Palmer, R. S., 1962. *Handbook of North American Birds.* Yale Univ. Pr., New Haven.

G   Peterson, R. T., 1967. The Galápagos, eerie cradle of new species. *Natn. geogr. Mag.* 131 (4): 540–85.

S   Ridgway, R., 1896. Birds of the Galápagos Archipelago. *Proc. U. S. natn. Mus.* 19: 459–670.

S   ——, 1919. The birds of North and Middle America. *Bull. U. S. natn. Mus.* 50 (8): 1–852.

S   Rothschild, W., 1898. Untitled. *Bull. Br. Orn. Club* 7: 51–53.

S   —— and Hartet, E., 1899. A review of the ornithology of the Galápagos Islands. With notes on the Webster-Harris expedition. *Novit. zool.* 6: 85–205.

S   —— and ——, 1902. Further notes on the fauna of the Galápagos Islands. Notes on the birds. *Novit. zool.* 9: 381–418.

S Salvin, O., 1876. On the avifauna of the Galápagos Archipelago. *Trans. zool. Soc. Lond.* 9: 447–510.

S Schauensee, R. M. de, 1966. *The Species of Birds of South America and Their Distribution.* Philadelphia, Academy of Natural Sciences; distributed by Livingston Publ. Co., Narbeth, Pa.

G Shipman, J. C., 1962. *William Dampier, Seaman–Scientist.* Univ. of Kansas Publ. Library series, 15.

S Snodgrass, R. E. and Heller, E., 1904. Papers from the Hopkins-Stanford Galápagos expedition, 1898–1899. XVI. Birds. *Proc. Wash. Acad. Sci.* 5: 231–372.

S* Swarth, H. S., 1931. The avifauna of the Galápagos Islands. *Occ. Pap. Calif. Acad. Sci.* 18: 5–299.

S Voous, K. H., 1960. *Atlas of European Birds.* Nelson, London.

G Wallace, A. R., 1880. *Island Life.* Macmillan, London.

CHAPTER 8

S Abs, M., Curio, E., Kramer, P. and Niethammer, J., 1965. Zur Ernahrungsweise der Eulen auf Galápagos. *J. Orn., Lpz.* 106: 49–57.

S Amadon, D., 1966. Insular adaptive radiation among birds. *In:* R. I. Bowman (ed.), *Proc. Symp. Galápagos int. scient. Project:* 18–29. Univ. California Pr., Berkeley and Los Angeles.

S Bock, W. J., 1963. Morphological differentiation and adaptation in the Galápagos finches. *Auk* 80: 20–7.

S* Bowman, R. I., 1961. Morphological differentiation and adaptation in the Galápagos Finches. *Univ. Calif. Publs. Zool.* 58: 1–302.

S ——, 1963. Evolutionary patterns in Darwin's finches. *Occ. Pap. Calif. Acad. Sci.* 44: 107–40.

G ——, 1965. Darwin's finches. *Pacif. Discovery* 18 (5): 10–13.

G —— and Billeb, S. L., 1965. Blood-eating in a Galápagos finch. *Living Bird:* 29–44.

S Curio, E., 1964. Zur geographischen Variation des Feinderkennens einiger Darwinfinken (*Geospizidae*). *Verh. dt. zool. Ges., Kiel* 41: 466–92.

S ——, 1965. Galápagos–Prüffeld der Evolutions forschung. *Umschau* 18: 562–67.

G ——, 1966. How finches react to predators. *Animals* 9 (3): 142–43.

S —— and Kramer, P., 1964. Vom Mangrovefinken (*Cactospiza heliobates* S & H). *Z. Tierpsychol.* 21 (2): 223–34.

S —— and ——, 1965. On plumage variation in male Darwin's finches. *Bird-Banding* 36 (1): 27–44.

G Darwin, C., 1845. *Journal of researches into the natural history and geology of the countries visited during the voyage of H.M.S. Beagle round the world.* 2nd edition. Ward, Lock & Co., London.

G ——, 1872. *The origin of species by means of natural selection, or the preservation of favoured races in the struggle for life.* 6th edition. Oxford Univ. Pr., London.

S DeBenedectis, P. A., 1966. The bill-brace feeding behaviour of The Galápagos finch *Geospiza conirostris. Condor* 68: 206–8.

G Eibl-Eibesfeldt, I., 1961. *Galápagos—Noah's Ark of the Pacific.* Doubleday, New York.

G ——, 1966. Darwin's finches. *Animals* 9 (3): 137–39.

S —— and Sielmann, H., 1961. Uber den Werkzenggebrauch des Spechtfinken *Camarhynchus pallidus. Z. Tierpsychol.* 18 (3): 343–46.

S —— and ——, 1962. Beobachtungen am Spechtfinken *Cactospiza pallida. J. Orn., Lpz.* 103 (1): 92–101.

G Fosberg, F. R., 1965. Natural bird refuges in the Galápagos. *Elepaio* 25: 60–67.

G Gifford, E. W., 1919. Field notes on the land birds of the Galápagos Islands and of Cocos Island, Costa Rica. *Proc. Calif. Acad. Sci.* ser. 4, 2 (2) (13): 118–258.

S Gould, J., 1837. Remarks on a series of "ground finches" from Mr. Darwin's Collection, with descriptions of new species. *Proc. zool. Soc. Lond.* (5): 4–7.

S ——, 1841. Birds. Part III of: *The zoology of the voyage of H.M.S. Beagle under the command of Captain Fitzroy, R.N., during the years 1832 to 1836.* Smith, Elder & Co., London.

S ——, 1843. Descriptions of nine new species of birds collected during the recent voyage of H.M.S. *Sulphur. Proc. zool. Soc. Lond.* 1843: 103–6.

S ——, 1844. Birds. *In: The zoology of the voyage of H.M.S. Sulphur, under the command of Captain Sir Edward Belcher,*

R.N., C.B., F.R.G.S., etc. during the years 1836–42. Smith, Elder & Co., London.

S   Hamilton, T. H. and Rubinoff, I., 1963. Isolation, endemism and multiplication of species in the Darwin finches. *Evolution* 17 (4): 388–403.

S   —— and ——, 1964. On models predicting the abundance of species and endemics of the Darwin finches in the Galápagos archipelago. *Evolution* 18 (2): 339–42.

S   —— and ——, 1967. On predicting insular variation in endemism and sympatry for the Darwin finches in the Galápagos archipelago. *Amer. Nat.* 101: 161–72.

G   Harris, M. P., 1968. Egg-eating by Galápagos mockingbirds. *Condor* 70 (3): 269–70.

G   Kinsey, E. C., 1942. The breeding of Galápagos finches in California. *Avicult. Mag.* ser. 5, (8): 125–37.

S   Lack, D., 1940. Evolution of the Galápagos finches. *Nature* 146: 324–27.

S*   ——, 1945. The Galápagos finches (Geospizinae): A study in variation. *Occ. Pap. Calif. Acad. Sci.* 21: 1–152.

S   ——, 1946. The names of the Geospizinae (Darwin's finches). *Bull. Br. Orn. Club* 67: 15–22.

G*   ——, 1947. *Darwin's finches*. Cambridge Univ. Pr., London.

G   ——, 1953. Darwin's finches. *Scient. Am.* April, 1953: 3–7.

G   Lack, D., 1969. Subspecies and sympatry in Darwin's finches. *Evolution* 23 (2): 252–63.

S   Lowe, P. R., 1936. The finches of the Galápagos in relation to Darwin's conception of species. *Ibis* ser. 13, 6: 310–21.

S   MacArthur, R. and Levins, R., 1967. The limiting similarity, convergence and divergence of coexisting species. *Amer. Nat.* 101: 377–85.

S   Orr, R. T., 1942. Darwin's finches. *Bull. N. Y. zool. Soc.* 45 (6): 142–45.

S   ——, 1945. A study of captive Galápagos finches of the genus *Geospiza*. *Condor* 47: 177–201.

G   Peterson, R. T., 1967. The Galápagos, eerie cradle of new species. *Natn. geogr. Mag.* 131 (4): 540–85.

S   Ridgway, R., 1896. Birds of the Galápagos Archipelago. *Proc. U. S. natn. Mus.* 19: 459–670.

S   Rothschild, W., 1898. A comunication. *Bull. Br. Orn. Club* 7: 51–53.

S   —— and Hartet, E., 1899. A review of the ornithology of the Galápagos Islands. With notes on the Webster-Harris expedition. *Novit. zool.* 6: 85–205.

S   —— and ——, 1902. Further notes on the fauna of the Galápagos Islands. Notes on the birds. *Novit. zool.* 9: 381–418.

S   Sammalisto, L., 1966. Censusing Darwin's finches. *Notic. Galápagos* 7–8: 13–17.

S   Selander, R. K., 1962. Feeding adaptations in Darwin's finches. *Evolution* 16: 391–93.

S   Snodgrass, R. E., 1902. The relation of the food to the size and shape of the bill in the Galápagos genus *Geospiza*. *Auk* 19: 367–81.

S   ——, 1903. Notes on the anatomy of *Geospiza*, *Cocornis*, and *Certhidea*. *Auk* 20: 402–17.

G   —— and Heller, E., 1904. Papers from the Hopkins-Stanford Galápagos expedition, 1896–1899. XVI. Birds. *Proc. Wash. Acad. Sci.* 5: 231–372.

S†   Stresemann, E., 1936. Zur Frage der Artibildung in der Gattung *Geospiza*. *Orgaan Club ned. Vogelk.* 9: 13–21.

S   Swarth, H. S., 1929. A new bird family (*Geospizidae*) from the Galápagos Islands. *Proc. Calif. Acad. Sci.* ser. 4, 18: 29–43.

S   ——, 1931. The avifauna of the Galápagos Islands. *Occ. Pap. Calif. Acad. Sci.* 18: 5–299.

S   ——, 1934. The bird fauna of the Galápagos Islands in relation to species formation. *Biol. Rev.* 9: 214–34.

S   Thornton, I. W. B., 1967. The measurement of isolation on archipelagos, and its relation to insular faunal size and endemism. *Evolution* 21 (4): 842–49.

CHAPTER 9

S   Allen, J. A., 1892. On a small collection of mammals from the Galápagos Islands, collected by Dr. G. Baur. *Bull. Am. Mus. nat. Hist.* 4: 47–50.

S   Bartholomew, G. A., 1966. Interaction of physiology and behavior under natural conditions. *In:* R. I. Bowman (ed.), *Proc. Symp. Galápagos int. scient. Project:* 39–45. Univ. California Pr., Berkeley and Los Angeles.

BIBLIOGRAPHY

S   Beaufort, F. de, 1963. Les cricetines des Galápagos. Valeur du genre *Nesoryzomys*. *Mammalia* 27: 338–40.

G   Brosset, A., 1963. Statut actuel des mammifères des îles Galápagos. *Mammalia* 27: 323–38.

S   Eibl-Eibesfeldt, I., 1955. Ethologische Studien am Galápagos–Seelowen. Z. *Tierpsychol.* 12 (2): 286–303.

S   Heller, E., 1904. Mammals of the Galápagos Archipelago, exclusive of the Cetacea. *Proc. Calif. Acad. Sci.* ser. 3, 3: 233–50.

S   King, J. E., 1954. The otariid seals of the Pacific coast of America. *Bull. Br. Mus. nat. Hist., Zool.* 2: 309–37.

G   Leleup, N., 1965. Commentaires sur le sanctuaire zoologique des Galápagos. *Africa-Tervuren* 9 (3–4): 85–91.

G   Lévêque, R., 1963. Le statut actuel des vertébrés rares et menacés de l'archipel des Galápagos. *Terre Vie* 110: 397–430.

GS   Nelson, B., 1968. *Galápagos: islands of birds.* Longmans, Green & Co., London.

S   Niethammer, J., 1964. Contribution à la connaissance des mammifères terrestres de l'île Indefatigable (Santa Cruz), Galápagos. *Mammalia* 28 (4): 593–606.

S   Orr, R. T., 1938. A new rodent of the genus *Nesoryzomys* from the Galápagos Islands. *Proc. Calif. Acad. Sci.* ser. 4, 23: 303–6.

G   ——, 1965. Barrington Island. *Pacif. Discovery* 18: 23–27.

S*   ——, 1966. Evolutionary aspects of the mammalian fauna of the Galápagos. *In:* R. I. Bowman (ed.), *Proc. Symp. Galápagos int. scient. Project:* 276–81. Univ. California Pr., Berkeley and Los Angeles.

S   Osgood, W. H., 1929. A new rodent from the Galápagos Islands. *Field Mus. nat. Hist. Publ. Zool.* ser. 17: 21–24.

S   Peterson, R. L., 1966. Recent mammal records from the Galápagos Islands. *Mammalia* 30 (3): 441–43.

S   Sivertsen, E., 1953. A new species of sea lion, *Zalophus wollebaeki*, from the Galápagos Islands. *K. norske Vidensk. Selsk. Forh.* 26: 1–3.

S†   ——, 1954. A survey of the eared seals (family Otariidae) with remarks on the antarctic seals collected by M/K "Norvegia" in 1928–1929. *Det Norske Videnskaps-Akademi i Oslo, Sci. Results Norwegian Antarctic Exped.* 36: 1–76.

S Thomas, O., 1899. Descriptions of new neotropical mammals. *Ann. Mag. nat. Hist.* ser. 7, 4: 278–88.

S Townsend, C. H., 1934. The fur seal of the Galápagos Islands. *Zoologica, N. Y.* 18 (2): 47–49.

G Ziswiler, V., 1967. *Extinct and vanishing animals*. Longmans, Green & Co., London.

CHAPTER 10

G Agassiz, A., 1892. General sketch of the expedition of the *Albatross* from February to May, 1891. The Galápagos Islands. *Bull. Mus. comp. Zool. Harv.* 23 (1): 56–74.

S Asahina, S., 1968. Insect dispersal as observed by a weather ship on the northwestern Pacific. *Abstr. Pap. Xlllth int. Congr. Ent., Moscow:* 16.

S Berland, L., 1935. Premier résultats de mes recherches en avion sur la faune et la flore atmosphériques. *Annls. Soc. ent. Fr.* 104: 73–96.

S Cain, S. A., 1944. *Foundations of Plant Geography*. Harper, New York.

G Carlquist, S., 1965. *Island Life*. Natural History Pr., New York.

S ——, 1967. The biota of long-distance dispersal. V. Plant dispersal to Pacific islands. *Bull. Torrey bot. Club* 94 (3): 129–62.

S Cruden, R. W., 1966. Birds as agents of long-distance dispersal for disjunct plant groups of the temperate western hemisphere. *Evolution* 20: 517–32.

S Dammermann, K. W., 1948. The fauna of Krakatau. *Verh. K. ned. Akad. Wet., Afd. Natuurk.* (2) sect. 44: 1–594.

S Darlington, P. J. Jr., 1938. The origin of the fauna of the Greater Antilles, with discussion of dispersal of animals over water and through the air. *Q. Rev. Biol.* 13: 274–300.

S ——, 1957. *Zoogeography: the Geographical Distribution of Animals*, John Wiley & Sons, New York.

S Darwin, C., 1872. *The origin of species by means of natural selection, or the preservation of favoured races in the struggle for life.* 6th edition. Oxford Univ. Pr., London.

S Dorst, J., 1962. *The Migrations of Birds*. Houghton Mifflin, Boston.

S† Dunnet, G. M., 1964. Distribution and host relationships of fleas in the Antarctic and Subantarctic. *In:* Carrick, Holdgate and

Prevost (eds.), *Biologie Antarctique-Antarctic Biology*. Hermann, Paris.

S   Eliasson, U., 1968. Studies in Galápagos plants. V. Some new botanical records from the archipelago. *Sv. Bot. Tidskr.* 62 (1): 243–48.

S   Elton, C. S., 1925. The dispersal of insects to Spitsbergen. *Trans. R. ent. Soc. Lond.* 1925: 289–99.

S   Falla, R. A., 1960. Oceanic birds as dispersal agents. *Proc. R. Soc.* B 152: 655–59.

S   Fisher, R. A., 1954. Retrospect of the criticisms of the theory of natural selection, *In:* J. Huxley, A. C. Hardy, and E. B. Ford, (eds.), *Evolution as a Process*. George Allen & Unwin, London.

S   Fosberg, F. R., 1948. Derivation of the flora of the Hawaiian Islands. *In:* E. C. Zimmerman, *Insects of Hawaii, I. Introduction*. Univ. Hawaii Pr., Honolulu.

S   ——, 1963. Plant dispersal in the Pacific. *In:* J. L. Gressit, (ed.), *Pacific Basin Biogeography*. Bishop Museum Pr., Honolulu.

S   Freeman, J. A., 1945. Studies on the distribution of insects by aerial currents. The insect population of the air from ground level to 300 feet. *J. Anim. Ecol.* 14: 128–54.

S   French, R. A., 1964 (1965). Long range dispersal of insects in relation to synoptic meteorology. *Proc. XIIth int. Congr. Ent., London* 6: 418–19.

S   Gislen, T., 1948. Aerial plankton and its conditions of life. *Biol. Rev.* 23: 109–26.

S   Glick, P. A., 1939. The distribution of insects, spiders, and mites in the air. *Tech. Bull. U. S. Dept. Agric.* 673: 1–150.

S   ——, 1957. Trapping insects by airplane in southern Texas. *Tech. Bull. U. S. Dept. Agric.* 1158: 1–27.

S   Good, R. d'O., 1953. *The geography of flowering plants*. 2nd edition. Longmans, Green & Co., London.

S   Gregory, P. H., 1961. *The microbiology of the atmosphere*. Interscience, New York.

G   Gressitt, J. L., 1954. *Insects of Micronesia I. Introduction*. Bishop Museum Pr., Honolulu.

S*   ——, 1961. Problems in the zoogeography of Pacific and Antarctic insects. *Pacif. Insects Monogr.* 2: 1–94.

S   ——, Leech, R. E. and O'Brien, C. W., 1960. Trapping of airborne insects in the Antarctic area. *Pacif. Insects* 2 (2): 245–50.

S ——— and Nakata, S., 1958. Trapping of air-borne insects on ships on the Pacific. *Proc. Hawaii. ent. Soc.* 16 (3): 363–65.

S* ——— and Yoshimoto, C., 1963. Dispersal of animals in the Pacific. *In:* J. L. Gressitt (ed.), *Pacific Basin Biogeography.* Bishop Museum Pr., Honolulu.

S Gulick, A., 1932. Biological peculiarities of oceanic islands. *Q. Rev. Biol.* 7: 405–27.

G Guppy, H. B., 1906. *Observations of a naturalist in the Pacific between 1891 and 1899. Volume 2. Plant dispersal.* Macmillan, London.

S ———, 1925. Dispersal of butterflies and other insects. *Nature* 116: 543.

S Hardy, A. C. and Milne, P. S., 1937. Insect drift over the North Sea. *Nature* 139: 510–11.

S ——— and ———, 1938. Studies in the distribution of insects by aerial currents. *J. Anim. Ecol.* 7: 199–229.

S Hartmann, G., 1964. Contribution to discussion. *In:* Carrick, Holdgate and Prevost (eds.), *Biologie Antarctique—Antarctic Biology.*

S Hely, P. C., 1960. Dispersal of White Wax Scale (*Ceroblastes destructor* Newst.) by wind. *J. Aust. Inst. agric. Sci.* 26 (4): 355–56.

S Herring, J. L., 1958. Evidence for hurricane transport and dispersal of aquatic Hemiptera. *Pan-Pacif. Ent.* 34: 174–75.

S* Holdgate, M. W., 1965. The fauna of the Tristan da Cunha Islands. *Phil. Trans. R. Soc.* B 249: 361–402.

S Johnson, C. G., 1957a. The distribution of insects in the air and the empirical relation of density to height. *J. Anim. Ecol.* 26: 479–94.

S ———, 1957b. The vertical distribution of aphids in the air and the temperature lapse rate. *Q. Jl. R. met. Soc.* 83: 194–201.

S ———, 1960. A basis for a general system of insect migration and dispersal by flight. *Nature* 186: 348–50.

G ———, 1963. The aerial migration of insects. *Scient. Am.* December 1963: 2–8.

S Lack, D. and Venables, L. S. V., 1940. Migratory limicoline birds in the Galápagos. *Ibis* 82: 730–31.

S   Leston, D., 1957. Spread potential and the colonization of islands. *Syst. Zool.* 6: 41–46.

S   Lévêque, R., Bowman, R. I. and Billeb, S. L., 1966. Migrants in the Galápagos area. *Condor* 68 (1): 81–101.

S   Lindroth, C. H., 1968. Colonization of a new island Surtsey off Iceland. *Abstr. Pap. XIIIth int. Congr. Ent., Moscow:* 148.

S   MacArthur, R. H. and Wilson, E. O., 1967. *The Theory of Island Biogeography.* Princeton Univ. Pr., Princeton, N.J.

S   Maher, L. J., 1964. *Ephedra* pollen in sediments of the Great Lakes region. *Ecology* 45: 391–400.

S   Malone, C. R. and Proctor, V. W., 1965. Dispersal of *Marsilea micronata* by water birds. *Am. Fern J.* 55: 167–70.

S   Matthew, W. D., 1915. Climate and evolution. *Ann. N. Y. Acad. Sci.* 24: 171–318.

S   Mayr, E., 1965. The nature of colonizations in birds. *In:* H. G. Baker and G. L. Stebbins (eds), *The Genetics of Colonizing Species.* Academic Pr., New York.

S   Muller, A., 1871. On the dispersal of non-migratory insects by atmospheric agencies. *Trans. ent. Soc. Lond.* 1871: 175–86.

S   Myers, G. S., 1953. Ability of amphibians to cross sea barriers, with especial reference to Pacific zoogeography. *Proc. 7th Pacif. Sci. Congr., New Zealand.* 4: 19–27.

S   Polunin, N., 1960. *Introduction to plant geography.* Longmans, Green & Co., New York.

G   Powers, S., 1911. Floating islands. *Pop. Sci. Mon.* 79: 303–7.

S   Ridley, H. N., 1930. *The dispersal of plants throughout the world.* Reeve and Co., Ashford, Kent.

S   Setchell, W. A., 1926. Les migrations des oiseaux et la dissemination des plantes. *C.r. somm. Séanc. Soc. Biogéogr.* 3: 54–57.

S   Smith, A. G., 1966. Land snails of the Galápagos. *In:* R. I. Bowman (ed.), *Proc. Symp. Galápagos int. scient. Project:* 240–51. Univ. California Pr., Berkeley and Los Angeles.

S   Stephens, S. G., 1958. Salt water tolerance of seeds of *Gossypium* species as a possible factor in seed dispersal. *Am. Nat.* 92: 83–92.

S   ——, 1966. The potentiality for long-range dispersal of cotton seeds. *Am. Nat.* 100: 199–210.

S   —— and Rick, C. M., 1966. Problems on the origin, dispersal and establishment of the Galápagos cottons. *In:* R. I. Bowman (ed.), *Proc. Symp. Galápagos int. scient. Project:* 201–8. Univ. California Pr., Berkeley and Los Angeles.

S   Sykes, W. R. and Godley, E. J., 1968. Transoceanic dispersal in *Sophora* and other genera. *Nature* 218: 495–96.

S   Taylor, B. W., 1954. An example of long distance dispersal. *Ecology* 35 (4): 569–72.

S   ——, 1960. Mortality and viability of insect migrants high in the air. *Nature* 186: 410.

S   Thorne, R. F., 1963. Biotic distribution patterns in the tropical Pacific. *In:* J. L. Gressitt (ed.), *Pacific Basin Biogeography.* Bishop Museum Pr., Honolulu.

S   Van Dyke, E. C., 1953. The Coleoptera of the Galápagos Islands. *Occ. Pap. Calif. Acad. Sci.* 22: 1–181.

S   Van Zwaluwenburg, R. H., 1942. Notes on the temporary establishment of insect and plant species on Canton Island. *Hawaii. Plrs'. Rec.* 46 (2): 49–52.

S   Visher, S. S., 1925. Tropical cyclones and the dispersal of life from island to island in the Pacific. *Am. Nat.* 59: 70–78.

S   Wace, N. M. and Dickson, J. H., 1965. The terrestrial botany of the Tristan da Cunha Islands. *Phil. Trans. R. Soc.* B 249: 273–360.

G   Wallace, A. R., 1880. *Island Life.* Macmillan, London.

G   Wheeler, W. M., 1916. Ants carried in a floating log from the Brazilian coast to San Sebastian Island. *Psyche* 23: 180–83.

S   ——, 1919. The ants of the Galápagos Islands. *Proc. Calif. Acad. Sci.* ser. 4, 2: 259–310.

D   Whitaker, T. W. and Carter, G. F., 1961. A note on the longevity of seed of *Lagenaria siceraria* (Mol.) Standl. after floating in sea water. *Bull. Torrey bot. Club* 88: 104–6.

S   Williams, C. B., 1957. Insect migration. *A. Rev. Ent.* 2: 163–80.

S   Williams, F. X., 1911. The butterflies and hawk-moths of the Galápagos Islands. *Proc. Calif. Acad. Sci.* ser. 4, 1: 289–322.

S   Wodzicki, K., 1965. The status of some exotic vertebrates in the ecology of New Zealand. *In:* H. G. Baker and G. L. Stebbins (eds.), *The Genetics of Colonizing Species.* Academic Pr., New York.

S† Wollaston, T. V., 1877. *Coleoptera Sanctae-Helenae.* John van Voorst, London.

G   Wood Jones, F., 1910. *Coral and atolls.* Lovell Reeve & Co., London.

S   Yasumatsu, K. and Nakao, S., 1957. Experiments of the dispersal of the crawling larvae of some Coccoidea (*Homoptera*) by air currents. (English summary). *Sci. Bull. Fac. Agric. Kyushu Univ.* 16: 203–19.

S   Yoshimoto, C. M. and Gressitt, J. L., 1959, 1960, 1961. Trappings of air-borne insects on ships on the Pacific. Part 2. *Proc. Hawaii. ent. Soc.* 17 (1): 150–55. Parts 3, 4. *Pacif. Insects* 2 (2): 239–43, 3 (4): 556–58.

S   ——, Gressitt, J. L. and Mitchell, C. J., 1962. Trapping of air-borne insects in the Pacific-Antarctic area. 1. *Pacif. Insects* 4 (4): 847–58.

S   ——, —— and Wolff, T., 1962. Air-borne insects from the Galathea Expedition. *Pacif. Insects* 4 (2): 269–91.

S   Zimmerman, E. C., 1942. Distribution and origin of some Eastern Oceanic insects. *Am. Nat.* 76 (764): 280–307.

G*   ——, 1948. *Insects of Hawaii. I. Introduction.* Univ. Hawaii Pr., Honolulu.

CHAPTER 11

S   Baker, H. G., 1955. Self-compatibility and establishment after "long-distance" dispersal. *Evolution* 9: 347–49.

S   ——, 1967. Support for Baker's Law—as a rule. *Evolution* 21 (4): 853–56.

S   Bailey, S. F., 1967. A collection of Thysanoptera from the Galápagos Islands. *Pan-Pacif. Ent.* 43: 203–10.

S   Bowman, R. I., 1961. Morphological differentiation and adaptation in the Galápagos finches. *Univ. Calif. Publs. Zool.* 58: 1–302.

G   Carlquist, S., 1965. *Island Life.* Natural History Pr., New York.

S   ——, 1966a. The biota of long-distance dispersal. II. Loss of dispersibility in Pacific Compositae. *Evolution* 20 (1): 30–48.

S   ——, 1966b. The biota of long-distance dispersal. IV, Genetic systems in the floras of oceanic islands. *Evolution* 20 (4): 433–55.

S   ——, 1967. The biota of long-distance dispersal. V. Plant dispersal to Pacific Islands. *Bull. Torrey bot. Club.* 94 (3): 129–62.

G   Elton, C. S., 1958. *The ecology of invasions by animals and plants*. Methuen, London.

S   Fosberg, F. R., 1948. Derivation of the flora of the Hawaiian Islands. *In:* E. C. Zimmerman, *Insects of Hawaii. Introduction.* Univ. Hawaii Pr., Honolulu.

S   Holdgate, M. W., 1965. The fauna of the Tristan da Cunha Islands. *Phil. Trans. R. Soc.* B 249: 361–402.

S   Lack, D., 1947. *Darwin's finches.* Cambridge Univ. Pr., London.

S   Linsley, E. G., 1966. Pollinating insects of the Galápagos Islands. *In:* R. I. Bowman (ed.), *Proc. Symp. Galápagos int. scient. Project:* 225–32. Univ. California Pr., Berkeley and Los Angeles.

S   ——, Rick, C. M. and Stephens, S. G., 1966. Observations on the floral relationships of the Galápagos carpenter bee (Hymenoptera: Apidae). *Pan-Pacif. Ent.* 42 (1): 1–18.

S   MacArthur, R. H. and Wilson, E. O., 1963. An equilibrium theory of insular zoogeography. *Evolution* 17 (4): 373–87.

S   —— and ——, 1967. *The Theory of Island Biogeography.* Princeton Univ. Pr., Princeton, N.J.

S   Rick, C. M., 1966. Some plant-animal relations on the Galápagos Islands. *In:* R. I. Bowman (ed.), *Proc. Symp. Galápagos int. scient. Project:* 215–24. Univ. California Pr., Berkeley and Los Angeles.

S   Stebbins, G. L., 1957. Self fertilization and population variability in the higher plants. *Am. Nat.* 91: 337–54.

S   Thorne, R. F., 1963. Biotic distribution patterns in the tropical Pacific. *In:* J. L. Gressitt (ed.), *Pacific Basin Biogeography.* Bishop Museum Pr., Honolulu.

S   Williams, F. X., 1926. The bees and aculeate wasps of the Galápagos Islands. *Proc. Calif. Acad. Sci.* ser. 4, 2: 347–57.

CHAPTER 12

S   Baker, H. G., 1965. Characteristics and modes of origin of weeds. *In:* H. G. Baker and G. L. Stebbins (eds.), *The genetics of colonizing species.* Academic Pr., New York and London.

S   —— and Stebbins, G. L., (eds.) 1965. *The genetics of colonizing species.* Academic Pr., New York and London.

S   Bowman, R. I., 1961. Morphological differentiation and adaptation in the Galápagos finches. *Univ. Calif. Publs. Zool.* 58: 1–302.

S   Brown, W. L. and Wilson, E. O., 1956. Characters displacement. *Syst. Zool.* 5: 49–64.

G   Carlquist, S., 1965. *Island Life.* Natural History Pr., New York.

S   Carson, H. L., 1965. Chromosomal morphism in geographically widespread species of *Drosophila*. *In:* H. G. Baker and G. L. Stebbins (eds.), *The genetics of colonizing species.* Academic Pr., New York and London.

S   Curio, E., 1968. Some observations on the "Four-eyed" Blenny of the Galápagos Islands, *Dialommus fuscus* (Pisces: Clinidae). *Notic. Galápagos.* 12: 13–17.

S   Darlington, P. J. Jr., 1943. Carabidae of mountains and islands: data on the evolution of isolated faunas, and on atrophy of wings. *Ecol. Monogr.* 13: 37–61.

S   Dirsh, V. M., 1969. Acridoidea of the Galápagos Islands. (Orthoptera). *Bull. Br. Mus. nat. Hist.* (Ent.). 23 (2): 27–51.

S   Dobzhansky, Th., 1960. Evolution and environment. *In:* S. Tax (ed.), *Evolution after Darwin* Vol. 1. Univ. Chicago Pr., Chicago.

S   ——, 1963. Biological evolution in island populations. *In:* F. R. Fosberg (ed.), *Man's Place in the Island Ecosystem.* Bishop Museum Pr., Honolulu.

S   —— and Pavlovsky, O., 1957. An experimental study of interaction between genetic drift and natural selection. *Evolution* 11: 311–19.

S   Fraser, A., 1965. Colonization and genetic drift. *In:* H. G. Baker and G. L. Stebbins (eds.), *The genetics of colonizing species.* Academic Pr., New York and London.

S   Hardy, D. E., 1960. Diptera. *Insects Hawaii* 10: 1–368.

S   Hebard, M., 1920. Dermoptera and Orthoptera. *Proc. Calif. Acad. Sci.* ser. 4, 2, Part 2 (1f): 311–46.

S   Holdgate, M. W., 1965. The fauna of the Tristan da Cunha Islands. *Phil. Trans. R. Soc.* B 249: 361–402.

S   Hosgood, S. and Parsons, P. A., 1967. The exploitation of genetic heterogeneity among the founders of laboratory populations of *Drosophila* prior to directional selection. *Experientia* 23: 1066.

G   Kramer, P., 1966. The behavior of the Rock Crab, *Grapsus grapsus* L. on Galápagos. *Notic. Galápagos* 7–8: 18–20.

S   Lack, D., 1969. Subspecies and sympatry in Darwin's finches. *Evolution* 23 (2): 252–63.

S Lewontin, R. C., 1965. Selection for colonizing ability. *In:* H. G. Baker and G. L. Stebbins (eds.), *The genetics of colonizing species.* Academic Pr., New York and London.

S MacArthur, R. H. and Wilson, E. O., 1967. *The Theory of Island Biogeography.* Princeton Univ. Pr., Princeton, N.J.

S Mayr, E., 1954. Change of genetic environment and evolution. *In:* J. Huxley, A. C. Hardy and E. B. Ford (eds.), *Evolution as a Process.* George Allen & Unwin, London.

S ——, 1963. *Animal species and evolution.* Harvard Univ. Pr., Cambridge, Mass.

S Miller, A. H., 1966. Animal evolution on islands. *In:* R. I. Bowman (ed.), *Proc. Symp. Galápagos int. scient. Project:* 10–17. Univ. California Pr., Berkeley and Los Angeles.

S Parsons, P. A., 1970. Genetic Heterogeneity in natural populations of *Drosophila melanogaster* for ability to withstand desiccation. *Theor. and appl. Gent.* 40: 261–66.

S Usinger, R. L. and Ashlock, P. D., 1966. Evolution of orsilline insect faunas on oceanic islands (Hemiptera, Lygaeidae). *In:* R. I. Bowman (ed.), *Proc. Symp. Galápagos int. scient. Project:* 233–35. Univ. California Pr., Berkeley and Los Angeles.

S Van Denburgh, J. and Slevin, J. R., 1913. The Galápagoan lizards of the genus *Tropidurus;* with notes on the iguanas of the genera *Conolophus* and *Amblyrhynchus. Proc. Calif. Acad. Sci.* ser. 4, 2 (1): 133–202.

S Van Valen, L., 1965. Morphological variation and width of ecological niche. *Am. Nat.* 99: 377–90.

S Wace, N. M. and Dickson, J. H., 1965. The terrestrial botany of the Tristan da Cunha Islands. *Phil. Trans. R. Soc.* B 249: 273–360.

S† Wagner, M., 1868. *Die Darwin'sche Theorie und das Migrationsgesetz der Organismen.* Duncker and Humblot, Leipzig.

S Wilson, E. O., 1959. Adaptive shift and dispersal in a tropical ant fauna. *Evolution* 13: 122–44.

S ——, 1961. The nature of the taxon cycle in the Melanesian ant fauna. *Am Nat.* 95: 169–93.

G Zimmerman, E. C., 1963. Nature of the land biota. *In:* F. R. Fosberg (ed.), *Man's Place in the Island Ecosystem.* Bishop Museum Pr., Honolulu.

CHAPTER 13

G   Acosta Solis, M., 1963. Protection and conservation problems on the Galápagos Islands. *Occ. Pap. Calif. Acad. Sci.* 44: 141–46.

G   ——, 1966. Problems of conservation and economic development of the Galápagos. *In:* R. I. Bowman (ed.), *Proc. Symp. Galápagos int. scient. Project:* 282–85. Univ. California Pr., Berkeley and Los Angeles.

S   Brosset, A., 1963a. Statut actuel de la faune aux îles Galápagos. *Notic. Galápagos* 1: 5–8.

S   ——, 1963b. Statut actuel des mammifères des îles Galápagos. *Mammalia* 27: 323–38.

G   Dorst, J., 1963. Future scientific studies in the Galápagos Islands. *Occ. Pap. Calif. Acad. Sci.* 44: 147–54.

G   Eibl-Eibesfeldt, I., 1959. *Survey on the Galápagos Islands.* UNESCO, Paris.

S   Eliasson, U., 1968. On the influence of introduced animals on the natural vegetation of the Galápagos Islands. *Notic. Galápagos* 11: 19–21.

G   Grant, M., 1928. Conservation of wild life. *Bull. N. Y. Zool. Soc.* 31 (5): 147–48.

G†   Hailman, J. P., 1963. Two views on conservation in the Galápagos. II. *Phila. herp. Soc. Bull.* 11: 72–74.

S   Harris, M. P., 1970. The biology of an endangered species, the Dark-rumped Petrel (*Pterodroma phaeopygia*) in the Galápagos Islands. *Condor* 72 (1): 76–84.

G   Koford, C. B., 1966. Economic resources of the Galápagos Islands. *In:* R. I. Bowman (ed.), *Proc. Symp. Galápagos int. scient. Project:* 286–90. Univ. California Pr., Berkeley and Los Angeles.

S   Leleup, N., 1965. Commentaires sur le sanctuaire zoologique des Galápagos. *Africa-Tervuren* 9 (3-4): 85–91.

S   Lévêque, R., 1963a. Le statut actuel des vertébrés rares et menacés de l'archipel des Galápagos. *Terre Vie* 4: 397–430.

S   ——, 1963b. The status of some rarer Galápagos birds. *Bull. int. Coun. Bird Preserv.* 9: 96–98.

S   Lowe, P. R., 1934. On the need for the preservation of the Galápagos fauna. Birds. *Proc. Linn. Soc., Lond.* 146: 84–89.

S   MacArthur, H. R. and Wilson, E. O., 1967. *The Theory of Island Biogeography*. Princeton Univ. Pr., Princeton, N.J.

G   Moore, R. T., 1935. The protection and conservation of the zoological life of the Galápagos Archipelago. *Science* 82 (2135): 519–21.

S   Parker, H. W., 1934. On the need for the preservation of the Galápagos fauna. Reptiles. *Proc. Linn. Soc., Lond.* 146: 80–84.

G   Snow, D. W., 1966a. Research station in the Galápagos. *Oryx* 7 (6): 275–76.

G   ——, 1966b. The giant tortoises of the Galápagos Islands. Their present status and future chances. *Oryx* 7 (6): 277–90.

G   Street, P., 1961a. *Vanishing Animals*. Faber & Faber, London.

G   ——, 1961b. Can the giant tortoise survive? *Discovery* 21–22: 158–60.

G   Svenson, H. K., 1963. Opportunities for botanical study in the Galápagos Islands. *Occ. Pap. Calif. Acad. Sci.* 44: 53–58.

G   Townsend, C. H., 1924. Impending extinction of the Galápagos tortoises. *Bull. N. Y. Zool. Soc.* 27 (2): 55–56.

G   ——, 1925. The Galápagos tortoises in their relation to the whaling industry. *Zoologica, N. Y.* 4 (3): 55–135.

S   ——, 1934. The fur seal of the Galápagos Islands. *Zoologica, N. Y.* 18 (2): 47–49.

G   Wintour, C. J., 1900. The strange hunt of the wild hound. *Wide World Mag.* 5 (26): 200–3.

GS Zimmerman, E. C., 1948. *Insects of Hawaii. I. Introduction.* Univ. Hawaii Pr., Honolulu.

G   ——, 1963. Nature of the land biota. *In:* F. R. Fosberg, (ed.), *Man's Place in the Island Ecosystem*. Bishop Museum Pr., Honolulu.

G   Ziswiler, V., 1967. *Extinct and vanishing animals*. Longmans, Green & Co., London.

INDEX

Index

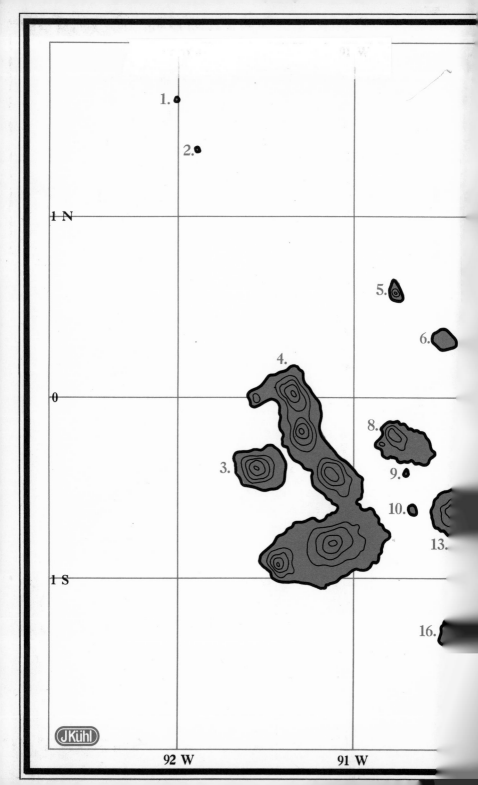

1.●

2.●

1 N

5.●

6.●

4.

0

8.●

3.●

9.●

10.●

13.

1 S

16.

JKühl

92 W   91 W